**SEPUP**

# Science

## INDIANA EDITION ▶ GRADE 8

SEPUP

# Science

## INDIANA EDITION ▶ GRADE 8

SCIENCE
EDUCATION FOR
PUBLIC
UNDERSTANDING
PROGRAM

UNIVERSITY OF CALIFORNIA AT BERKELEY
LAWRENCE HALL OF SCIENCE **LHS**

**LaB-aiDS**

RONKONKOMA, NEW YORK

## This book is a compilation of the following SEPUP publications:

### Issues and Physical Science

Studying Materials Scientifically
Chemistry of Materials
Plate Tectonics

### Issues and Life Science

Genetics
Evolution

### Issues and Earth Science

Weather and Atmosphere

This project was supported, in part, by the
National Science Foundation
Opinions expressed are those of the authors
and not necessarily those of the Foundation.

3 4 5 6 7 8 9        11 12 13 14 15

**SEPUP**
Lawrence Hall of Science
University of California at Berkeley
Berkeley CA 94720-5200

e-mail: sepup@berkeley.edu
Website: www.sepuplhs.org

Published by:

**LaB-aiDS**

17 Colt Court
Ronkonkoma NY 11779
Website: www.lab-aids.com

## A Letter to 8th Grade Indiana Science Students,

As you examine the activities in this book, you may wonder, "Why does this book look so different from other science books I've seen?" The reason is simple: it is a different kind of science program, and only some of what you will learn can be seen by leafing through this book!

This program uses several kinds of activities to teach physical, life and earth science concepts. For example, you will observe and test the properties of elements and compounds. You will model the atoms and molecules that make up these substances. You will design and conduct investigations to explore how different earth surfaces are heated by the Sun's energy and how they cool. You will also investigate how reproduction is essential for the continuation of every species and is the mechanism for transmitting genetic information. You will explore a model of how species compete for food. A combination of laboratories, investigations, readings, models, debates, role plays, and projects will help you uncover the nature of science and the relevance of science to your interests.

You will find that important scientific ideas come up again and again in different activities. You will be expected to do more than just memorize these concepts: you will be asked to explain and apply them. In particular, you will improve your decision-making skills, using evidence and weighing outcomes to decide what you think should be done about scientific issues facing society.

How do we know that this is a good way for you to learn? In general, research on science education supports it. In particular, the activities in this book were tested by hundreds of students and their teachers, and they were modified on the basis of their feedback. In a sense, this entire book is the result of an investigation: we had people test our ideas, we interpreted the results, and we revised our ideas! We believe the result will show you that learning more about science is important, enjoyable, and relevant to your life.

This student book is a compilation of SEPUP publications, customized to align to the Indiana Core Content Expectations, for Science Grade 8. The sequence of units provided below indicates the order that they appear in this publication. Please note that due to the nature of this compilation, a "Unit" letter may seem to appear out of sequence.

# Contents

## LAB-AIDS Correlation to
## INDIANA CORE CONTENT EXPECTATIONS FOR SCIENCE
## Grade 8

This document illustrates how curricula from LAB-AIDS are used to address the Indiana Core Content Expectations for Science, Grade 8, Science. Each heading tells the unit (s) that aligns to that particular content. The formative analysis question numbering in the last column shows that the student response addresses the Core Content Expectation.

*Note: SEPUP lessons come in several types including Investigations, View and Reflect, Reading, Laboratory, Talking it Over, Role Play, Modeling, Project*

## Grade 8 RECOMMENDED SCOPE AND SEQUENCE

### ISSUES & PHYSICAL SCIENCE (IAPS) UNITS

Studying Materials Scientifically (25 days)

Chemistry of Materials (45 days)

### ISSUES & LIFE SCIENCE (IALS) UNITS

Genetics (40 days)

Evolution (25 days)

### ISSUES & EARTH SCIENCE (IAPS) UNIT

Weather and Atmosphere (35 days)

For a total of 170 days

# GRADE 8 - CORE STANDARD 1 - PHYSICAL SCIENCE

Core Standard:  Describe how atomic structure determines chemical properties and how atoms and molecules interact. *This group of indicators map to the "Studying Materials Scientifically" (SMS) and "The Chemistry of Materials" (CM) SEPUP Units ...the issues of household chemical safety and product life cycles provide context.*

| INDIANA INDICATOR | UNIT TITLE - ACTIVITY NUMBER(S) | INDIANA ASSESSMENT BLUEPRINT |
|---|---|---|
| 8.1.1  Explain that all matter is composed of particular arrangements of atoms and approximately one hundred elements. | IAPS: CM - 15, 16, 17 | 16 AQ 1, AQ 4 17 Procedure |
| 8.1.2  Understand that elements are organized on the periodic table based on atomic number. | IAPS: CM - 15, 16 | 15 AQ 5 (UC) |
| 8.1.3  Explain how the arrangement of atoms and molecules determines chemical properties of substances. | IAPS: CM - 15, 16, 17, 19, 20, 21 | 16 AQ 1, 4 17 Procedure 19 AQ 1, 2 20 AQ 1, 4 21 AQ 2, 3 |
| 8.1.4  Describe the structure of an atom and relate the arrangement of electrons to how that atom interacts with other atoms. | IAPS: CM - 15, 15A, 16, 17 (we frame as bonding) | 15A All AQ 16 AQ 1, AQ 4 17 Procedure |
| 8.1.5  Explain that atoms join together to form molecules and compounds and illustrate with diagrams the relationship between atoms and compounds and/or molecules. | IAPS: CM - 16, 17, 21 | 16 AQ 1-4 17 AQ 5-6 21 AQ 2, 3 IB 9, 10, 11 |
| 8.1.6  Explain that elements and compounds have characteristic properties such as density, boiling points and melting points that remain unchanged regardless of the sample size. | IAPS: SMS - 6, 7, 8, 9, 10  CM - 18 | 7 AQ 1, 3 8 AQ 1, 3 9 AQ 1, 3 10 Procedure  18 AQ 2, 3 and Extension |
| 8.1.7  Explain that chemical changes occur when substances react and form one or more different products, whose physical and chemical properties are different from those of the reactants. | IAPS: CM - 19, 20, 21, 23 | 19 AQ 1, 2 20 AQ 2, 3 21 AQ 2, 3 23 AQ 1 IB 12, 13 |
| 8.1.8  Demonstrate that in a chemical change, the total number of each kind of atom in the product are the same as in the reactants and that the total mass of the reacting system is conserved. | IAPS: CM - 25 | 25 Procedure and AQ 2, 3 |

## GRADE 8 - CORE STANDARD 2 - EARTH AND SPACE SYSTEMS

**Core Standard:** Explain how the sun's energy heats the air, land, and water driving the processes that result in wind, ocean currents, and the water cycle. *This group of indicators mostly maps to the "Weather and Atmosphere" (WA) SEPUP Unit ...the issue of how weather affects communities provides context.* Other indicators are met with Activities from "Chemistry of Materials (CM), and Evolution (EVO).

**Core Standard:** Describe how human activities have changed the land, water, and atmosphere.

| INDIANA INDICATOR | UNIT TITLE - ACTIVITY NUMBER(S) | INDIANA ASSESSMENT BLUEPRINT |
|---|---|---|
| 8.2.1 Recognize and demonstrate how the sun's energy drives convection in the atmosphere and in bodies of water, which results in ocean currents and weather patterns. | IAES: WA - 55, 58, 68 | 55 AQ 3 58 AQ 1, AQ 3 68 AQ 2 IB 6, 7 |
| 8.2.2 Describe and model how water moves through the earth's crust, atmosphere, and oceans in a cyclic way, as liquid, vapor, and solid. | IAES: WA - 60. 62 | 60 AQ 2 62 Procedure, AQ 1, AQ 4 IB 3, 6, 15 |
| 8.2.3 Describe the characteristics of ocean currents and identify their effects on weather patterns. | IAES: WA - 57, 58 | 57 AQ 3, AQ 4 58 AQ 2, Stopping to Think 2 IB 10 |
| 8.2.4 Describe the physical and chemical composition of the atmosphere at different elevations. | IAES: WA - 64, 66 | 64 Procedure, AQ 1-4 66 AQ 2 IB 4, 5 |
| 8.2.5 Describe the conditions that cause Indiana weather and weather-related events such as tornadoes, lake effect snow, blizzards, thunderstorms, and flooding. | IAES: WA - 52, 58, 69 | 52 Procedure 58 Stopping to Think 3 69 AQ 1 C IB 16 |
| 8.2.6 Identify, explain, and discuss some effects human activities have on the biosphere, such as air, soil, light, noise and water pollution. | IAPS: CM - 23, 24, 26, 28<br><br>IAES: WA - 65 | 23 AQ 3 24 AQ 6, Extension 26 AQ 4-5 28 AQ 3<br><br>65 AQ 1, 2, 3 |
| 8.2.7 Recognize that some of Earth's resources are finite and describe how recycling, reducing consumption and the development of alternatives can reduce the rate of their depletion. | IAPS: CM - 27, 28, 29<br><br>IAES: WA - 70 | 27 AQ 2, AQ 3, Extension 28 AQ 2, AQ 3 29 AQ 1, AQ 2<br><br>70 AQ 2, 3 |
| 8.2.8 Explain that human activities, beginning with the earliest herding and agricultural activities, have drastically changed the environment and have affected the capacity of the environment to support native species. Explain current efforts to reduce and eliminate these impacts and encourage sustainability. | IALS: EVO - 89, 101<br><br>Spiral from 6th Grade ECO - 72, 73, 87, 88 | 89 AQ 1 101 AQ 1<br><br>88 AQ 1-3 |

# GRADE 8 - CORE STANDARD 3 - LIFE SCIENCE

**Core Standard:** Understand the predictability of characteristics being passed from parents to offspring. *This group of indicators map to the "Genetics" (G) SEPUP Unit ...the issue of genetic disease provides context.*

**Core Standard:** Explain how a particular environment selects for traits that increase the likelihood of survival and reproduction by individuals bearing those traits. *This group of indicators map to the "Evolution" (EVO) SEPUP Unit... the issue of saving endangered species provides context.*

| INDIANA INDICATOR | UNIT TITLE - ACTIVITY NUMBER(S) | INDIANA ASSESSMENT BLUEPRINT |
|---|---|---|
| 8.3.1 Explain that reproduction is essential for the continuation of every species and is the mechanism by which all organisms transmit genetic information. | IALS: G - 57, 63 | 57 AQ 2 |
| 8.3.2 Compare and contrast the transmission of genetic information in sexual and asexual reproduction. | IALS: G - 57 | 57 AQ 1, AQ 2 IB 3, 4, 8, 11, 16, 24 |
| 8.3.3 Explain that genetic information is transmitted from parents to offspring mostly by chromosomes. | IALS: G - 63, 64 | 63 Informal through discussion 64 AQ 6 |
| 8.3.4 Understand the relationship between deoxyribonucleic acid (DNA), genes, and chromosomes. | IALS: G - 63 | 63 AQ 1 (UC) IB 9 |
| 8.3.5 Identify and describe the difference between inherited traits and physical and behavioral traits that are acquired or learned. | IALS: G - 54, 55, 56, 64 | 54 AQ 2, AQ 3 55 AQ 1, AQ 2 56 AQ 7 64 AQ 2, AQ 3 IB 27 |
| 8.3.6 Observe anatomical structures of a variety of organisms and describe their similarities and differences. Use the data collected to organize the organisms into groups and predict their relatedness. | IALS: EVO - 98, 99 Spirals from 6th Grade Ecology - 75, 76 Spirals from 7th Grade Cell Biology - 44, 45 | 98 Reflection Question 6 99 AQ 1-5 and Extension 76 AQ 1, 2 44 AQ 1-3 |
| 8.3.7 Recognize and explain that small genetic differences between parents and offspring can accumulate in successive generations so that descendants may be different from their ancestors. | IALS: EVO - 94, 97 | 94 AQ 3, AQ 4 97 AQ 2 IB 30, 40b, 41 |
| 8.3.8 Examine traits of individuals within a population of organisms that may give them an advantage in survival and reproduction in a given environments or when the environment changes. | IALS: EVO - 95, 96 | 95 Procedure, AQ 3 96 Procedure, AQ 4 IB 20, 21, 38 |
| 8.3.9 Describe the effect of environmental changes on populations of organisms when their adaptive characteristics put them at a disadvantage for survival. Describe how extinction of a species can ultimately result. | IALS: EVO - 89, 96, 101 | 89 AQ 1 96 AQ 4, AQ 7 101 AQ 1, AQ 4, AQ 5 IB 3, 18, 22 |
| 8.3.10 Recognize and describe how new varieties of organisms have come about from selective breeding. | IALS: G - 58, 58A, 60, 61 | 58A All AQ |

# GRADE 8 - CORE STANDARD 4 - SCIENCE, TECHNOLOGY AND ENGINEERING

**Core Standard:** Identify the appropriate materials to be used to solve a problem based on their specific properties and characteristics. *This group of indicators map to the "Studying Materials Scientifically (SMS)" and "The Chemistry of Materials (CM)" SEPUP Units ...the issues of household chemical safety and product life cycles provide context.

| INDIANA INDICATOR | UNIT TITLE - ACTIVITY NUMBER(S) | INDIANA ASSESSMENT BLUEPRINT |
|---|---|---|
| 8.4.1 Understand how the strength of attractive forces between particles in a material helps to explain many physical properties of the material, such as why different materials exist as gases, liquids or solids at a given temperature. | IAPS: SMS - 6, 7, 7A | 6 AQ 1 and Teacher Extension 7 AQ 1, 3 and Teacher Extension 7A All AQ |
| 8.4.2 Rank the strength of attractions between the particles of room-temperature materials. | IAPS: SMS - 6, 7, 7A | 7A All AQ |
| 8.4.3 Investigate the properties (mechanical, chemical, electrical, thermal, magnetic, and optical) of natural and engineered materials. | IAPS: SMS - 6, 7, 7A<br><br>CM - 12, 13, 14, 15, 18, 20, 21 | 6 Procedure, AQ 1 7 Procedure, AQ 1 7A All AQ<br><br>12 Procedure, AQ 4, 5 13 Procedure, AQ 3, 4 14 Procedure, AQ 4 15 Procedure AQ 1, 3, 4, 5 18 Procedure, AQ 4 20 AQ 2, 3, 4 21 AQ1, 2, 3 IB 20, 21 |

# GRADE 8 - PROCESS STANDARDS

**The Nature of Science** - Students gain scientific knowledge by observing the natural and constructed world, performing and evaluating investigations and communicating their findings. These principles should guide student work and be integrated into the curriculum along with the content standards on a daily basis.

| INDIANA INDICATOR | UNIT TITLE | ACTIVITY NUMBERS |
|---|---|---|
| A.1 Make predictions and develop testable questions based on research and prior knowledge. | IAPS:<br>SMS | 2, 3, 8 |
| | CM | 12, 15, 25 |
| | IALS:<br>G | 55, 58, 59, 64, 66, 68, 70 |
| | EVO | 90, 91, 93, 95, 96, 99 |
| | IAES:<br>WA | 50, 52, 54, 55, 61, 63, 65, 68, 69 |
| A.2 Plan and carry out investigations as a class, in small groups or independently often over a period of several class lessons. | IAPS:<br>SMS - SEPUP Throughout<br>CM - SEPUP Throughout | Exemplar - 3<br>Exemplar - 12 |
| | IALS:<br>G - SEPUP Throughout<br>EVO - SEPUP Throughout | Exemplar - 64<br>Exemplar - 90 |
| | IAES:<br>WA - SEPUP Throughout | Exemplar - 51 |
| A.3 Collect quantitative data with appropriate tools or technologies and use appropriate units to label numerical data. | IAPS:<br>SMS | 8, 9, 10 |
| | CM | 24, 25 |
| | IALS:<br>G | 54 |
| | EVO | 92, 99 |
| | IAES:<br>WA | 51, 55, 61, 68 |
| A.4 Incorporate variables that can be changed, measured or controlled. | IAPS:<br>CM | 18, 24, 25, 26, 27, 28 |
| | IALS:<br>G | 64 |
| | IAES:<br>WA | 55 |
| A.5 Use the principles of accuracy and precision when making measurement. | IAPS:<br>SMS | 8, 9, 10 |
| | CM | 18, 19, 24, 25, 26, 27 |
| | IALS:<br>G | 54 |
| | EVO | 92, 99 |
| | IAES:<br>WA | 55, 61, 67, 68 |

# GRADE 8 - PROCESS STANDARDS, CONTINUED

| INDIANA INDICATOR | UNIT TITLE | ACTIVITY NUMBERS |
|---|---|---|
| A.6 Test predictions with multiple trials. | IALS:<br>G | 59, 64 |
| | IAES:<br>WA | 67 |
| A.7 Keep accurate records in a notebook during investigations. | IAPS:<br>SMS - SEPUP Throughout<br>CM - SEPUP Throughout | Exemplar - 6<br>Exemplar - 14 |
| | IALS:<br>G - SEPUP Throughout<br>EVO - SEPUP Throughout | Exemplar - 64<br>Exemplar - 99 |
| | IAES:<br>WA - SEPUP Throughout | Exemplar - 67 |
| A.8 Analyze data, using appropriate mathematical manipulations as required, and use it to identify patterns and make inferences based on these patterns. | IAPS:<br>SMS | 6, 7, 8, 9, 10, 11 |
| | CM | 12, 14, 15, 18, 22, 24, 25, 27, 28, 29 |
| | IALS:<br>G | 54, 55, 59, 60, 61, 62, 64, 66 |
| | EVO | 92, 95, 96, 98, 100 |
| | IAES:<br>WA | 51, 52, 53, 54, 55, 56, 64, 65, 68, 69, 70 |
| A.9 Evaluate possible causes for differing results (valid data). | IAPS:<br>SMS | 11 |
| | CM | 14, 25 |
| | IALS:<br>G | 54, 58, 59, 60, 62, 64 |
| | EVO | 93, 96, 99 |
| | IAES:<br>WA | 55, 61, 63, 67 |
| A.10 Compare the results of an experiment with the prediction. | IAPS:<br>SMS | 2, 8, 10 |
| | CM | 12, 25 |
| | IALS:<br>G | 59, 62, 64, 68, 70 |
| | EVO | 95, 96 |
| | IAES:<br>WA | 55, 61, 63, 67 |
| A.11 Communicate findings using graphs, charts, maps and models through oral and written reports. | IAPS:<br>SMS | 7, 10, 11 |
| | CM | 22, 27, 29 |
| | IALS:<br>G | 58, 62, 64 |
| | IAES:<br>WA | 67, 68, 69, 70 |

**The Design Process** - As citizens of the constructed world, students will participate in the design process. Students will learn to use materials and tools safely and employ the basic principles of the engineering design process in order to find solutions to problems.

| INDIANA INDICATOR | UNIT TITLE | ACTIVITY NUMBERS |
|---|---|---|
| B.1  Identify a need or problem to be solved. | IAPS:<br>SMS<br>CM<br><br>IALS:<br>G<br>EVO<br><br>IAES:<br>WA | <br><br>1, 4, 10, 11<br>12, 13, 22, 29<br><br><br>56, 67, 68, 71<br>89, 99, 100, 101<br><br><br>67, 70 |
| B.2  Brainstorm potential solutions. | IAPS:<br>SMS<br>CM<br><br>IALS:<br>G<br>EVO<br><br>IAES:<br>WA | <br><br>1, 4, 10, 11<br>12, 13, 22, 29<br><br><br>56, 67, 68, 71<br>89, 99, 100, 101<br><br><br>67, 70 |
| B.3  Document the design throughout the entire design process so that it can be replicated in a portfolio/notebook with drawings including labels. | IAPS:<br>SMS<br>CM<br><br>IALS:<br>EVO<br><br>IAES:<br>WA | <br><br>5<br>12, 13, 22, 29<br><br><br>99<br><br><br>67 |
| B.4  Select a solution to the need or problem. | IAPS:<br>SMS<br>CM<br><br>IALS:<br>G<br>EVO<br><br>IAES:<br>WA | <br><br>5, 11<br>12, 13, 22, 29<br><br><br>56, 67, 68, 71<br>89, 99, 100, 101<br><br><br>67 |
| B.5  Select the most appropriate materials to develop a solution that will meet the need. | IAPS:<br>SMS<br>CM<br><br>IALS:<br>EVO<br><br>IAES:<br>WA | <br><br>5<br>12, 13, 22, 29<br><br><br>99<br><br><br>55, 61, 63, 67 |
| B.6  Create the solution through a prototype. | IAPS:<br>SMS<br>CM<br><br>IALS:<br>EVO<br><br>IAES:<br>WA | <br><br>5<br>12, 13<br><br><br>99<br><br><br>67 |

## The Design Process, continued

| INDIANA INDICATOR | UNIT TITLE | ACTIVITY NUMBERS |
|---|---|---|
| B.7 Test and evaluate how well the solution meets the goal. | IAPS:<br>SMS<br>CM<br><br>IALS:<br>EVO<br><br>IAES:<br>WA | 5, 11<br>13 Extension<br><br><br>99<br><br><br>67 |
| B.8 Evaluate and test the design using measurement. | IAPS:<br>SMS<br>CM<br><br>IAES:<br>WA | 5<br>13 Extension<br><br><br>67 |
| B.9 Present evidence using mathematical representations (graphs, data tables). | IAPS:<br>SMS<br>CM<br><br>IALS:<br>G<br>EVO<br><br>IAES:<br>WA | 6, 7, 8, 10<br>12, 13, 22, 29<br><br><br>56, 67, 68, 71<br>99<br><br><br>67 |
| B.10 Communicate the solution including evidence using mathematical representations (graphs, data tables), drawings or prototypes. | IAPS:<br>SMS<br>CM<br><br>IALS:<br>G<br>EVO<br><br>IAES:<br>WA | 6, 7, 8, 10<br>12, 13, 22, 29<br><br><br>56, 67, 68, 71<br>89, 99, 100, 101<br><br><br>67 |
| B.11 Redesign to improve the solution based on how well the solution meets the need. | IAPS:<br>SMS<br>CM<br><br>IALS:<br>EVO<br><br>IAES:<br>WA | 5<br>13 Extension<br><br><br>99 Extension<br><br><br>67 |

# KEY SKILLS MATRIX FOR GRADE 8 INDIANA

## INQUIRY SKILLS

| | Unit A Studying Materials Scientifically | Unit B The Chemistry of Materials | Unit D Genetics | Unit F Evolution | Unit E Weather and Atmosphere | Total Opportunities to Practice Skills |
|---|---|---|---|---|---|---|
| Makes observations | 1, 3, 5-10 | 14, 15-17, 20, 22, 24-28 | 54, 58-60, 62, 64-66, 69, 70 | 90, 91, 93, 95-97, 100 | 51, 53–57, 59, 61, 64–69 | 48 |
| Identifies data | 1, 2, 6-11 | 12-16, 18-29 | 54, 56-60, 62, 64-71 | 89, 91-98, 101 | 50–70 | 71 |
| Analyzes data | 2, 6-11 | 12-16, 18-29 | 54, 56-68, 70, 71 | 89, 91-101 | 50–59, 60–70 | 63 |
| Makes/ interprets data tables | 6, 7, 8, 9, 10 | 12, 14, 17-20, 22, 26-28 | 54, 59-70 | 91, 95, 96, 98, 100 | 51, 55, 56, 59, 61, 63–65, 67–70 | 45 |
| Makes/ interprets graphs | | 12, 22 | 54 | 95, 96, 98 | 51, 52, 55, 70 | 10 |
| Identifies/ controls a variable | | 18, 24-28 | 64 | | 55 | 8 |
| Makes a prediction/ hypothesis | 2, 8 | 25 | 55, 58, 59, 64, 66, 68, 70 | 90, 91, 93-96, 99 | 50, 52, 54, 55, 61, 63, 65, 68, 69 | 26 |
| Designs an investigation | 3, 10 | (only in extensions) 18,27 | 64 | | 51, 55, 67 | 8 |
| Creates/uses models | | 17, 19, 20, 26 | 58, 59, 65, 69, 70 | 92, 93, 95, 96 | 53–55, 59, 61–63, 67 | 21 |
| Evaluates models | | 20 | 58, 59, 69 | 92, 95, 96 | 62, 67 | 9 |
| Makes evidence-based decisions | 6, 7, 9-11 | 12, 14, 18, 24-28 | 67, 68, 70, 71 | 89, 93, 99, 100, 101 | 57, 63, 65, 68–70 | 28 |
| Revises predictions or explanations based on evidence | 6-10 | 29 | 55, 58, 59, 62, 66, 68, 70 | 91, 93, 95, 96, 99, 100 | 61, 65, 68–70 | 24 |
| Total Opportunities to Practice Skills | 42 | 76 | 72 | 62 | 107 | 287 |

# LITERACY AND COMMUNICATION SKILLS

| | Unit A Studying Materials Scientifically | Unit B The Chemistry of Materials | Unit D Genetics | Unit F Evolution | Unit E Weather and Atmosphere | Total Opportunities to Practice Skills |
|---|---|---|---|---|---|---|
| Reads for information | 2, 4, 6-8, 11 | 12-16, 18, 21, 23, 27–29 | 56-63, 66-69, 71 | 89, 94, 97-99, 101 | 50, 51, 53, 57, 58, 60, 62, 65, 66, 70 | 46 |
| Communicates orally | 1-11 | 12-17, 20, 22, 24-29 | 54, 57-66, 71 | 89, 91-101 | 53–57, 65, 67–70 | 57 |
| Communicates in writing | 1-3, 6-11 | 12, 13, 16-18, 20, 21, 24, 27-29 | 54-59, 61-65, 67, 70, 71 | 89, 91-94, 96-99, 101 | 50–53, 57, 58, 60, 62, 65–70 | 58 |
| Describes observations | 1, 3, 6-10 | 14, 15, 17-20, 22, 24-28 | 54, 57-65, 70 | 90-96, 99, 100 | 51, 53–57, 59, 61–65, 67, 68, 70 | 52 |
| Writes explanations | 1, 2, 7, 8-11, | 14-16, 18–22, 24-29 | 55-71 | 89-100 | 50, 52–59, 61–70 | 69 |
| Makes presentations | | 13, 15, 29 | | | 62, 65, 67, 69, 70 | 8 |
| Uses diagrams or sketches | 8 | 13, 17, 20, 21-32, 36, 39 | 60, 61, 63, 65-69 | 89-94, 99 | 54–57, 60, 62, 64, 67–70 | 44 |
| Formulates operational definitions | 6, 7, 8 | 13-15, 17, 19, 20, 24-27 | 55, 59-61, 66, 67 | 93 | 50, 53, 55, 59, 60, 62–64, 67, 68 | 30 |
| Listens to others | 1-11 | 12-15, 17, 19, 20, 22, 24-29 | 55-64, 66, 68-71 | 89-96, 98-101 | 50–57, 60, 62, 63, 65, 67–70 | 67 |
| Works collaboratively | 1-11 | 12-15, 17-20, 22, 24-29 | 54-59, 62, 64, 65-70 | 90-96, 98-100 | 50–57, 60–63, 65, 67–70 | 66 |
| Keeps a science journal | 1-11 | 12-20, 22, 24, 26-28 | 54-71 | 89-101 | 50, 51, 53–56, 64–70 | 68 |
| Total Opportunities to Practice Skills | 72 | 133 | 128 | 92 | 139 | 564 |

## INFORMATION ORGANIZING AND PROCESSING SKILLS

| | Unit A Studying Materials Scientifically | Unit B The Chemistry of Materials | Unit D Genetics | Unit F Evolution | Unit E Weather and Atmosphere | Total Opportunities to Practice Skills |
|---|---|---|---|---|---|---|
| Categorizes/ sorts information | 2, 6-11 | 12-15,18-22, 26-29 | 59-62, 65-70 | 89-100 | 50–54, 56, 57, 59, 60, 62-70 | 60 |
| Sequences information | 8 | 13 | 57, 58, 63, 69 | 89, 91-96, 98, 99 | | 30 |
| Summarizes information | 2, 11 | 12-14, 18-22, 26-29 | 54, 56-62, 64, 66-71 | 89-96, 98-101 | | 41 |
| Differentiates observations/ inferences | 3 | | 58, 64, 66 | 90, 91, 93, 101 | | 16 |
| Differenti- ates evidence/ opinion | 6, 7, 11 | 18, 24, 26, 29 | 60, 67-71 | 99, 100 | | 15 |
| Draws/ analyzes con- cept maps | | | | 97 | | 1 |
| Creates/ uses other graphic organizers | 2 | 13, 15 | 57, 61, 62, 66, 67 | 94 | | 9 |
| Total Opportunities to Practice Skills | 15 | 32 | 43 | 41 | 18 | 149 |

## LABORATORY/MATH SKILLS

| | Unit A Studying Materials Scientifically | Unit B The Chemistry of Materials | Unit D Genetics | Unit F Evolution | Unit E Weather and Atmosphere | Total Opportunities to Practice Skills |
|---|---|---|---|---|---|---|
| Uses tools correctly | 6-11 | 14, 18, 19, 24-28 | 54, 55, 62, 64 | 90, 92 | 55, 59 ,61, 63, 67 | 25 |
| Uses apprprte. tools to measure | 6-11 | 18, 19, 24-27 | 54 | 92, 93, 99 | 51, 55, 58, 61, 63, 67 | 22 |
| Uses SI measurements | 8-10 | 18, 19, 25 | 54 | 92, 93, 99 | 50–57, 61, 63 | 20 |
| Calculates mean, median, mode | | | | | 51, 54, 64 | 3 |
| Determines a scale | | 24 | 54, 62, 64 | 92, 95, 96 | | 7 |
| Uses graphs appropriately | | 12, 22 | 54 | 95, 96, 98 | 51–53, 55, 70 | 11 |
| Follows procedures | 2, 5-10 | 14, 18, 19, 22, 24-28 | 54-59, 61, 64-70 | 90-96, 98, 99 | 51–55, 58, 61–65, 67-70 | 54 |
| Total Opportunities to Practice Skills | 22 | 29 | 24 | 23 | 44 | 142 |

## COMPUTER SKILLS

| | Unit A Studying Materials Scientifically | Unit B The Chemistry of Materials | Unit D Genetics | Unit F Evolution | Unit E Weather and Atmosphere | Total Opportunities to Practice Skills |
|---|---|---|---|---|---|---|
| Gathers information or conducts research | | 13, 15, 16 | 56-59, 62, 64, 67, 69, 71 | 89, 99, 101 | 51, 61, 64, 68, 70 | 20 |
| Uses a simulation of scientific phenomena | | | 57, 61, 63 | | 64, 68 | 5 |
| Total Opportunities to Practice Skills | 0 | 3 | 12 | 3 | 7 | 25 |

# ISSUES
# & Physical Science

## STUDYING MATERIALS SCIENTIFICALLY

SCIENCE™
EDUCATION FOR
PUBLIC
UNDERSTANDING
SEPUP PROGRAM

UNIVERSITY OF CALIFORNIA AT BERKELEY
LAWRENCE HALL OF SCIENCE

## LAB-AIDS®
INCORPORATED
RONKONKOMA, NEW YORK

This book is part of SEPUP's middle school science course sequence:

## Issues and Earth Science

Studying Soils Scientifically
Rocks and Minerals
Erosion and Deposition
Plate Tectonics
Weather and Atmosphere
The Earth in Space
Exploring the Solar System

## Issues and Life Science

Experimental Design: Studying People Scientifically
Body Works
Cell Biology and Disease
Genetics
Ecology
Evolution
Bioengineering

## Issues and Physical Science

Studying Materials Scientifically
The Chemistry of Materials
Water
Energy
Force and Motion

**Additional SEPUP instructional materials include:**
CHEM-2 (Chemicals, Health, Environment and Me): Grades 4–6
SEPUP Modules: Grades 7–12
*Science and Sustainability*: Course for Grades 9–12
Science and Global Issues Biology: Course for Grades 9–12

 This material is based upon work supported by the National Science Foundation under Grants No. 9252906 and No. 0099265. Any opinions, findings, and conclusions or recommendations expressed in this material are those of the authors and do not necessarily reflect the views of the National Science Foundation.

*For photo and illustration credits, see page A-54, which constitutes an extension of this copyright page.*

**SEPUP**
Lawrence Hall of Science
University of California at Berkeley
Berkeley CA 94720-5200

e-mail: sepup@berkeley.edu
Website: www.sepuplhs.org

Published by:

INCORPORATED

17 Colt Court
Ronkonkoma NY 11779
Website: www.lab-aids.com

## A Letter to *Issues and Physical Science* Students

As you examine the activities in this book, you may wonder, "Why does this book look so different from other science books I've seen?" The reason is simple: it is a different kind of science program, and only some of what you will learn can be seen by leafing through this book!

*Issues and Physical Science* uses several kinds of activities to teach science. For example, you will observe and test the properties of elements and compounds. You will model the atoms and molecules that make up these substances. You will design and conduct investigations to explore energy transfer. You will investigate the motion of a cart on a ramp, and apply what you learn to the physics of automobile accidents and safety features. A combination of laboratories, investigations, readings, models, debates, role plays, and projects will help you uncover the nature of science and the relevance of physical science to your interests.

You will find that important scientific ideas come up again and again in different activities throughout the book. You will be expected to do more than just memorize these concepts: you will be asked to explain and apply them. In particular, you will improve your decision-making skills by using evidence to weigh outcomes and to decide what you think should be done about the scientific issues facing our society.

How do we know that this is a good way for you to learn? In general, research on science education supports it. In particular, the activities in this book were tested by hundreds of students and their teachers, and then modified on the basis of their feedback. In a sense, this entire book is the result of an investigation: we had people test our ideas, we interpreted the results, and we then revised our ideas! We believe the result will show you that learning more about science is important, enjoyable, and relevant to your life.

*SEPUP Staff*

### ISSUES & PHYSICAL SCIENCE PROJECT

Director (2003–2007): Barbara Nagle

Director (2001–2002): Herbert D. Thier

**Unit A Authors**

Manisha Hariani

Sara Dombkowski

Din Seaver

### OTHER CONTRIBUTORS

Lee Trampleasure, Janet Bellantoni, Kathy Burke, Kate Haber, Donna Markey, Barbara Nagle

### CONTENT AND SCIENTIFIC REVIEW

Dr. Tanya Faltens, Lawrence Hall of Science, University of California, Berkeley

### PRODUCTION

Production Coordinator: Ayse Frosina

SEPUP Publications Coordinator: Miriam Shein

Design and Composition: Seventeenth Street Studios

Photo Research: Seventeenth Street Studios

Editing: Trish Beall

Administrative Assistance: Roberta Smith, Ezequiel Gonzalez

### FIELD TEST CENTERS

This course is a revision of *Issues, Evidence and You.* The following centers participated in field testing the original course or the revised materials. We are extremely grateful to the center directors and teachers who taught the program. These teachers and their students contributed significantly to improving the course.

#### IEY CENTERS

*Alaska:* Donna York (Director), Kim Bunselmeyer, Linda Churchill, James Cunningham, Patty Dietderich, Lori Gillam, Gina Ireland-Kelly, Mary Klopfer, Jim Petrash, Amy Spargo

*California–San Bernardino County:* Dr. Herbert Brunkhorst (Director), William Cross, Alan Jolliff, Kimberly Michael, Chuck Schindler

*California–San Diego County:* Mike Reeske and Marilyn Stevens (Co-Directors), Pete Brehm, Donna Markey, Susan Mills, Barney Preston, Samantha Swann

*California–San Francisco Area:* Stephen Rutherford (Director), Michael Delnista, Cindy Donley, Judith Donovan, Roger Hansen, Judi Hazen, Catherine Heck, Mary Beth Hodge, Mary Hoglund, Mary Pat Horn, Paul Hynds, Margaret Kennedy, Carol Mortensen, Bob Rosenfeld, Jan Vespi

*Colorado:* John E. Sepich (Director), Mary Ann Hart, Lisa Joss, Geree Pepping-Dremel, Tracy Schuster, Dan Stebbins, Terry Strahm

*Connecticut:* Dave Lopath (Director), Harald Bender, Laura Boehm, Antonella Bona-Gallo, Joseph Bosco, Timothy Dillon, Victoria Duers, Valerie Hoye, Bob Segal, Stephen Weinberg

*Kentucky–Lexington Area:* Dr. Stephen Henderson and Susie Nally (Co-Directors), Stephen Dilly, Ralph McKee II, Barry Welty, Laura Wright

*Kentucky–Louisville Area:* Ken Rosenbaum (Director), Ella Barrickman, Pamela T. Boykin, Bernis Crawford, Cynthia Detwiler, Denise Finley, Ellen Skomsky

*Louisiana:* Dr. Sheila Pirkle (Director), Kathy McWaters, Lori Ann Otts, Robert Pfrimmer, Eileen Shieber, Mary Ann Smith, Allen (Bob) Toups, Dorothy Trusclair

*Michigan:* Phillip Larsen, Dawn Pickard, and Peter Vunovich (Co-Directors), Ann Aho, Carolyn Delia, Connie Duncan, Kathy Grosso, Stanley Guzy, Kevin Kruger, Tommy Ragonese

*New York City:* Arthur Camins (Director), Eddie Bennett, Steve Chambers, Sheila Cooper, Sally Dyson

*North Carolina:* Dr. Stan Hill and Dick Shaw (Co-Directors), Kevin Barnard, Ellen Dorsett, Cameron Holbrook, Anne M. Little

*Oklahoma:* Shelley Fisher (Director), Jill Anderson, Nancy Bauman, Larry Joe Bradford, Mike Bynum, James Granger, Brian Lomenick, Belva Nichols, Linda Sherrill, Keith Symcox, David Watson

*Pennsylvania:* Dr. John Agar (Director), Charles Brendley, Gregory France, John Frederick, Alana Gazetski, Gill Godwin

*Washington, D.C.:* Frances Brock and Alma Miller (Co-Directors), Vasanti Alsi, Yvonne Brannum, Walter Bryant, Shirley DeLaney, Sandra Jenkins, Joe Price, John Spearman

*Western New York:* Dr. Robert Horvat and Dr. Joyce Swartney (Co-Directors), Rich Bleyle, Kathaleen Burke, Al Crato, Richard Duquin, Lillian Gondree, Ray Greene, Richard Leggio, David McClatchey, James Morgan, Susan Wade

## REVISION CENTERS

*Buffalo, New York:* Kathaleen Burke (Director), Robert Baxter, Robert Tyrell

*Charleston County, South Carolina:* Rodney Moore (Director), Deborah Bellflower, Liz Milliken, Donna Ouzts, Gail Wallace

*Lemon Grove, California:* Samantha Swann (Director), Lyn Ann Boulette, Amber Lunde

*Vista, California:* Donna Markey (Director)

*Winston-Salem/Forsyth County, North Carolina:* Jim Bott (Director), Kathy Boyer, Jason Felten, Bill Martin

# Contents

# Studying
# Materials
# Scientifically

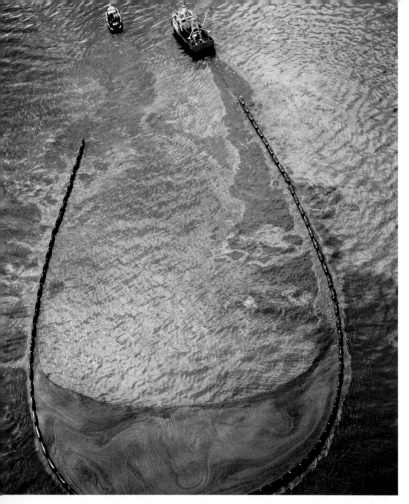

# Studying Materials Scientifically

**K**ai, did you hear about those barrels they found by the baseball field yesterday?"

"No, what happened?" Kai stopped. She had been hurrying to get ready for the baseball game.

"They found barrels full of chemicals near the field, so they cancelled the game," Gabriela grumbled.

"What? I gave up going to the movies so I could play today."

"The town started digging into that empty lot next to the baseball field to build the new playground. When they cleared out the brush and garbage, they found at least ten old corroded barrels full of stuff."

"Do they know what is in them?" asked Kai.

"Nope, so they have to call in a hazardous materials team to open the barrels. I heard my uncle talking about it last night with my Dad. My uncle works for the company that will come in and do the testing," Gabriela continued. "The testing will be done today and thus, the game is cancelled."

"Really, well that's kind of scary," Kai responded. "We have been playing there since we were little. What if the stuff in the barrels is hazardous? How are they going to figure out what it is?"

"I think they'll take samples, and do some tests," said Gabriela.

• • •

Our world is filled with substances. The liquids we drink, air we breathe, and the roads we walk on are all made from different combinations of substances. The substances people use to make products are called materials. Each material has unique properties. For example, we can identify gold by its shiny characteristic metallic color. But how can these properties help to identify unknown samples? In this unit you will look at how substances can be identified based on their chemical and physical properties. You will learn how to handle potentially hazardous substances with care as you study materials scientifically.

VIEW AND REFLECT

**Y**ou *are cleaning out a cabinet at home and you find an old jar filled with what appears to be a mixture of rusty pieces of metal and a thick oily liquid. What should you do? Is it safe to dump it out? How could you figure out what to do with it if you're not sure what it is?*

In this unit you will work with an unlabeled jar filled with a mixture of substances. When you don't know the contents of a container, it is best to assume they are hazardous. **Hazardous materials** (HAZ-ur-dus ma-TEER-ee-uls) are substances that pose a danger to the health and safety of living organisms. They can cause injury or even death. People who are trained to clean up or dispose of hazardous materials are often members of a hazardous materials, or "hazmat," team. Before working with potentially hazardous chemicals in this unit, you will learn how to handle and identify them.

CHALLENGE ⟶ **How should unidentified materials be handled?**

## PROCEDURE

1. Watch a segment about hazardous materials on the SEPUP DVD, "Hazardous Materials."

2. In your science notebook, make a list titled "Handling an Unknown Substance." As you watch the DVD, list the steps the hazmat team takes when approaching and handling the unidentified barrel.

3. Watch the DVD again. Record any additional precautions the hazmat team took that you did not list in your notebook in Step 2.

4. Compare your list with the lists of the other members of your group. As you do this:

   • Listen to and consider the precautions listed by others.

   • If you disagree about a precaution, explain to the rest of the group why you disagree.

5. Add to the list in your notebook any new ideas that your group members proposed.

## ANALYSIS

 1. Based on what you observed on the DVD, make a list of safety precautions you would take if you found a jar of unidentified substances at home.

2. If you found a jar filled with unidentified substances at school, would you handle it differently than you would at home? Add to your list from Question 1 any additional safety precautions you would take.

 3. How could you identify the contents of an unlabeled jar? Explain ways to identify the jar's contents.

4. Could you determine the contents of the unlabeled jar through observation alone? Explain.

---

Key to Analysis Icons

= Answer the question by yourself.

= Discuss with your partner.

= Discuss with your group.

= Discuss the question in class.

If you found an unlabeled container in your home, how would you know whether its contents were hazardous? A hazmat team assumes the contents are hazardous until it identifies the properties of each substance, and you should do the same. Since substances can be hazardous in many different ways, it is important to be prepared for the dangers they pose.

Hazardous materials, like those in the barrel in the last activity, are transported daily throughout the United States. Whenever they are shipped in large volumes, they must be labeled according to their class of hazard, as the U.S. Department of Transportation (D.O.T.) requires.

In science classes you will encounter a variety of potentially hazardous substances. Some are more hazardous than others. To prepare to work with them, you will learn how to choose and use safe methods.

CHALLENGE ⟶ **What types of hazards do certain substances pose?**

*DOT labels posted on vehicles and containers alert people to the dangers of the substances inside.*

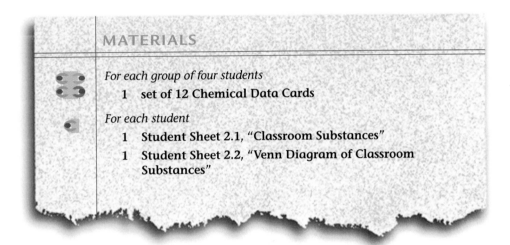

**MATERIALS**

*For each group of four students*

   1   set of 12 Chemical Data Cards

*For each student*

   1   Student Sheet 2.1, "Classroom Substances"

   1   Student Sheet 2.2, "Venn Diagram of Classroom Substances"

## PROCEDURE

1. Look at the table on the next page that shows the labels that the D.O.T. requires on hazardous materials. You may have seen some of these labels on large trucks or on storage containers. Discuss what each label reveals about the material.

2. Divide the set of Chemical Data Cards in half. You and your partner will work with six of the cards.

3. With your partner, read the six cards. Consider places where you might have encountered the substances on each card.

4. Familiarize yourself with each of the substances the cards describe as you fill out Student Sheet 2.1, "Classroom Substances." For each substance, list:

   • The hazard class(es) it belongs to.

   • The safety precautions people should take when using this substance.

5. When you have finished the six cards, switch sets with the other pair in your group and repeat Steps 3 and 4.

6. Work with your group to sort all 12 substances according to the hazard class(es) you assigned to each in Step 4.

7. Record the results of your sorting on Student Sheet 2.2, "Venn Diagram of Classroom Substances."

## Labeling Hazardous Materials

| Class | Label | Description of class | Examples |
|---|---|---|---|
| Biohazard | | Can cause infection or disease in living organisms. | Tools used for medical treatment and procedures, disease-causing microorganisms and viruses |
| Corrosive | | Liquids that chemically wear away at solid materials. | Sulfuric acid, bleach, oven cleaners |
| Explosive | | Materials that cause sudden release of pressure, gas, or heat when exposed to a change in pressure or temperature. | Nitroglycerin, TNT, gases stored under pressure |
| Flammable | | Liquids that catch on fire when exposed to a spark, flame, or heat source. | Gasoline, paint thinner, paints, acetone, ethanol, kerosene |
| Flammable solid | | Materials that ignite in the presence of oxygen or when exposed to water or humidity. | Magnesium metal, sulfur, naphthalene (ingredient in moth balls) |
| Gas | | Gases stored under pressure that are flammable, toxic, or explosive. | Propane, butane |
| Oxidizer (reactive) | | Materials that react chemically to cause other materials to burn. | Hair bleach and laundry bleach products, certain pool chemicals |
| Radioactive | | Materials that release nuclear energy that causes damage to living organisms. | Used or unused nuclear fuel, uranium ore, radon |
| Toxic | | Materials that are poisonous if inhaled, ingested, or absorbed through skin. | Insecticides, brake and transmission fluids, household cleaners |

## ANALYSIS

1. Which substances from Student Sheet 2.1, "Classroom Substances," fall into more than one hazard class?

2. Explain in detail the safety guidelines you would follow when working with potassium hydroxide.

3. Of the substances listed on Student Sheet 2.1, which do you think poses the greatest hazard to the health of humans and animals? Explain.

4. If a shipment of sodium borate were sent to your classroom, which hazard label(s) do you think would be on the box?

PROBLEM SOLVING

When a hazmat team works with an unknown substance, the team first tries to identify it, after taking care of any immediate hazards. The substance could be a **mixture**—a combination of two or more pure substances that can be physically separated. It is essential for the team to know what is in the mixture so that they can determine how to store and dispose of its different substances.

The first step in identifying an unknown substance is to take a sample of each part of the mixture. In this activity, you will design a three-part plan to:

- separate the liquid and solid substances.
- separate the different liquids.
- separate and clean the different solids.

CHALLENGE

**How can you separate the substances in a mixture?**

## MATERIALS

*For each group of four students*

1 plastic cup with lid, containing unidentified mixture
2 pairs of plastic forceps
2 droppers
1 funnel
2 pieces of filter paper
1 metal screen
1 piece of steel wool
1 SEPUP tray
3 small plastic cups with lids
1 cup of water
   paper towels

*For each student*

1 pair of safety goggles

## SAFETY

Wear safety goggles while working with chemicals. Do not touch the mixture or bring it into contact with your eyes or mouth. Keep the lid on the cup. Wash your hands after completing the activity.

## PROCEDURE

1. Your teacher will provide you with a sealed sample of an unidentified mixture. With your group, carefully examine the sample.

2. Record in your science notebook your observations about the mixture and each substance it contains. Be as descriptive as possible.

3. With your group, discuss ways to separate the different substances and the safety precautions you will need to take. Be sure to consider the tools available to you in the materials list.

4. Work with your group to create a procedure for safely separating the substances. In your plan, be sure to:

   • List materials or tools you will use.

   • Explain each step in detail.

   • Describe safety precautions you will take.

5. Record the procedure in your science notebook.

6. Because the solids and liquids were mixed together, the solids may still have some liquid on them. Discuss with your group how you can remove the liquid.

7. Record these additional steps in your science notebook.

8. Obtain your teacher's approval of your plan.

## ANALYSIS

1. Based on your observations, how many substances do you think there are in the unidentified mixture? Explain.

2. Compare your plan with the plans of others in your class. What ideas do they have for separating the substances that you did not think to include in your plan?

3. What safety precautions will you take when separating the mixture?

4. What is the purpose of separating the different substances in the mixture?

5. You are walking down the sidewalk and see a puddle of green, oily liquid on the ground. Could you identify the contents of the puddle through observation alone?

ROLE PLAY

**O**ne way to reduce the risk of household hazardous chemicals is to dispose of them when they are no longer needed. But how can you handle and get rid of them without harming yourself, others, or the environment? In this activity you will read about Hassan, who must decide how to dispose of the contents of an unlabeled jar he found when cleaning at home.

CHALLENGE ⟹ **How should unwanted household hazardous materials be handled?**

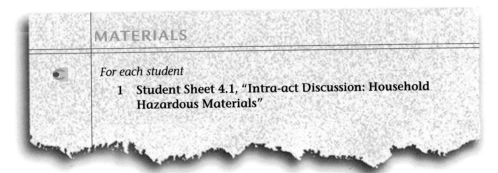

MATERIALS

*For each student*
1 Student Sheet 4.1, "Intra-act Discussion: Household Hazardous Materials"

## PROCEDURE

1. Assign one of the following roles to each person in your group. Note that there are two roles that change from Act 1 to Act 2. Two people should be ready to change to new roles for Act 2.

   Act 1
   - Hassan, a middle school student
   - Mother, head of purchasing for Community Hospital
   - Maya, his 12-year-old sister
   - Grandfather

   Act 2
   - Hassan
   - Mother
   - Mark Chu, Director of Waste Collection Center
   - Karen Greenbach, Environmental Engineer

2. In your group, read the role-play aloud. As you read, think about what each character is saying.

3. With your group, discuss the types of products you might find at home that could pose a hazard.

4. Mark whether you agree or disagree with the statements on Student Sheet 4.1, "Intra-act Discussion: Household Hazardous Materials." Then predict what you think other members of your group will say.

5. Discuss the statements with your group. Have each person share and explain his or her opinion about each statement.

# HAZARDOUS MATERIALS AT HOME

## Act 1: At Hassan's Home

**Mother:** Hassan, did you finish cleaning out the cabinet? I want to put the new cleaning supplies there when you're done.

**Hassan:** Almost. I found this jar filled with oily stuff. I have no idea what it is.

**Grandfather:** The people who lived here before sure left a lot behind. You'd think they were running a chemical factory. What is it?

**Hassan:** I really can't tell. Most of the jars don't have labels, or the labels are so faded I can't read them. This jar is filled with an oily mess with pieces of metal and something else in it.

**Maya:** Can I see?

**Hassan:** Be careful! It might be dangerous. How do you think I should get rid of it?

**Grandfather:** Why don't you just dump it down the drain?

**Maya:** But what if it's hazardous? We learned at school that a lot of the things we buy to clean our homes and take care of our gardens contain chemicals that are bad for us and the environment.

**Mother:** Some household products can be very reactive, toxic, or flammable. At the hospital, I work with other department heads to be sure we make good decisions about the hazardous products we use.

**Hassan:** Why would a store sell cleaning products if they're harmful? They're being diluted with water when you put them down the drain. Doesn't that take away any hazard?

*It is estimated that in most homes in the United States there are 10 to 40 liters (3 to 10 gallons) of hazardous materials in household products.*

**Grandfather:** That's what I think. I always wash everything down the sink, or throw it in the garbage. They treat wastewater don't they? And the garbage is taken to a dump, so what's the harm in that?

**Mother:** All those chemicals dumped down the drain build up. Imagine all the homes around the world over 20 years—that's a lot of cleaning supplies in the water systems. These chemicals can do long-term harm to animals, organisms, and habitats.

**Grandfather:** I've been dumping cleaners down the drain for years.

**Mother:** But now we are more aware of how chemicals can affect us and other organisms. I read an article in last week's newspaper that said it is no longer legal to throw out batteries in the garbage. Batteries have to be recycled by dropping them off at a recycling center.

**Grandfather:** But batteries are made to be disposable. I don't see why they need to be recycled.

**Maya:** We learned about recycling batteries at school. They contain heavy metals that can leak into the ground if they sit in landfills.

**Mother:** *(looking at Grandfather)* That reminds me. Remember how Mama used to take our temperature with a mercury thermometer? It was filled with silvery metal. Once, when the thermometer broke, we played with the little metal beads of mercury liquid. Now liquid mercury is known to be hazardous and is not used in thermometers.

**Grandfather:** Who would have thought that it was harmful? Mercury was used in so many different products like batteries, light switches, and thermometers.

**Mother:** Not anymore. Research has shown that it is toxic. If you're exposed to it for long periods of time, it can affect your nervous system.

**Hassan:** But what should I do with the jar?

**Mother:** We need to figure out what it is. A postcard came in the mail last week announcing a "Household Hazardous Waste Drop-off Day" at the Waste Collection Center. Let's take it there and see if they can help us. We'll drive over after we drop your sister off at soccer practice.

*In 2005, regulations in more than 30 states prohibited throwing batteries in the trash. They can leak toxic chemicals that can harm organisms.*

*Household hazardous waste collection days are a way to safely dispose of latex paint, batteries, and other hazardous substances.*

## Act 2: At the Waste Collection Center

**Director Chu:** How can I help you?

**Hassan:** We'd like to know if we can dump this down the drain to get rid of it.

**Director Chu:** Do you know what it is?

**Hassan:** No, it wasn't labeled.

**Mother:** Hassan found it while he was cleaning out one of our cupboards at home. It looks like it has been there for a long time.

**Director Chu:** It will take some testing, but we will identify what is in it. Then we will know how to dispose of it. This is Karen Greenbach, our environmental engineer, who is an expert on testing methods. *(Turning to Karen)* Karen, we have an unlabeled jar here. Can you help these people?

**Karen Greenbach:** I'd be happy to. We will send it to a lab where it will be separated. Then they will run tests to identify each of the parts.

**Hassan:** If it was bought in a store, wouldn't it be safe to just throw it out?

**Director Chu:** Sometimes the chemicals that are toxic, flammable, or corrosive are what make a product work. There aren't strict regulations about what is put in household products, so it is important to consider what hazards they pose when you are buying, using, and throwing them out.

**Mother:** When people buy products for their homes they usually choose what is most affordable and the best at doing the job. They don't often take into account the health or environmental hazards they might cause.

Director Chu: There have been many cases of people mixing and storing products incorrectly and getting hurt. It's important to know what you're working with and to consider their hazards.

Karen: The next step with your jar will be for us to send it to a lab to determine what is in it. It looks like a mixture of several liquids and some solids.

Hassan: Then what will you do with it once the parts have been identified?

Karen: If it is not hazardous, we will dilute it and pour it down the drain. But if it is hazardous, we will package it and put it in a special hazardous waste land-fill. These sites are made so that hazardous material contained in them will not leak into the ground and groundwater.

Mother: Thank you for helping us.

Hassan: We have to tell Grandpa: No more dumping everything down the drain!

## ANALYSIS

1. In what ways can household products be harmful?

2. Give an example of a product that can no longer be discarded in the garbage. Explain why this is no longer allowed.

3. Where in people's homes do you think they are likely to have the greatest number of potentially hazardous products?

4. **Reflection:** Why do you think there are now more regulations about the use and disposal of hazardous substances than there were 20 to 40 years ago?

## EXTENSION

When is your community holding a hazardous waste drop-off day? See if you can locate information in your area about when and where to take potentially hazardous materials.

LABORATORY

**T**o properly dispose of the unidentified mixture found in the jar, you need to identify the substances it contains. In this activity, you will follow the separation procedure that you developed in Activity 3, "Developing a Separation Plan." Once the substances are separated, you will be able to perform tests to determine the identity of the liquids. Since you do not yet know what the substances are, treat them as if they are hazardous.

CHALLENGE ➡ **How can the substances in the mixture be separated?**

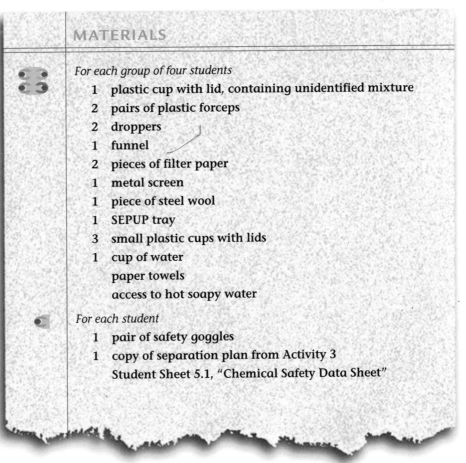

**MATERIALS**

*For each group of four students*

- 1 **plastic cup with lid, containing unidentified mixture**
- 2 **pairs of plastic forceps**
- 2 **droppers**
- 1 **funnel**
- 2 **pieces of filter paper**
- 1 **metal screen**
- 1 **piece of steel wool**
- 1 **SEPUP tray**
- 3 **small plastic cups with lids**
- 1 **cup of water**
  **paper towels**
  **access to hot soapy water**

*For each student*

- 1 **pair of safety goggles**
- 1 **copy of separation plan from Activity 3**
  **Student Sheet 5.1, "Chemical Safety Data Sheet"**

*Identifying an unknown substance in the field often takes several steps to first isolate a sample and identify its contents.*

**SAFETY**

Wear safety goggles while working with chemicals. Clean up any spills immediately. Do not touch the mixture or bring it into contact with your eyes or mouth. Wash your hands after completing the activity.

## PROCEDURE

1. Your teacher will return to you the cup that contains a sample of the unidentified mixture.

2. Review with your group your written procedure for safely separating the parts of the mixture. Be sure you have included all essential safety procedures.

3. Work with your group to follow your procedure to separate the solids from the liquids, and then clean the solids. If you need to change any steps as you work, be sure to record the new steps in your procedure.

4. Place the cleaned, separated solids in a small plastic cup with a lid. You will test them in Activity 7, "Identifying Solids."

5. Separate the liquids, placing them into two separate small plastic cups. You will perform tests in Activity 6, "Identifying Liquids," to find out what the liquids are.

6. For each substance you isolated from the mixture, start an entry on Student Sheet 5.1, "Chemical Safety Data Sheet." You will fill in more information about each substance in future activities.

## ANALYSIS

1. What changes did you have to make to your separation procedure while you were performing the procedure? Why?

2. What safety precautions did you take while working with the unidentified mixture?

3. How would you separate:

   a. oil and vinegar?

   b. salt and iron shavings?

   c. salt and sand?

LABORATORY

**N**ow you will investigate the liquids' physical and chemical properties. **Physical properties** are characteristics that can be observed or measured about a substance without changing it into something else in the process. Color, texture, and appearance are some of the physical properties you will determine in this activity. **Chemical properties** are traits of a substance that you find by seeing if it reacts in certain ways with other chemicals. You will do tests for the chemical properties of corrosiveness and toxicity. Assume the liquids are hazardous until you identify them.

CHALLENGE ⟹ **What are the liquids in the mixture?**

*After an oil tanker accident, the crude oil floats on top of seawater because it is less dense. An inflatable barrier can then be used to separate the oil, which has different properties than the seawater.*

## MATERIALS

*For each group of four students*

1  small cup of Liquid A
1  small cup of Liquid B
1  dropper bottle of ethanol
1  dropper bottle of potassium thiocyanate
2  plastic vials with lids
1  pH color scale

*For each pair of students*

1  pair of plastic forceps
1  dropper
1  SEPUP tray
2  cobalt chloride paper strips
2  pieces of pH paper
   paper towels
   access to hot soapy water

*For each student*

1  pair of safety goggles
   Student Sheet 5.1, "Chemical Safety Data Sheet"

## SAFETY

Wear safety goggles while working with chemicals. Clean up any spills immediately. Do not touch the mixture or any part of it, and do not bring it into contact with your eyes or mouth. Wash your hands after completing the activity.

## PROCEDURE

1. Review the information contained in Table 1, "Tests to Identify Liquids" on the next page. It lists the tests that you will use to gather evidence about the liquids you separated from the mixture. Listen carefully as your teacher demonstrates the procedure for each test.

## Table 1: Tests to Identify Liquids

| Test | Procedure | Interpreting test results |
|------|-----------|---------------------------|
| Appearance | Examine the liquid. Observe its color, transparency, and thickness. | Describe your observations in detail. |
| Miscible in water | 1. Add 50 drops of water to a vial.<br>2. Add 10 drops of the liquid being tested.<br>3. Secure the top on the vial.<br>4. Observe. | If the liquid beads up or forms a separate layer on the top or bottom of the water, it is NOT MISCIBLE in water.<br><br>If the liquid mixes, it is MISCIBLE in water. |
| Miscible in ethanol | 1. Add 50 drops of ethanol to a vial.<br>2. Add 10 drops of the liquid being tested.<br>3. Secure the top on the vial.<br>4. Observe. | If the liquid beads up or forms a separate layer on the top or bottom of the ethanol, it is NOT MISCIBLE in ethanol.<br><br>If the liquid mixes, it is MISCIBLE in ethanol. |
| Contains water | 1. Place a dropperful of the liquid to be tested in a clean cup in the SEPUP tray.<br>2. Dip a piece of cobalt chloride paper into the liquid.<br>3. Remove it, and place it on a paper towel.<br>4. Observe. | If the paper remains blue, water is NOT PRESENT in the liquid.<br><br>If the paper turns pink, water is PRESENT in the liquid. |
| Corrosive | 1. Place a dropperful of the liquid to be tested in a cup in the SEPUP tray.<br>2. Dip a strip of pH paper into the liquid.<br>3. Remove and place it on a paper towel.<br>4. Match the color of the moistened strip to the pH color scale. | If the pH is 3–11, the solution is NOT CORROSIVE.<br><br>If the pH is less than 3 or greater than 11, the solution is CORROSIVE. |
| Toxic | 1. Place a dropperful of the liquid to be tested in a cup in the SEPUP tray.<br>2. Add 1 drop of potassium thiocyanate solution.<br>3. Observe. | If the solution does not turn red, the liquid is NOT TOXIC.<br><br>If the solution turns red, the liquid is TOXIC. |

2. In your notebook, create a table similar to the one shown below, "Properties of Separated Liquids," to record the results of your work.

Properties of Separated Liquids

| Test | Liquid A | Liquid B |
|---|---|---|
| Appearance | | |
| Miscible in water | | |
| Miscible in ethanol | | |
| Contains water | | |
| Corrosive | | |
| Toxic | | |

3. Work with your partner to test the liquids. Record the results of each test in your table.

4. Follow your teacher's directions for cleanup.

## ANALYSIS

1. Look at Table 2, "Information on Selected Liquids," on the next page.

   a. Compare the information from this activity with the information in the table. Look for similarities.

   b. Based on their properties, what are the identities of Liquid A and Liquid B?

   c. Support your answers with at least three pieces of evidence for each liquid.

2. Based on the information in Table 2, would you label Liquid A or Liquid B from the mixture as hazardous?

3. Using evidence from this activity, add the following to Student Sheet 5.1 for Liquid A and Liquid B:

   a. The name of the liquid you identified.

   b. Under "Hazards," write yes or no for those categories that apply.

## Table 2: Information on Selected Liquids

| Type of liquid | Appearance | Miscible in water | Miscible in ethanol | Contains water | Corrosive | Flammable | Toxic |
|---|---|---|---|---|---|---|---|
| **Iodine solution** (used in disinfectants) | Transparent, yellow to brown liquid | Yes | Yes | Yes | Not corrosive | Not flammable | Toxic |
| **Iron nitrate solution** (used in garden fertilizers, vitamins) | Transparent, orange liquid | Yes | Yes | Yes | Corrosive | Not flammable | Toxic |
| **Isooctane** (used in fuels) | Transparent, colorless liquid | No | No | No | Not corrosive | Flammable | Toxic |
| **Lauric acid solution** (used in soaps and shampoo) | Transparent, colorless liquid | No | Yes | No | Not corrosive | Flammable | Slightly toxic |
| **Mineral oil** (used in furniture oils, baby oils, cleaning products) | Transparent, colorless to pale yellow liquid | No | No | No | Not corrosive | Flammable | Not toxic |
| **Citric acid solution** (used in foods, household cleaners) | Transparent, colorless or pale yellow liquid | Yes | Yes | Yes | Slightly corrosive at very high concentrations | Not flammable | Not toxic |

**LABORATORY**

**N**ow you will test and identify the solid substances. The solids appear to be metal and plastic, but you need more information to determine what they are made of. The tests that you used for identifying the liquids do not help to identify solids. So in this activity, you will perform a set of different tests to determine the physical and chemical properties of the solids. This information will help you identify the solids. Assume the solids are hazardous until you identify them.

**CHALLENGE** ⟹ **What are the solids in the mixture?**

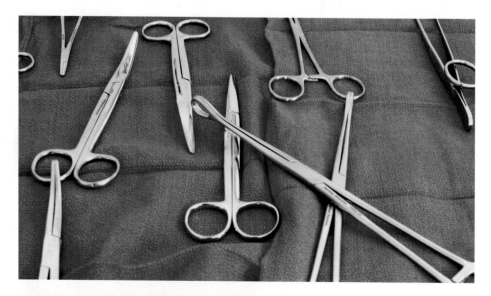

*Easy-to-rip candy wrappers and durable surgical scissors are both made of silver-colored metal. However, the unique physical properties of the metals are quite different and, as a result, the scissors are much stronger than the wrapper.*

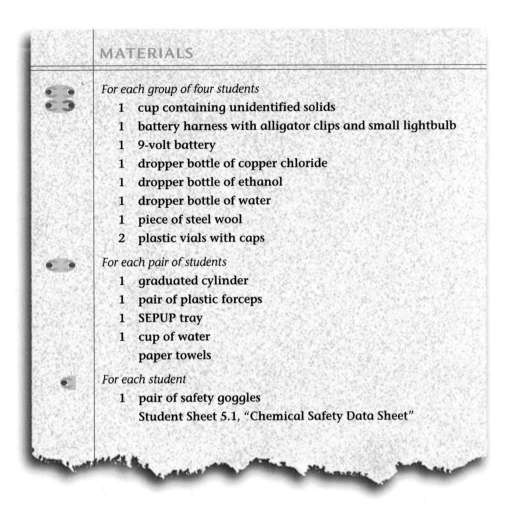

## MATERIALS

*For each group of four students*

1  cup containing unidentified solids
1  battery harness with alligator clips and small lightbulb
1  9-volt battery
1  dropper bottle of copper chloride
1  dropper bottle of ethanol
1  dropper bottle of water
1  piece of steel wool
2  plastic vials with caps

*For each pair of students*

1  graduated cylinder
1  pair of plastic forceps
1  SEPUP tray
1  cup of water
   paper towels

*For each student*

1  pair of safety goggles
   Student Sheet 5.1, "Chemical Safety Data Sheet"

*Scientists can identify types of rock from the moon, based on their chemical and physical properties.*

### SAFETY

**Wear safety goggles while working with chemicals. Clean up any spills immediately. Do not touch the mixture or any parts of the mixture, and do not bring them into contact with your eyes or mouth. Wash your hands after completing the activity.**

## PROCEDURE

1. Review the information contained in Table 1, "Tests to Identify Solids." It describes tests that you will use to gather evidence about the solids you separated from the mixture. Listen carefully as your teacher demonstrates the procedure for each test.

2. In your notebook, create a table similar to "Properties of Separated Solids," shown below. Decide with your class what you will call each type of solid. Record these names in the top row of your table.

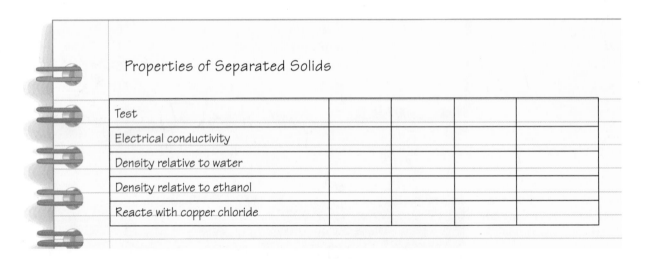

Properties of Separated Solids

| Test | | | | |
|------|---|---|---|---|
| Electrical conductivity | | | | |
| Density relative to water | | | | |
| Density relative to ethanol | | | | |
| Reacts with copper chloride | | | | |

3. Be sure each solid is prepared for testing. If a solid has a coating, gently clean the surface with steel wool, rinse it, and dry it well.

4. Work with your partner to test one of the solids. Record the results of each test in your table.

5. Rinse and dry each solid, and place it back in its container.

6. Work with your partner to repeat Steps 4 and 5 for each type of solid from the mixture.

7. Follow your teacher's directions for cleanup.

## Table 1: Tests to Identify Solids

| Test | Procedure | Interpreting test results |
|---|---|---|
| Electrical conductivity | 1. Snap the battery into the battery harness with lightbulb.<br>2. Attach the clips on opposite ends of the solid being tested.<br>3. Observe the bulb. | If the bulb does not light, the material does NOT CONDUCT electricity.<br><br>If the bulb lights, the material CONDUCTS electricity. |
| Density relative to water | 1. Put 5 mL of water into a vial.<br>2. Gently place the solid being tested in the vial.<br>3. Secure the cap on the vial and gently shake.<br>4. Observe. | If the solid floats, it is LESS DENSE than water.<br><br>If the solid sinks, it is MORE DENSE than water. |
| Density relative to ethanol | 1. Put 5 mL of ethanol into a vial.<br>2. Gently place the solid being tested in the vial.<br>3. Secure the cap on the vial and gently shake.<br>4. Observe. | If the solid floats, it is LESS DENSE than ethanol.<br><br>If the solid sinks, it is MORE DENSE than ethanol. |
| Reacts with copper chloride | 1. Place the solid being tested in a cup of the SEPUP tray.<br>2. Place 5 drops of copper chloride on the solid.<br>3. Observe for signs of chemical reaction.<br><br>Signs of a reaction may include a color change, bubbling, temperature change, or precipitate forming.<br><br>Note: If a reaction does occur, use the forceps to dip the solid in water to stop the reaction. | If no signs of a reaction are visible, the solid does NOT REACT with copper chloride.<br><br>If one or more signs of a reaction are visible, the solid REACTS with copper chloride. |

## ANALYSIS

1. Look at Table 2, "Information on Selected Solids," on the next page.

   a. Compare your data with the information in the table. Look for similarities.

   b, Based on their properties, what are the solids?

   c. Support your answer with at least three pieces of evidence for each solid.

2. Were you able to identify what material each solid was made of? Explain.

3. In this activity you performed four tests on each solid. List which test(s) identified:

   a. physical properties of the solids?

   b. chemical properties of the solids?

4. Using evidence from this activity, add the following to Student Sheet 5.1 for each type of solid:

   a. The name of the solid material you identified.

   b. Under "Hazards," write yes or no for those categories that apply.

5. You have been asked to submit a report to your state's Hazmat Training Center explaining the safety procedures you followed while identifying the solids. Write a letter to the hazmat director that explains:

   a. all safety steps taken during this activity.

   b. why each was necessary.

*This equipment, including a meter, is being used to test the conductivity of a sample. Which materials from Table 3 would you predict conduct electricity?*

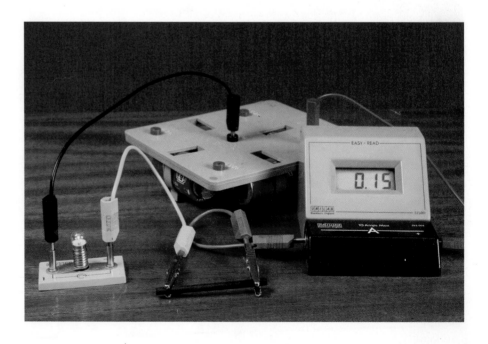

## Table 2: Information on Selected Solids

| Type of solid | Physical description | Conducts electricity | Density relative to water | Density relative to ethanol | Reacts with copper chloride | Hazards |
|---|---|---|---|---|---|---|
| **Plastics** | | | | | | |
| High-density polyethylene (HDPE) | Plastic, produced in different colors, shapes, and sizes | No | Floats | Sinks | No | None |
| Polystyrene (PS) | Plastic, produced in different colors, shapes, and sizes | No | Sinks | Sinks | No | None |
| Polyvinyl chloride (PVC) | Plastic, produced in different colors, shapes, and sizes | No | Sinks | Sinks | No | None |
| **Metals** | | | | | | |
| Aluminum | Silver gray metal | Yes | Sinks | Sinks | Yes | None |
| Beryllium | Silver gray metal | Yes | Sinks | Sinks | Yes | Toxic |
| Iron | Silver gray metal | Yes | Sinks | Sinks | Yes | None |
| Magnesium | Silver gray metal | Yes | Sinks | Sinks | Yes | Flammable |
| Zinc | Silver gray metal | Yes | Sinks | Sinks | Yes | Flammable, toxic |

LABORATORY

**H**ow much space does each of the substances in the unlabeled mixture occupy? One way to describe this is to measure each substance's volume. **Volume** is the amount of space a material takes up. The material can be a solid, liquid, or a gas. You use volume measurements in your daily life to describe amounts of things such as one gallon of gas, two liters of soda, or one quart of milk. The metric system units scientists use to measure volume are the liter (L) and the cubic meter ($m^3$). Smaller volumes are often measured in milliliters (mL) or cubic centimeters ($cm^3$). The table on the next page shows metric units used to measure mass, length, and volume that you will use in this unit along with the English units commonly used in the United States.

In this activity, you will focus on measuring the volume of solid objects using two different methods—measurement and calculation and water displacement. This will prepare you to determine the volume of the metallic solids from the mixture.

CHALLENGE

**How do you measure the volume of a solid object?**

*What volume of liquid is currently in the measuring cup? This glass measuring cup, commonly found in home kitchens, measures volume in both English and metric units.*

## Units of Measurement

|  | Common metric units | Common English units |
|---|---|---|
| Length | Centimeter (cm)<br>Meter (m)<br>Kilometer (km) | Inch (in)<br>Foot (ft)<br>Yard (yd)<br>Mile (Mi) |
| Mass | Gram (g)<br>Kilogram (kg) | Ounce (oz)<br>Pound (lb) |
| Volume | Milliliter (ml)<br>Liter (l)<br>Cubic centimeter (cm$^3$)<br>Cubic meter (m$^3$) | Cup (c)<br>Quart (qt)<br>Gallon (g) |

## MATERIALS

*For each group of four students*

1  set of six objects:
   light gray cube
   dark gray cube
   light gray cylinder
   dark gray cylinder
   light gray bar
   dark gray bar

*For each pair of students*

1  pair of plastic forceps
1  50-mL graduated cylinder
1  pipette
1  calculator
   supply of water
   paper towels

*For each student*

1  pair of goggles
1  metric ruler
   Student Sheets 8.1a and 8.1b, "Two Methods to Measure Volume"

### SAFETY

**Review the Procedure and decide on appropriate safety measures for working with the unknown solids. If you do not know what material an object is made from, assume it is hazardous until you prove otherwise.**

## PROCEDURE

1. Record on Student Sheet 8.1a, "Two Methods to Measure Volume," the letter on your group's cup of objects.

2. Remove the six objects from the cup so that you can observe each one.

3. Predict the order of the six objects from least to greatest volume. Record your predicted order in your notebook.

4. Watch your teacher demonstrate how to measure the volume of an object using two methods:
   - measurement and calculation
   - water displacement

5. Divide the six objects into two sets so that each pair in your group gets either the light gray set or the dark gray set. Each pair will begin by measuring the volumes of the three objects in one set.

6. Decide which method listed in Step 4 above is best for determining the volume of each object.

7. Determine the volume of each object. Record your data and calculations on Student Sheet 8.1b.

8. Exchange objects with the other pair of students in your group, and repeat Steps 6 and 7.

9. Compare your data for each object with the results found by the other pair of students in your group. If you think any of your results are inaccurate, repeat your measurements and calculations.

10. Based on your data, list the six objects from least to greatest volume. Record the measured volume of each of the six objects in your notebook.

## ANALYSIS

1. Choose one of the objects from Student Sheet 8.1b. Which method—water displacement or measurement and calculation—did you use to determine its volume? Explain why you chose that method.

2. Look at the way you ordered the objects by volume in Step 3. Compare this with the measured volumes you recorded in your notebook in Step 10. Were they the same? Explain.

3. Copy the three lists of measurements shown below. Pay close attention to the units that follow each number.

    | List 1 | List 2 | List 3 |
    |--------|--------|--------|
    | 150 mL | 2 mL | 1 L |
    | 11 mL | 801 mL | 999 mL |
    | 200 mL | 27 $cm^3$ | 998 $cm^3$ |

    a. Cross out the smallest volume in each list.

    b. Circle the largest volume in each list.

4. How would you measure the volume of:

    a. a cardboard shoebox?

    b. a plastic pen?

    c. an irregularly shaped stone?

    d. a child's wooden block?

    e. some orange juice?

    f. the two metallic solids from your mixture?

5. In this activity, you were working with unidentified materials. Explain the safety steps you took when working with the solids.

6. How would you explain volume to a 10-year-old?

    - Include at least two examples that would be familiar to a child and that would clarify your explanation.

    - Include a diagram to help you explain your ideas.

LABORATORY

**D**ensity is a physical property that describes the mass of a substance per unit of volume. It is one of many physical properties of a substance that can be useful when trying to identify what a substance is made from. In previous activities you determined whether substances were more or less dense than water, alcohol, and saltwater. This was comparison of one substance to another. But to calculate the exact density of a material, it is necessary to make measurements of a substance's mass and volume. Then you can calculate density by using the following formula:

$$\text{Density} = \frac{\text{mass}}{\text{volume}}$$

You now know how to measure volume. Once you have also measured an object's mass, you can calculate its density. The **mass** of an object describes how much matter is in the object. An object with greater mass has more matter than an object with less mass. Mass is measured in the metric unit grams (g), or related units such as kilograms (kg).

In this activity you will measure mass so that you can calculate the density of different materials. This is determining **quantitatively** (kwan-ta-TAY-tive-lee)—with numbers. Because pure substances have characteristic densities, you can use the calculated density to identify the type of material an object is made from.

CHALLENGE   ➡    **How can you use the mass and volume of an object to calculate its density?**

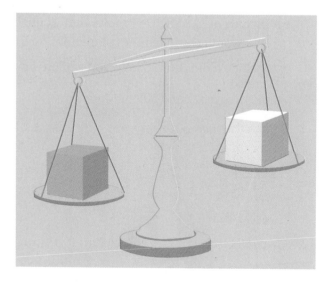

*The objects on the balance have the same volume, but different masses.*

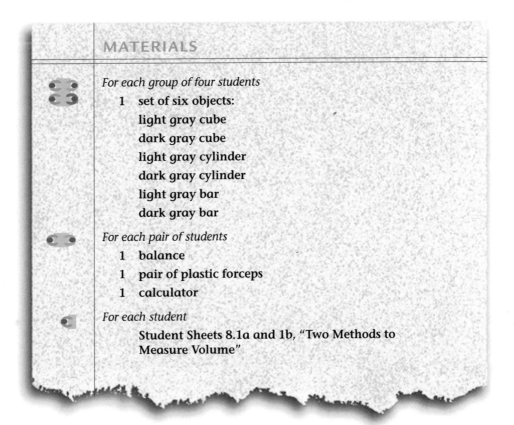

**MATERIALS**

*For each group of four students*
1 set of six objects:
   light gray cube
   dark gray cube
   light gray cylinder
   dark gray cylinder
   light gray bar
   dark gray bar

*For each pair of students*
1 balance
1 pair of plastic forceps
1 calculator

*For each student*
   Student Sheets 8.1a and 1b, "Two Methods to Measure Volume"

## SAFETY

Review the procedure, and decide on appropriate safety measures for working with the unknown solids. If you do not know what material an object is made from, assume it is hazardous until you prove otherwise.

## PROCEDURE

### Part A: Measuring Mass

1. Obtain the same set of objects you used in Activity 8, "Measuring Volume."

2. In your science notebook, create a data table similar to Table 1, "Mass, Volume, and Density of Six Objects," on the next page. You will use it to record your data and calculations.

3. Divide the six objects into two sets so that each pair in your group has either the light gray set or the dark gray set. Each pair will begin by determining the masses of the three objects in one set.

4. Use a balance to find the mass of each object to the nearest 0.1 gram (g). Record your data in your table.

5. Exchange objects with the other half of your group, and repeat Step 4.

## Part B: Calculating Density

6. In Table 1, record the volume of each object from Student Sheet 8.1b, "Two Methods to Measure Volume."

7. Work with your partner to calculate the density of each object, dividing its mass by its volume. Record this data in your table.

$$\text{Density} = \frac{\text{mass}}{\text{volume}}$$

8. Compare your results with the results of the other pair of students in your group. If you think any of your results are inaccurate, repeat your measurements and your calculations.

Table 1: Mass, Volume, and Density of Six Objects

| Object | Mass (g) | Volume (cm³ or mL) | Density calculation | Density (g/cm³ or g/mL) |
|---|---|---|---|---|
| Light gray bar | | | | |
| Dark gray bar | | | | |
| Light gray cube | | | | |
| Dark gray cube | | | | |
| Light gray cylinder | | | | |
| Dark gray cylinder | | | | |

## Part C: Using Density to Identify Materials

9. Now that you have calculated the density of several objects, you will use this to identify the material each of the objects is made from. In your science notebook, make a table similar to Table 2, "Identifying Objects' Material Using Density."

Table 2: Identifying Objects' Material Using Density

| Name of object | Density calculated | Closest density from Table 3 | Object's material |
|---|---|---|---|
|  |  |  |  |

10. In your new table, fill in the name and density calculated for each object from Table 1, "Mass, Volume, and Density of Six Objects."

11. Compare the densities you calculated in Table 2 with the densities shown in Table 3, "Densities of Selected Solids," on the next page. Find the density closest to the density of each object, and enter that in Table 2.

12. Identify the material that might make up each of the six objects.

    Hint: Look for the material that has a density closest to the density that you determined for each object. Write the density and the material of this object in Table 2.

*This bowling ball and balloon have very similar volumes, but because the bowling ball has more mass per volume, it is more dense.*

## ANALYSIS

1.  What material is each metallic solid made of? Use data from this activity to support your explanation.

2.  Now that you have identified what each solid is made of, look at the hazards for each in Table 2, "Information on Selected Solids," in Activity 7. What safety precautions must you take when working with these materials?

3.  A block of wood is 4 cm wide, 5 cm long, and 10 cm high. It weighs 100 grams.

    a.  Calculate its volume.

    b.  Calculate its density.

    c.  Will the block sink or float in water? Explain. (Remember, the density of water is 1.0 g/cm³.)

    d.  Imagine cutting the block into two exactly equal halves. Calculate the volume, mass, and density of each piece.

    e.  How do the densities of the new pieces compare with the density of the original block? Use your answer to Question 3d and a diagram to illustrate your answer.

| Table 3: Densities of Selected Solids | |
|---|---|
| **Type of solid material** | **Density (g/cm³)** |
| **Plastics** | |
| High-density polyethylene (HDPE) | 0.95 |
| Polystyrene (PS) | 1.1 |
| Polyvinyl chloride (PVC) | 1.3 |
| **Metals** | |
| Magnesium | 1.7 |
| Beryllium | 1.9 |
| Aluminum | 2.7 |
| Titanium | 4.5 |
| Zinc | 7.1 |
| Iron | 7.9 |
| Tungsten | 19.4 |

In Activity 9, "Measuring Mass, Calculating Density," you saw that determining the density of an object can help determine the material it is made from. In this activity, you will use density to identify the remaining two unknown metallic solids you separated from the unidentified mixture. Once you have identified the parts of the mixture, you will use the information you collected to create a hazard label for it.

**CHALLENGE**

**How can you use density to identify solids?**

*Density is one of the many properties of materials that can be found in reference tables.*

## MATERIALS

*For each group of four students*

1 cup containing metallic solids separated from the mixture in Activity 5, "Separating the Mixture"

*For each pair of students*

1 50-mL graduated cylinder
1 metric ruler
1 cup of water
1 pair of plastic forceps
1 pipette
1 calculator
1 balance
paper towels
1 Material Safety Data Sheet (MSDS) booklet

*For each student*

1 pair of safety goggles
Student Sheet 10.1, "More Density Data"
Student Sheet 5.1, "Chemical Safety Data Sheet"
Table 3, "Densities of Selected Solids" from Activity 9

### SAFETY

Review the procedure, and decide on appropriate safety measures for working with the unknown solids.

## PROCEDURE

### Part A: Identify Solids Using Density

1. Look at the two metallic solids you separated from the unlabeled mixture. Discuss with your partner how to best calculate the density of the metal solids. Be sure to consider the tools included in the materials list.

2. Work with your partner to create a procedure for determining the density of each solid. In your plan, be sure to:

   • List the materials or tools you will use.

   • Explain each step in detail.

   • Describe safety precautions you will take.

3. Record the procedure in your science notebook.

Data for Two Metallic Solids

| Name of object | Mass (g) | Volume (cm³ or mL) | Density (g/cm³ or g/mL) | Object's material |
|---|---|---|---|---|
| | | | | |
| | | | | |

4. Make a data table similar to the one above. You will use it to record your data during your investigation.

5. Obtain your teacher's approval of your plan.

6. With your group, decide which pair will work with which object first.

7. Conduct your investigation for that object, and record your results in your data table. Be sure to include units of measurement for each measurement you record.

8. Switch objects with the other pair in your group. Repeat Step 7.

9. Compare your density calculations with those of the other pair in your group. Are your measurements the same? If not, perform additional calculations to verify the density of each solid.

10. Use the densities you calculated to determine the material each object is made of. To do this:

   a. Look at the information in Table 3, "Densities of Selected Solids," on page A-40 in Activity 9.

   b. Find the density in the table that is closest to the density you calculated for each solid.

   c. Record the name of the material in the column, "Object's material."

## Part B: More Density Data

11. Look at Student Sheet 10.1, "More Density Data." The data shown was measured by a lab that made additional measurements of the two metallic pieces from the mixture. The lab took several mass and volume measurements using instruments with more precision.

12. Using the mass and volume measurements on Student Sheet 10.1, calculate the density for each set of data. Record your answers on Student Sheet 10.1.

13. Compare the densities determined by the lab with your measurements from "Data for Two Metallic Solids." With your group, determine the amount of variation, and discuss the reasons for the variations.

14. Using both the data on Student Sheet 10.1, and your measurements, identify the material each metallic piece is made from. To do this, look once again at the density values, "Densities of Selected Solids," on page A–40 in Activity 9. Use this information to determine the type of materials the objects are made from.

### Part C: Constructing a Label for the Unlabeled Mixture

15. With your partner, make a label for the unlabeled mixture.

16. As you design a label, consider:

    a. What information from your Chemical Data Sheets will you include?

    b. What directions about handling, storage, and disposal of the mixture will you include?

    Note: If you wish to include storage and disposal guidelines on your label, refer to the Material Safety Data Sheet booklet for information about each substance.

## ANALYSIS

1. Based on your density calculations and the data on Student Sheet 10.1, what are the two metallic solids from the unlabeled mixture? Provide evidence from the activity to support your answer.

   Hint: Compare values with those listed in "Densities of Selected Solids" on page A-40 of Activity 9.

2. How many substances were in the unlabeled mixture? What were they?

3. Review your answer to Analysis Question 1 in Activity 3, "Plan to Separate the Mixture." How close was your prediction about the number of substances in the unlabeled mixture?

4. **Reflection:** What are the three most important things you learned in this unit about identifying and studying materials scientifically?

*TALKING IT OVER*

**Y**ou are the Safety Officer for Sunnyvale Hospital. Your job responsibilities include monitoring procedures and products used for cleaning the hospital. When you choose cleaning products to be used by the hospital, you must know how they are stored and disposed of, and be aware of any hazards they pose to the cleaning staff who use them daily.

*You have been asked to evaluate information about four window-cleaning products. You will analyze the trade-offs of selecting one product rather than another. This means you will consider the benefits and drawbacks of each and choose one to purchase for the hospital.*

*As you evaluate the products, keep the following in mind:*

- *The glass cleaner you choose will be stored in a locked room that is located next to the hospital's boiler room. This makes the room very warm in winter months.*

- *The cleaner will be kept in a large cabinet that also contains other cleaning products including bleach used to disinfect laundry and hospital surfaces.*

- *The hospital recently started a recycling program. All containers used by the hospital are recycled if possible.*

**CHALLENGE** ➡ **Which glass cleaner will you select for the hospital?**

*Cleaning products are used in homes every day. But when used in different settings, like hospitals, potential hazards may change.*

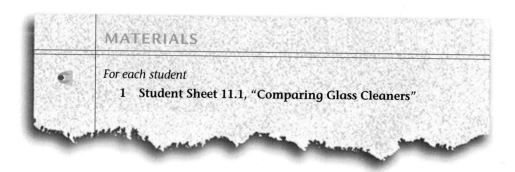

**MATERIALS**

*For each student*

1  **Student Sheet 11.1, "Comparing Glass Cleaners"**

## PROCEDURE

1. On the next page are descriptions of possible ingredients in glass cleaners. Review this information to familiarize yourself with these ingredients.

2. With your group, read the product information provided for each of the four glass cleaners on pages A-48 and A-49. Use this information to help decide which cleaner to select for the hospital. As you read, make a list of the categories of information in the labels.

3. Compare your list with the factors shown in the left-hand column of Student Sheet 11.1, "Comparing Glass Cleaners." If there are factors in your list that are not listed on the student sheet, add them to the left-hand column.

4. Record information about each cleaner on the student sheet. You will use this information to compare the glass cleaners.

5. Decide which of the four glass cleaners you will select for the hospital. Begin by re-reading the introduction to this activity. Based on how the cleaner will be used, stored, and disposed of, decide which three factors are the most important in making your decision. Draw a star to the left of the three factors you selected on the student sheet.

6. With your group discuss which product you will purchase. Consider the evidence and trade-offs for selecting each product. Remember to listen to and consider the ideas of the other members of your group. If you disagree with the other members of your group, explain why you disagree.

## What's in a Cleaner?
### Possible Ingredients in Glass Cleaners

**Ammonia** *(ah-MOAN-ya)* is good at dissolving grease. Because it kills microorganisms it is a disinfectant. If mixed with bleach it releases toxic vapors.

**2-Butoxyethanol** *(2 bew-tox-ee-ETH-an-all)* is a transparent, colorless liquid that has a fruit-like odor. It is a solvent, which dissolves dirt. It is also a disinfectant. It can be listed under several names, including butyl cellusolve, butyl glycol, and butyl oxitol.

**Coloring** is added to make a cleaning product pleasing to the eye. Coloring does not add to the cleaning ability of the product.

**Fragrances,** such as pine, lemon, or floral, are sometimes added so the cleaning solution does not have an unpleasant chemical smell, or to help get rid of bad odors in a house or other building. They do not add to the cleaning power of the product.

**Isobutane** *(eye-so-BEW-tane)* is added in aerosol spray cans, not because it helps to rid surfaces of dirt, but because it helps force the cleaning solution out of the spray nozzle. It is very flammable.

**Isopropanol** *(eye-so-PRO-pa-nol)* is a solvent that is good at dissolving grease and disinfecting surfaces. It is the main ingredient in rubbing alcohol.

**Surfactants** *(sur-FAK-tants)* break up the surface tension of water. They are added to cleaners to prevent streaking or spotting as the cleaned surface dries.

**Water** is the main ingredient of most cleaners. It provides a liquid base for the other ingredients.

## ANALYSIS

1. Which cleaner have you selected?

   a. State your decision.

   b. Support your decision with as many pieces of evidence from the activity as you can.

   c. Discuss the trade-offs of your decision.

2. Did the physical characteristics of each product affect your decision? Explain.

3. Which factors were the most important in making your decision? Explain.

**INGREDIENTS:**
ISOPROPANOL 12%
SURFACTANT 10%
WATER 78%

**CLEANING ABILITY:** 80%*
*Based on customer satisfaction surveys.

**COST:** $6.25 FOR 1 GALLON

**ENVIRONMENTAL IMPACT:** MEDIUM

## PRODUCT A: MATERIAL SAFETY DATA SHEET

| Physical Characteristics | Transparent red liquid<br>Floral scent<br>Miscible in water<br>Density 0.99 g/mL | |
|---|---|---|
| **Toxicity** | 1 | **Scale:** 3 – high risk |
| | | 2 – moderate risk |
| **Flammability** | 0 | 1 – slight risk |
| | | 0 – no risk |
| **Warning Label** | Keep out of reach of children. Avoid eye and skin contact. | |
| **Health Effects** | May cause eye and skin irritation. | |
| **First Aid** | **Eye contact:** Flush eyes with water immediately.<br>**Skin contact:** Wash contaminated area thoroughly with soap and water.<br>**Ingestion:** Drink lots of water.<br>If pain or discomfort persists, call a doctor immediately. | |
| **Handling** | It is always good to wear gloves and goggles when handing chemicals. | |
| **Storage** | Keep out reach of children. | |
| **Disposal** | Pour down the drain with plenty of water. Recycle container. | |

## PRODUCT B: MATERIAL SAFETY DATA SHEET

| Physical Characteristics | Transparent colorless liquid in aerosol spray can.<br>Ammonia scent<br>Miscible in water<br>Density 0.99 g/mL | |
|---|---|---|
| **Toxicity** | 1 | **Scale:** 3 – high risk |
| | | 2 – moderate risk |
| **Flammability** | 3 | 1 – slight risk |
| | | 0 – no risk |
| **Warning Label** | **DANGER:** Reacts with chlorine bleach to form toxic gas.<br>**WARNING:** Extremely flammable. Do not use near flames or sparks. Avoid contact with eyes. Breathing of vapors can be toxic. | |
| **Health Effects** | Breathing in vapors can cause irritation of nose and lungs. | |
| **First Aid** | **Eye contact:** Flush eyes with water immediately.<br>**Inhalation:** Move to fresh air.<br>If pain or discomfort persists, call a doctor immediately. | |
| **Handling** | Keep away from eyes. Use in a well-ventilated area. | |
| **Storage** | Store in a cool, well-ventilated area in closed containers away from heat, and open flames. | |
| **Disposal** | Place in trash ONLY if can is empty. | |

**INGREDIENTS:**
AMMONIA 5%
2-BUTOXYETHANOL 5%
ISOBUTANE
(PROPELLANT) 5%
WATER 85%

**CLEANING ABILITY:** 95%*
*Based on customer satisfaction surveys.

**COST:** $10.25 FOR 6 12-OZ CANS

**ENVIRONMENTAL IMPACT:** HIGH

**INGREDIENTS:**

| | |
|---|---|
| ISOPROPANOL | 6% |
| 2-BUTOXYETHANOL | 4% |
| SURFACTANT | 10% |
| WATER | 80% |

**CLEANING ABILITY:** 90%*

*Based on customer satisfaction surveys.

**COST:** $6.65 FOR 1 GALLON

**ENVIRONMENTAL IMPACT:** HIGH

## PRODUCT C: MATERIAL SAFETY DATA SHEET

| | |
|---|---|
| **Physical Characteristics** | Transparent colorless liquid<br>Citrus scent<br>Miscible in water<br>Density 0.99 g/mL |
| **Toxicity** | 1    **Scale:** 3 – high risk |
| **Flammability** | 1    2 – moderate risk<br>1 – slight risk<br>0 – no risk |
| **Warning Label** | **CAUTION:** Slightly flammable. Store away from heat, flame, and sources of sparks. |
| **Health Effects** | Slightly toxic. If ingested, drink lots of water and contact a physician. |
| **First Aid** | **Eye contact:** Flush eyes with water immediately.<br>Ingestion: Drink lots of water.<br>If pain or discomfort persists, call a doctor immediately. |
| **Handling** | Keep away from eyes. |
| **Storage** | Store in a cool, well-ventilated area in closed containers away from heat, and open flames. |
| **Disposal** | Pour down the drain with plenty of water. Recycle container. |

## PRODUCT D: MATERIAL SAFETY DATA SHEET

| | |
|---|---|
| **Physical Characteristics** | White, cloudy liquid<br>Ammonia scent<br>Miscible in water<br>Density 0.90 g/mL |
| **Toxicity** | 1    **Scale:** 3 – high risk |
| **Flammability** | 1    2 – moderate risk<br>1 – slight risk<br>0 – no risk |
| **Warning Label** | **DANGER:** Reacts with chlorine bleach to form toxic gas. |
| **Health Effects** | Slightly toxic. If ingested, drink lots of water, and contact a physician. Inhaling vapors can damage mouth, nose, throat, and lungs. |
| **First Aid** | **Eye contact:** Flush eyes with water immediately.<br>**Inhalation:** Move to fresh air.<br>**Ingestion:** Drink lots of water.<br>If pain or discomfort persists, call a doctor immediately. |
| **Handling** | Avoid contact with eyes. Work with in a well ventilated area. |
| **Storage** | Store in a cool, well ventilated area in closed containers away from heat and open flames. |
| **Disposal** | Pour down drain with plenty of water. Recycle container. |

**INGREDIENTS:**

| | |
|---|---|
| AMMONIA | 10% |
| WATER | 90% |

**CLEANING ABILITY:** 85%*

*Based on customer satisfaction surveys.

**COST:** $6.95 A GALLON

**ENVIRONMENTAL IMPACT:** LOW

# Index

# The Chemistry of Materials

*B*

# The Chemistry of Materials

Janice and her father walked into the cell phone store. It was time to buy new phones. As they headed for the long row of the latest models, she noticed a sign: "Go green! Turn in your old phone and get 15% off a new phone!"

"Wow!" She thought, "I have my old phone, so I can turn it in for recycling. That's an easy 15% discount!"

They continued along the row of phones. The signs for one group displayed a logo with three green arrows in a triangle. It reminded Janice of the recycling symbol on the bottoms of plastic bottles. She noticed that the three phones with this symbol were cheaper than other phones with similar features. "I wonder why these are cheaper?" she asked. Just then the salesperson came by. Janice asked, "Excuse me, could you please tell me what this green symbol means?"

"If a phone carries a green label, it fits green criteria." the salesperson said. "That means that its materials or the way it was manufactured are less harmful to the environment than a standard phone."

"The green phones are so much cheaper than the others!" Janice said in amazement.

"Yes, isn't it great? The government offers lower taxes to electronics companies that meet green standards. They can sell their products for less."

"Yow," thought Janice, "not only do I need to choose a phone, but I have to think about the environment too."

• • •

The scenario you just read about does not exist—yet. When we buy a cell phone, there is no label that describes how much waste, some of it toxic, was created in manufacturing the phone. But should there be? When you buy a new product, do you think about what materials it is made of? How it was manufactured? What will happen to it when you no longer have a use for it? In this unit you will consider these questions as you investigate the chemistry of materials. With this information, you will be able to analyze the environmental impact of a product and decide which products to purchase.

Consider the world around you. The book in your hands, the floor underneath your feet—each is made from a type of material. The word "material" can have several meanings. To a scientist, a **material** is a type of solid matter used to make things. For example, clothing, homes, and computers are all made from different materials. **Materials scientists** and **materials engineers** study materials and design new ones. When they design these materials, some of the things they think about are:

- How will they be used?
- What resources are needed to make them?
- What will happen to them when they are no longer useful?

For example, think about the materials that can be used to make containers for drinks. Until 1947, almost all drink containers in the United States were made of glass. Consumers could return glass milk and soft drink bottles and have their deposits paid back, and the drink bottling companies would clean and refill the bottles to sell again. Today, most drink containers are made mainly of aluminum, plastic, or glass. Each material has particular characteristics, or properties, that make it useful for holding drinks. Each material is made from specific resources and has a set of effects on the environment when it is discarded or recycled.

*You are a materials scientist working for a bottling company. The president of the company has asked you which type of material to use to make containers for a new drink brand. You decide to look for a material that will both work well and have the fewest bad effects on the environment. Should it be aluminum, glass, or plastic? How will you decide? What evidence will you use?*

CHALLENGE **Which is the best material for making a drink container?**

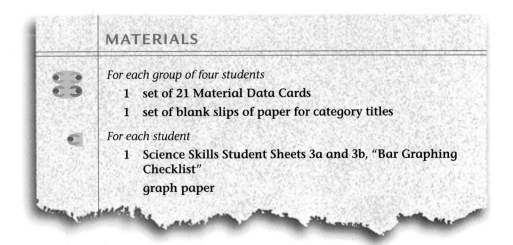

**MATERIALS**

*For each group of four students*

1   set of 21 Material Data Cards

1   set of blank slips of paper for category titles

*For each student*

1   Science Skills Student Sheets 3a and 3b, "Bar Graphing Checklist"

graph paper

## PROCEDURE

1. Prepare a data table for recording the advantages and disadvantages of each of the three materials—aluminum, glass, and plastic. Your table should fill an entire page in your science notebook. Give the table a title.

2. With your group:

   a. List the properties of each of the three materials—aluminum, glass, and plastic.

   b. Decide whether each property is an advantage or disadvantage if you are using the material to make a drink container.

   c. Record in your data table your decision from Step 2b.

3. Spread the Material Data Cards out on a table and read the information on each card.

4. Sort the cards into categories for comparing the three materials.

   • Listen to and consider the explanations and ideas of other members of your group.

   • If you disagree with other members of your group, explain why you disagree.

5. Create a title that describes each category of sorted cards. Write the title of each category on a slip of paper and place it above that group of cards.

6. Compare your categories with those of another group in the class. Discuss any differences in the way they sorted their cards.

7. If necessary, adjust your categories and titles based on your conversation with the other group.

8. Decide if the information on each card is an advantage or a disadvantage of the material it describes. Record these advantages and disadvantages in your data table.

9. Your teacher will assign you one of the categories. Prepare a bar graph comparing the three materials in that assigned category. Be sure to label the axes and title your graph.

## ANALYSIS

1. What two types of information do you think are the most important in deciding which material to use to make drink containers? Explain.

2. What additional information would you like to have about these materials? Explain.

3. Based on the information in your data table, which material is the best for making a drink container, from the viewpoint of each person listed below? Explain your answer for each of these people and support it with evidence from the activity.

    a. a consumer concerned with cost and convenience

    b. an environmentalist concerned with energy usage, litter, and problems with a bottle's impact on the environment

    c. a recycling-center owner who must handle all of the containers turned in for recycling

4. Did the graphs of the data help you make a decision about the advantages and disadvantages of each material? Explain.

5. What do you think is the best material to use to make drink containers? Write a letter or prepare a presentation to the president of the drink company describing your recommendation. Support your answer with evidence and identify the trade-offs of your decision.

READING

**W**hen deciding what material will be used to make a drink container, it can be helpful to think about what is needed to make the container, how it will be made, and what will happen to it when it is no longer being used. All of these stages together are called the **life cycle** of a product. One way of illustrating each stage in the cycle is a **life-cycle diagram.** Materials engineers use life-cycle diagrams when making decisions about a product. These diagrams show how the inputs and outputs from one stage relate to the inputs and outputs of other stages. Life-cycle diagrams can be used to make decisions that reduce the harm that manufacturing and disposing of a product might cause to the environment.

In this activity, you will read about the life cycle of a drink container. Then your group will construct a life-cycle diagram for that type of container. You will then be able to use the life-cycle diagram to determine ways to reduce the harm the container might cause to the environment.

CHALLENGE

**How can a life-cycle diagram be used to make a decision about a product?**

*Products like water bottles are a part of our everyday lives. It takes many steps to manufacture the material and produce the bottle.*

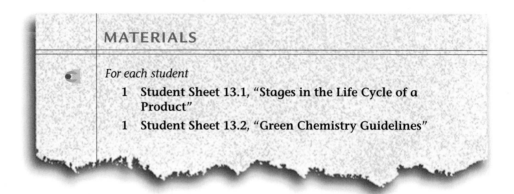

**MATERIALS**

*For each student*

1   Student Sheet 13.1, "Stages in the Life Cycle of a Product"

1   Student Sheet 13.2, "Green Chemistry Guidelines"

## PROCEDURE

1.  The stages in the life cycle of a glass bottle are described below. With your partner, read the description of the stages.

## The Life Cycle of a Glass Bottle

*Raw materials:* Raw materials come from the earth. They are substances that are used to manufacture a product. It takes energy of both humans and machinery to gather or mine raw materials for products. This may include cutting down trees to make paper or mining sand to make glass for a glass bottle.

Glass is a mixture of three main raw materials: silica sand, soda ash, and limestone. Energy to mine, gather, or collect the raw materials are inputs of this stage. These materials are mined from earth's surface. Recycling a product is one way to reduce the amount of new raw materials taken from the earth to produce new products.

*Raw materials of glass: sand, soda ash (sodium carbonate), limestone (calcium carbonate), yellow barium carbonate and brown iron oxide. The last two ingredients are added for color.*

*Manufacturing:* In the manufacturing stage a product or material is created. Raw materials and energy are inputs. To manufacture glass for a glass bottle the three main raw materials, silica sand, soda ash, and limestone, are heated to approximately 1500°C (2700°F) to make a liquid mixture. The molten mixture is then poured into a mold where it cools and becomes solid. Once cooled, the bottle is prepared for use. It is cleaned and, if necessary, a label is printed on it. Then it can be filled and used to hold a drink. The main product of this step is the glass bottle. Other products include the wastewater used to cool the glass, and other wastes that are

2. Your teacher will show and explain a life-cycle diagram that summarizes the stages below.

3. Your teacher will assign you one of the remaining types of drink containers. With your partner, read about the life cycle for the type of container you are assigned. As you read, record information about the life cycle on Student Sheet 13.1, "Stages in the Life Cycle of a Product."

4. Compare the information you have collected on your student sheet with that of the other pair in your group. If there are any differences in the information you have listed, consider adding new information to your sheet.

a result of the manufacturing process.

**Useful life:** During its useful life, the product is used for its intended purpose, or, perhaps, an unintended purpose. Products that are designed from more durable materials will have a longer useful life, reducing the overall energy and resources needed to replace them.

**End of life:** When a product is no longer useful, it is in its end-of-life stage. This is when it is thrown away. There are several end-of-life options for glass bottles. One is to sort discarded glass by color and clean and crush each color of glass separately since each is made by

*A pile of broken glass sitting by the smoke-stack of a recycling plant.*

adding slightly different material when the glass is made. The different pieces of glass can then be melted and reused to manufacture other glass products of the same color, such as brown jars or green bottles. An advantage of recycling glass is that manufactured glass melts at a lower temperature than the raw materials. This can save energy in the next round of manufacturing.

Finding ways to reuse a product extends its life and can reduce the need to make more products.

5. With your group, create a diagram of the life cycle for the drink container you were assigned. The purpose of your diagram is to show the connection between the stages of the life cycle. Decide the best way to illustrate this, and then make the life-cycle diagram on a piece of chart paper. Be sure to include the information you collected on Student Sheet 13.1, "Stages in the Life Cycle of a Product," on your life-cycle diagram.

## The Life Cycle of an Aluminum Can

*Raw materials:* Pure aluminum metal does not occur on the earth's surface. However, compounds that include aluminum are abundant. Aluminum-containing compounds are most easily mined from the earth's surface in a type of rock called bauxite.

Bauxite is ground up and mixed with a hot solution of sodium phosphate. This reaction changes the minerals chemically. Next they are exposed to an electrical current, which chemically changes the compounds into liquid aluminum metal. When the liquid is cooled it is molded into bars of solid aluminum. The process to this point is expensive and uses a large amount of energy. By the early 1900s, manufacturers realized that it is much cheaper to use recycled aluminum than to extract and process aluminum from bauxite.

*Manufacturing:* To produce aluminum cans, aluminum bars are transported to factories. There they are flattened and rolled into thin sheets. The sheets are pressed into cans.

*Useful life:* The useful life of an aluminum can starts when it is labeled, filled and sealed, and shipped to a store.

*End of life:* Once it is empty, the can is no longer useful, and the end-of-life stage begins. It might be recycled or tossed into a trash can to end up in a landfill. If recycled, the metal is crushed and melted to produce sheets of aluminum that can be used for new cans.

*(Above) Aluminum is isolated from bauxite, an ore shown in this photograph. (Below) An aluminum can factory where sheets of metal are cut and formed into cans.*

# The Life Cycle of a Plastic Bottle

*Raw materials:* Plastics are commonly made of hydrogen and carbon compounds called hydro-carbons. Petroleum and crude oil are the raw materials most frequently used to produce them. Oil or gas is pumped from the ground and transported to a processing factory.

Before oil can be used it is heated to temperatures greater than 9080°C (1800°F). This heating causes large molecules in the oil to break apart chemically or "crack" into smaller molecules. Specific types of these smaller molecules are combined with other chemicals, including some for color. At this stage the plastic is a hot liquid. The liquid is cooled to form pellets of plastic, each smaller than a marble.

Materials engineers are inventing ways to make plastics out of non-petroleum-based materials such as plant-derived materials. Drink containers may someday be made out of plant-based plastics.

*Manufacturing:* Next, machinery physically changes the pellets as it melts them and shapes them into plastic rods. The rods are placed into a mold and formed into bottles.

Once the bottles are filled, labeled, and packaged, they are shipped to stores to enter the useful-life portion of the life cycle.

*End of life:* When a plastic bottle has reached the end-of-life stage, one of several things occurs. The plastic may be put into a landfill where it will last for hundreds of years. Or, the plastic bottles can be recycled. If they are to be recycled, the bottles will be sorted (the number in the recycling symbol on the bottom of a bottle indicates its type of plastic). The sorted bottles are cleaned and shredded. The shreds can be reused, but only to make other products. For example, the plastic from water bottles can be recycled to make polar fleece materials for vests and jackets. It cannot be melted at a temperature that will allow it to be formed into new bottles. Other recycled plastics can be used to make detergent bottles, storm drains, paintbrushes, and even carpet fibers. Another end-of-life option is to reuse containers to hold things such as coins, or cooking supplies like flour and sugar. Reusing containers reduces the need for new plastic materials.

*(Above) Pellets can be made in any color. (Below) The bottle on the right was molded from one of the rods shown in the pile.*

## ANALYSIS

1. For the drink container you were assigned:

    a. What are its raw materials?

    b. Does the product have more than one end-of-life option? Explain.

2. Use your life-cycle diagram to explain what would happen to all of the other stages in the life cycle of the drink container if:

    a. the demand for the drink container increases.

    b. the raw materials used to make the product run out.

    c. materials engineers design a way to manufacture the container with less waste produced.

3. Explain why or why not a life-cycle diagram would be a useful tool for:

    a. the director of a drink company who wants to choose a container for a new drink.

    b. a materials scientist working to reduce the negative impact a drink container has on the environment.

    c. a person buying a bottle of sports drink in a store.

4. Look at the life cycle of a product shown on Student Sheet 13.1, "Stages in the Life Cycle of a Product." Using the "Green Chemistry Guidelines" on Student Sheet 13.2, make a list of ways to reduce the negative environmental impact of this product.

5. **Reflection:** Based on what you've learned in this activity, do you think that the life cycle of a product should be included on the label? Explain.

*Compacted bottles are ready for shredding, the next step in the plastic recycling process.*

# EXTENSION

Where do the raw materials come from to make products used in everyday life, such as CDs and plastic bags? What are the life cycles of these products? How many life-cycle stages does a cell phone have? Go to the *Issues and Physical Science* page of SEPUP website for links to the life cycles of different products. Use these and other Internet resources and books to find out about the life cycle of products. Then make a list of the ways to reduce the environmental harm that these products might cause.

LABORATORY

In the last activity, you compared glass, plastic, and aluminum—three materials that can be used to make drink containers. When designing a product, materials engineers consider the properties of materials to determine which is best to use. These properties can be grouped into two categories—physical and chemical. A **physical property** is one that you can identify without seeing if the material reacts with another substance. Examples of physical properties are color, hardness, and density. A **chemical property** describes how a material **reacts** with another substance, such as an acid or oxygen.

In this activity, you will test the physical and chemical properties of a variety of materials. You will then use this information to consider how those materials could best be used to make products.

CHALLENGE > **How do the properties of materials determine their uses?**

*Steel can be formed into many shapes, and is very durable. This makes it ideal for external building supports and stainless steel medical equipment.*

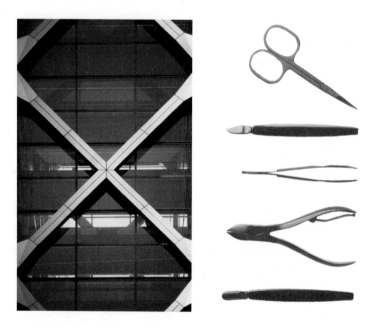

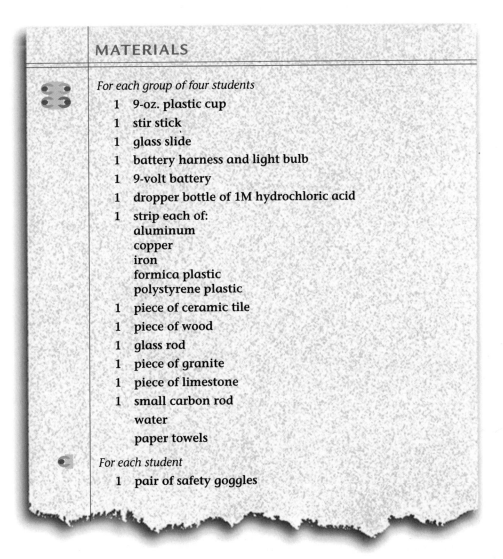

**MATERIALS**

*For each group of four students*

1   9-oz. plastic cup
1   stir stick
1   glass slide
1   battery harness and light bulb
1   9-volt battery
1   dropper bottle of 1M hydrochloric acid
1   strip each of:
    aluminum
    copper
    iron
    formica plastic
    polystyrene plastic
1   piece of ceramic tile
1   piece of wood
1   glass rod
1   piece of granite
1   piece of limestone
1   small carbon rod
    water
    paper towels

*For each student*

1   pair of safety goggles

**SAFETY**

Wear safety eyewear. If a material does not bend easily, do not use more force because you could break or tear it. Watch out for sharp edges.

## PROCEDURE

1.  Review how to test the properties of materials by examining the table, "Testing Physical and Chemical Properties," on the next page.

2.  You will test the properties of 11 materials. Make a data table in your science notebook to record your observations.

3.  Put the materials you have tested into groups based on their properties. Each group must have one, two, or more properties in common. Record your groupings in your science notebook.

## Testing Physical and Chemical Properties

**PHYSICAL PROPERTIES**

| Properties | Procedure | Interpreting test results |
|---|---|---|
| Color | 1. Observe the object material.<br><br>2. Record its color. | Describe your observations in detail. |
| Light transmission | 1. Hold the material above some printed material, such as the facing page.<br><br>2. Observe and record whether you can:<br>• see print clearly through the material.<br>• see the print, but it is blurry.<br>• not see the print. | It is TRANSPARENT if you can see through it clearly.<br><br>It is TRANSLUCENT if the print is blurry.<br><br>It is OPAQUE if you cannot see through it at all. |
| Luster | 1. Hold the material near a good source of light.<br><br>2. Observe how well light reflects off your material.<br><br>3. Record whether it is very shiny, somewhat shiny, or not shiny. | It is BRILLIANT if it reflects a lot of light and is very shiny.<br><br>It is GLASSY if it reflects some light and is somewhat shiny.<br><br>It is DULL if it does not reflect any light and is not shiny. |
| Texture | 1. Feel the material.<br><br>2. Record how it feels. | Describe your observations in detail. Words like *hard, soft, smooth, rough, grainy,* and others can be used to describe the texture of a material. |
| Flexibility | 1. Try to bend the material gently.<br><br>2. Record how easily it bends. | If it does not bend, it is NOT FLEXIBLE.<br><br>If it bends slightly, it is SOMEWHAT FLEXIBLE.<br><br>If it bends easily, it is VERY FLEXIBLE. |
| Hardness relative to glass | 1. Gently press the material across the surface of a glass slide.<br><br>2. If a mark appears, see if you can rub it away.<br><br>3. Record your observations. | If a scratch appears that is not easily rubbed away, the material is HARDER THAN GLASS.<br><br>If no scratch appears, or if the scratch is easily rubbed away, the material is SOFTER THAN GLASS. |

**PHYSICAL PROPERTIES** *(continued)*

| Properties | Procedure | Interpreting test results |
|---|---|---|
| Electrical conductivity | 1. Attach the bulb and battery assembly to opposite ends of the object.<br><br>2. Record whether the lightbulb lights.<br><br>3. Immediately disconnect the battery harness. | If the bulb does not light, the material does NOT CONDUCT electricity.<br><br>If the bulb lights, the material CONDUCTS electricity. |
| Density relative to water | 1. Fill the plastic cup half full of water, and place the material in the cup.<br><br>2. Check to see if the material sinks or floats. With your stir stick, push underwater any material that floats, and see if it returns to the surface.<br><br>3. As soon as you have recorded results, remove and dry the material. | If it floats, it is LESS DENSE than water.<br><br>If it sinks, it is MORE DENSE than water. |

**CHEMICAL PROPERTY**

| Properties | Procedure | Interpreting test results |
|---|---|---|
| Reaction to hydrochloric acid | 1. Place 2–3 drops of 1 M hydrochloric acid (HCl) on each material.<br><br>2. Observe and record the results.<br><br>3. As soon as you have recorded results, rinse the material in water and dry it. | If the material does not bubble or change in any way, it DOES NOT REACT with hydrochloric acid.<br><br>If the material bubbles or changes in any way, it REACTS with the hydrochloric acid. |

## ANALYSIS

1. Were your groupings the same as those of the other students? If they were different, explain how.

2. Should the shape of an object be considered a property of the material? Explain.

3. In this activity, you recorded the color of each material. Think of and explain two cases in which color does not help identify a material.

4. In your science notebook, make a copy of the table, "Selecting Materials for Products," shown below. For each product listed in the first column, complete the table by listing one material you tested that would work well and one that would *not* work well. Explain your reasons for each choice in the appropriate column.

Selecting Materials for Products

| Use of material | Materials that would work well | Reasons | Materials that would NOT work well | Reasons |
|---|---|---|---|---|
| Electrical wire | | | | |
| Garden statue | | | | |
| Toy boat | | | | |
| Tabletop | | | | |
| Inexpensive container for an acid, such as vinegar | | | | |

INVESTIGATION

In the last activity, you grouped selected materials based on their properties. Some of those materials were elements, while others were made of combinations of elements. An **element** is a substance that cannot be broken down into simpler substances by heating it or causing it to react with other chemicals.

Did you know that there are only 90 naturally occurring elements in our world, and scientists have made about 25 more elements in laboratories? That may seem like a lot, but think of it this way: everything—yes, everything—around you is made from one or more of these elements. In this activity you will investigate 14 of the 90 naturally occurring elements and think of ways to group them based on their chemical and physical properties.

CHALLENGE ➡ **How can elements be grouped based on their physical and chemical properties?**

*Samples of elements. Clockwise from upper center, they are chlorine (Cl), sulfur (S), mercury (Hg), copper (Cu), and silicon (Si).*

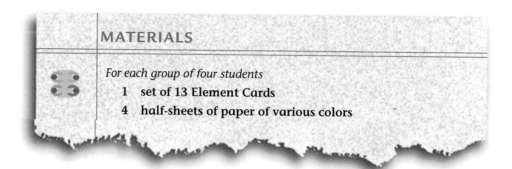

**MATERIALS**

*For each group of four students*
1   set of 13 Element Cards
4   half-sheets of paper of various colors

## PROCEDURE

1. With your group, spread the Element Cards out on a table. Each card provides the following information about an element:

   - Element symbol

   - Element name

   - Whether the element is a metal or nonmetal

   - Whether the element is solid, liquid, or gas at room temperature

   - Color

   - Atomic mass: the mass of the smallest particle (an atom) of the element

   - Reactivity: how likely the element is to react chemically with other elements

   - Number of bonds to hydrogen: the number of hydrogen atoms that usually combine chemically with this element when they react

2. Examine the information on each card carefully, noting similarities and differences among the elements.

3. Working together, sort the elements into at least three groups. Each group should have at least two similar properties. Agree on a classification system. As you work remember to:

   - Listen to and consider the explanations and ideas of your group.

   - If you disagree with other members of your group, explain why you disagree.

4. In your science notebook, list the groups you made and the common features of each. Be sure to record all the elements in each group.

5. Present your classification system to the class. As you look at other students' systems, observe similarities and differences between theirs and yours. Discuss your observations with your group.

6. Your group will receive four Element Family Cards. Each card describes a group of elements called a **family**. Based on the information on the Family Cards, place each element under a card.

7. Arrange the elements in each family in order from lowest atomic mass at the top to highest atomic mass at the bottom. Place the column on a half-sheet of paper.

8. Line up the four columns of elements to form a table, so that the elements are in columns and rows. Use the atomic masses of the elements to decide on an order for the holders.

9. In your notebook, record your new classification system, complete with:

   • family names

   • similar properties within each family

   • elements in each family in order of increasing atomic mass

## ANALYSIS

1. Which of the properties listed on the Element Cards are:

   **a.** physical properties?

   **b.** chemical properties?

2. How did your first classification system compare to the second classification with the Element Family Cards?

3. In what ways could grouping elements help scientists understand their properties?

4. Use the table of elements you constructed to find the family or families of elements that are:

   **a.** not usually reactive.

   **b.** highly reactive.

   **c.** all metals.

   **d.** all solids.

   **e.** all gases.

5. The element strontium (Sr) is below calcium (Ca) in Column 2 on the periodic table. Design an Element Card that shows the properties you predict for strontium.

## EXTENSION

Visit the *Issues and Physical Science* page of the SEPUP website for:

   • links to different versions of the periodic table.

   • the latest update on the number of elements.

READING

**M**aterials—both natural and human made—have unique properties. Some are made of one type of element, and some are made of combinations of elements. But what are elements made of, and how do they differ from each other?

Each element is made of tiny particles called **atoms.** A pure sample of an element contains many atoms of the same type. For example, the millions of iron atoms that make up a piece of iron metal are of the same type and have the characteristics of iron. Iron atoms, however, are very different from atoms of other elements, such as gold or oxygen. The properties of each element depend on its atoms.

Some elements are rarely found in a pure form. They tend to combine chemically, or **react**, with other elements. Scientists say that these elements are **reactive.** When elements react, they can form substances called **compounds.**

CHALLENGE ➤ **What are elements, and how do they relate to compounds?**

*Think of the world around you. Everything—from the air you breathe to the shoes you walk in—is made from elements or combinations of elements.*

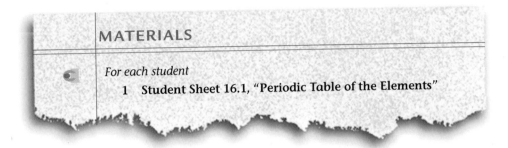

## MATERIALS

*For each student*
1   **Student Sheet 16.1, "Periodic Table of the Elements"**

# READING

## Discovering Elements

*When reading, answer the Stopping to Think questions in your mind. They can help you find out whether you understand the main ideas.*

The idea that everything on the earth is made of a basic set of elements began with the ancient Greeks more than 2,000 years ago. Greek philosophers thought that fire, earth, air, and water combined to make everything in the world.

Starting in the 1600s, early chemists realized that fire, earth, air, and water were not the basic building blocks of matter. They looked instead for substances that they could not break down into simpler substances. These substances are known today as the elements.

Some of the earliest known elements were carbon, gold, silver, copper, sulfur, tin, lead, mercury, and iron—all of them elements that occur in nature. Until the 1700s, very few new elements were discovered. But in the mid 1700s through the 1800s, chemists learned how to create chemical reactions and physical ways to separate pure elements. With these new techniques, they found dozens more elements. By 1869, approximately 63 elements were known. These included hydrogen, nitrogen, oxygen, sodium, and aluminum.

*Laboratory investigations in the 1700s similar to those shown in this illustration led to discoveries about the properties of elements.*

## STOPPING TO THINK 1

In what way were the ancient Greek philosophers right about elements?

In what way were the ancient Greek philosophers wrong?

## Mendeleev and the Periodic Table of the Elements

In 1869 the Russian scientist Dmitri Mendeleev (men-deh-LAY-eff) developed the ideas that led to the modern periodic table. Other scientists had some similar ideas, but Mendeleev made the most progress and published the first version of a table of the 63 elements known at the time.

Mendeleev collected information on the properties of those 63 elements and grouped them in a way similar to what you did in Activity 15, "Families of

### THE PERIODICITY OF THE ELEMENTS

| The Elements | Their Properties in the Free State | The Composition of the Hydrogen and Organo-metallic Compounds | Symbols and Atomic Weights | The Composition of the Saline Oxides | The Properties of the Saline Oxides | Small Periods or Series |
|---|---|---|---|---|---|---|

The elements listed include: Hydrogen, Lithium, Beryllium, Boron, Carbon, Nitrogen, Oxygen, Fluorine, Sodium, Magnesium, Aluminium, Silicon, Phosphorus, Sulphur, Chlorine, Potassium, Calcium, Scandium, Titanium, Vanadium, Chromium, Manganese, Iron, Cobalt, Nickel, Copper, Zinc, Gallium, Germanium, Arsenic, Selenium, Bromine, Rubidium, Strontium, Yttrium, Zirconium, Niobium, Molybdenum, Ruthenium, Rhodium, Palladium, Silver, Cadmium, Indium, Tin, Antimony, Tellurium, Iodine, Cæsium, Barium, Lanthanum, Cerium, Didymium, Ytterbium, Tantalum, Tungsten, Osmium, Iridium, Platinum, Gold, Mercury, Thallium, Lead, Bismuth, Thorium, Uranium.

Photo (left) of Russian chemist Dmitri Ivanovich Mendeleev (1834–1907) and a table (right) he developed based on the properties of elements. This reference was translated into English in 1891.

Elements." He used data that many other scientists had collected about the properties of each of the elements. When he arranged the elements according to their atomic masses and their physical and chemical properties, he noticed that there was a repeating—or periodic—pattern. For example, as the atomic mass increased from lithium to fluorine, the elements in between changed from metals to nonmetals and from solids to gases. He saw a similar pattern repeated from sodium to chlorine and again from potassium to bromine. Mendeleev predicted that there were more elements that would fit into gaps in his chart, the first version of what came to be known as a periodic table. He even used the patterns in the table to predict the properties of new elements.

Other scientists used Mendeleev's ideas and built on them to identify the elements he predicted. Later scientists found many more elements that follow the patterns he found. The modern version of the table is called the **Periodic Table of the Elements.** Based on new data about the elements, scientists around the world have agreed on some changes to the arrangement of the table.

## STOPPING TO THINK 2

How did Mendeleev build on other scientists' work?

How did other scientists build on Mendeleev's work?

## The Modern Periodic Table

Atomic number

Atomic mass

| 6 |
|---|
| **C** |
| carbon |
| 12.01 |

Today, there are more than 115 identified elements, and everything on earth is made of these elements. Look at the current periodic table shown below. Each element is represented by a symbol that includes either one uppercase letter, such as C for carbon, or an uppercase and a lowercase letter, such as Ca for calcium or Cu for copper. Each element shows an **atomic number** that corresponds to its order in the periodic table and an atomic mass, as shown in the example of the element carbon to the left.

**Periodic Table of the Elements**

| 1 | 2 | 3 | 4 | 5 | 6 | 7 | 8 | 9 | 10 | 11 | 12 | 13 | 14 | 15 | 16 | 17 | 18 |
|---|---|---|---|---|---|---|---|---|---|---|---|---|---|---|---|---|---|
| 1 H hydrogen 1.008 | | | | | | | | | | | | | | | | | 2 He helium 4.003 |
| 3 Li lithium 6.941 | 4 Be beryllium 9.012 | | | | | | | | | | | 5 B boron 10.81 | 6 C carbon 12.01 | 7 N nitrogen 14.01 | 8 O oxygen 16.00 | 9 F fluorine 19.00 | 10 Ne neon 20.18 |
| 11 Na sodium 22.99 | 12 Mg magnesium 24.31 | | | | | | | | | | | 13 Al aluminum 26.98 | 14 Si silicon 28.09 | 15 P phosphorus 30.97 | 16 S sulfur 32.07 | 17 Cl chlorine 35.45 | 18 Ar argon 39.95 |
| 19 K potassium 39.10 | 20 Ca calcium 40.08 | 21 Sc scandium 44.96 | 22 Ti titanium 47.88 | 23 V vanadium 50.94 | 24 Cr chromium 52.00 | 25 Mn manganese 54.94 | 26 Fe iron 55.85 | 27 Co cobalt 58.93 | 28 Ni nickel 58.69 | 29 Cu copper 63.55 | 30 Zn zinc 65.39 | 31 Ga gallium 69.72 | 32 Ge germanium 72.58 | 33 As arsenic 74.92 | 34 Se selenium 78.96 | 35 Br bromine 79.90 | 36 Kr krypton 83.80 |
| 37 Rb rubidium 85.47 | 38 Sr strontium 87.62 | 39 Y yttrium 88.91 | 40 Zr zirconium 91.22 | 41 Nb niobium 92.91 | 42 Mo molybdenum 95.94 | 43 Tc technetium (98) | 44 Ru ruthenium 101.1 | 45 Rh rhodium 102.9 | 46 Pd palladium 106.4 | 47 Ag silver 107.9 | 48 Cd cadmium 112.4 | 49 In indium 114.8 | 50 Sn tin 118.7 | 51 Sb antimony 121.8 | 52 Te tellurium 127.6 | 53 I iodine 126.9 | 54 Xe xenon 131.3 |
| 55 Cs cesium 132.9 | 56 Ba barium 137.3 | 57 La* lanthanum 138.9 | 72 Hf hafnium 178.5 | 73 Ta tantalum 180.9 | 74 W tungsten 183.9 | 75 Re rhenium 186.2 | 76 Os osmium 190.2 | 77 Ir iridium 190.2 | 78 Pt platinum 195.1 | 79 Au gold 197.0 | 80 Hg mercury 200.5 | 81 Tl thallium 204.4 | 82 Pb lead 207.2 | 83 Bi bismuth 208.9 | 84 Po polonium (209) | 85 At astatine (210) | 86 Rn radon (222) |
| 87 Fr francium (223) | 88 Ra radium (226) | 89 Ac~ actinium (227) | 104 Rf rutherfordium (257) | 105 Db dubnium (260) | 106 Sg seaborgium (263) | 107 Bh bohrium (262) | 108 Hs hassium (265) | 109 Mt meitnerium (266) | 110 Ds darmstadtium (271) | 111 Uuu (272) | 112 112 (277) | | 114 Uuq (296) | | 116 Uuh (298) | | 118 Uuo (?) |

| *Lanthanide Series | 58 Ce cerium 140.1 | 59 Pr praseodymium 140.9 | 60 Nd nenodymium 144.2 | 61 Pm promethium (147) | 62 Sm samarium (150.4) | 63 Eu europium 152.0 | 64 Gd gadolinium 157.3 | 65 Tb terbium 158.9 | 66 Dy dysprosium 162.5 | 67 Ho holmium 164.9 | 68 Er erbium 167.3 | 69 Tm thulium 168.9 | 70 Yb ytterbium 173.0 | 71 Lu luteium 175.0 |
|---|---|---|---|---|---|---|---|---|---|---|---|---|---|---|
| ~Actinide Series | 90 Th thorium 232.0 | 91 Pa protactinium (231) | 92 U uranium (238) | 93 Np neptunium (237) | 94 Pu plutonium (242) | 95 Am americium (243) | 96 Cm curium (247) | 97 Bk berkelium (247) | 98 Cf californium (249) | 99 Es einsteinium (254) | 100 Fm fermium (253) | 101 Md mendelevium (256) | 102 No nobelium (254) | 103 Lr lawrencium (257) |

**Shading Key**

A Solid at room temperature

A Liquid at room temperature

A Gas at room temperature

From the periodic table you can find out a lot about an element. For example, if you look at the element cesium (atomic number 55) on the periodic table shown on the next page, you will see that it is in the alkali metal column. From this you can assume that cesium is a highly reactive, soft metal. On this periodic table, you can also tell if an element is a metal or nonmetal, because a dark "stepped line" divides the table into metals to the left of the stepped line and nonmetals to its right.

### STOPPING TO THINK 3

Use the Periodic Table of the Elements on the next page to decide whether each of the following is a metal or a nonmetal: lithium (Li), carbon (C), sulfur (S), calcium (Ca), titanium (Ti), and bromine (Br).

Most elements are solid at room temperature. The 11 elements that are gases tend to appear on the right and near the top of the periodic table. Their symbols are white. There are two elements that are liquid at room temperature—mercury and bromine. Their symbols are shaded in gray. You might also notice that one of the newer synthesized elements, 112, is a liquid. This is interesting to note because it falls below the element mercury (atomic number 80), which is a liquid at room temperature.

You can also predict the chemical reactivity of an element based on its position in the periodic table. The **reactivity** of an element describes how likely it is to **react**, or combine, with other elements. An element that is very likely to react with other elements is described as highly **reactive**. This means that they will react with many other substances. The least reactive elements are the noble gases to the right. The most reactive metals are in the two columns to the far left of the periodic table. The most reactive nonmetals are in the halogen family in column 17.

### STOPPING TO THINK 4

Find magnesium on the periodic table.

- What is magnesium's chemical symbol?
- What family does magnesium belong to?
- Is magnesium a solid, a liquid, or a gas?

Based on its family, would you expect magnesium to be very reactive, somewhat reactive, or not reactive at all?

# Periodic Table of the Elements

**Color Key**
- Non-metals
- Alkali metals
- Alkaline earth metals
- Transition metals
- Rare earth metals
- Other metals
- Halogens
- Noble gases

| 1 | 2 | 3 | 4 | 5 | 6 | 7 | 8 | 9 | 10 | 11 | 12 | 13 | 14 | 15 | 16 | 17 | 18 |
|---|---|---|---|---|---|---|---|---|---|---|---|---|---|---|---|---|---|
| 1 **H** hydrogen 1.008 | | | | | | | | | | | | | | | | | 2 **He** helium 4.003 |
| 3 **Li** lithium 6.941 | 4 **Be** beryllium 9.012 | | | | | | | | | | | 5 **B** boron 10.81 | 6 **C** carbon 12.01 | 7 **N** nitrogen 14.01 | 8 **O** oxygen 16.00 | 9 **F** fluorine 19.00 | 10 **Ne** neon 20.18 |
| 11 **Na** sodium 22.99 | 12 **Mg** magnesium 24.31 | | | | | | | | | | | 13 **Al** aluminum 26.98 | 14 **Si** silicon 28.09 | 15 **P** phosphorus 30.97 | 16 **S** sulfur 32.07 | 17 **Cl** chlorine 35.45 | 18 **Ar** argon 39.95 |
| 19 **K** potassium 39.10 | 20 **Ca** calcium 40.08 | 21 **Sc** scandium 44.96 | 22 **Ti** titanium 47.88 | 23 **V** vanadium 50.94 | 24 **Cr** chromium 52.00 | 25 **Mn** manganese 54.94 | 26 **Fe** iron 55.85 | 27 **Co** cobalt 58.93 | 28 **Ni** nickel 58.69 | 29 **Cu** copper 63.55 | 30 **Zn** zinc 65.39 | 31 **Ga** gallium 69.72 | 32 **Ge** germanium 72.58 | 33 **As** arsenic 74.92 | 34 **Se** selenium 78.96 | 35 **Br** bromine 79.90 | 36 **Kr** krypton 83.80 |
| 37 **Rb** rubidium 85.47 | 38 **Sr** strontium 87.62 | 39 **Y** yttrium 88.91 | 40 **Zr** zirconium 91.22 | 41 **Nb** niobium 92.91 | 42 **Mo** molybdenum 95.94 | 43 **Tc** technetium (98) | 44 **Ru** ruthenium 101.1 | 45 **Rh** rhodium 102.9 | 46 **Pd** palladium 106.4 | 47 **Ag** silver 107.9 | 48 **Cd** cadmium 112.4 | 49 **In** indium 114.8 | 50 **Sn** tin 118.7 | 51 **Sb** antimony 121.8 | 52 **Te** tellurium 127.6 | 53 **I** iodine 126.9 | 54 **Xe** xenon 131.3 |
| 55 **Cs** cesium 132.9 | 56 **Ba** barium 137.3 | 57 **La\*** lanthanum 138.9 | 72 **Hf** hafnium 178.5 | 73 **Ta** tantalum 180.9 | 74 **W** tungsten 183.9 | 75 **Re** rhenium 186.2 | 76 **Os** osmium 190.2 | 77 **Ir** iridium 190.2 | 78 **Pt** platinum 195.1 | 79 **Au** gold 197.0 | 80 **Hg** mercury 200.5 | 81 **Tl** thallium 204.4 | 82 **Pb** lead 207.2 | 83 **Bi** bismuth 208.9 | 84 **Po** polonium (209) | 85 **At** astatine (210) | 86 **Rn** radon (222) |
| 87 **Fr** francium (223) | 88 **Ra** radium (226) | 89 **Ac~** actinium (227) | 104 **Rf** rutherfordium (257) | 105 **Db** dubnium (260) | 106 **Sg** seaborgium (263) | 107 **Bh** bohrium (262) | 108 **Hs** hassium (265) | 109 **Mt** meitnerium (266) | 110 **Ds** darmstadtium (271) | 111 **Uuu** (272) | 112 **112** (277) | 114 **Uuq** (296) | | 116 **Uuh** (298) | | | 118 **Uuo** (?) |

**\*Lanthanide Series**

| 58 **Ce** cerium 140.1 | 59 **Pr** praseodymium 140.9 | 60 **Nd** neodymium 144.2 | 61 **Pm** promethium (147) | 62 **Sm** samarium (150.4) | 63 **Eu** europium 152.0 | 64 **Gd** gadolinium 157.3 | 65 **Tb** terbium 158.9 | 66 **Dy** dysprosium 162.5 | 67 **Ho** holmium 164.9 | 68 **Er** erbium 167.3 | 69 **Tm** thulium 168.9 | 70 **Yb** ytterbium 173.0 | 71 **Lu** lutetium 175.0 |
|---|---|---|---|---|---|---|---|---|---|---|---|---|---|

**~Actinide Series**

| 90 **Th** thorium 232.0 | 91 **Pa** protactinium (231) | 92 **U** uranium (238) | 93 **Np** neptunium (237) | 94 **Pu** plutonium (242) | 95 **Am** americium (243) | 96 **Cm** curium (247) | 97 **Bk** berkelium (247) | 98 **Cf** californium (249) | 99 **Es** einsteinium (254) | 100 **Fm** fermium (253) | 101 **Md** mendelevium (256) | 102 **No** nobelium (254) | 103 **Lr** lawrencium (257) |
|---|---|---|---|---|---|---|---|---|---|---|---|---|---|

**Shading Key**
- A Solid at room temperature
- A Liquid at room temperature
- A Gas at room temperature

## Forming Compounds

Elements contain only one kind of atom. Other substances contain two or more types of atoms held together by chemical bonds. Bonds form when the atoms of one element are attracted to the atoms of one or more other elements. Substances with two or more types of atoms held together by bonds are called compounds. For example, the compound water forms when the elements hydrogen and oxygen react together. Sugars are chemical combinations of the elements carbon, hydrogen, and oxygen. Groups of differing atoms that are held together by chemical attraction are called **molecules.** The diagram below shows a water molecule, made of two hydrogen atoms and one oxygen atom.

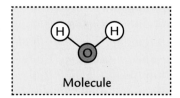

Molecule

*Water molecule*

There are more than 115 elements, and these elements can combine to form millions of compounds. To get an idea of how many, just look at a dictionary of the English language and think about how many words are formed from just 26 letters!

Compounds have different properties than the elements that form them. For example, the compound we call water is a liquid formed from two gases—hydrogen and oxygen. Table sugar is an edible white solid formed from a black solid (carbon) and the gases hydrogen and oxygen.

### STOPPING TO THINK 5

What are two ways that compounds are different from the elements that form them?

## Chemical Names and Formulas

Scientists have created a system for naming compounds. These names often identify the elements that make up the compound. For example, the full chemical name for table salt is "sodium chloride." This name tells you table salt contains sodium and chlorine. This is information about the compound that you would not have if you called it "table salt." Notice that the ending of "chlorine" is changed to "–ide" in the name of the compound. A **chemical formula** is a shorthand way to identify the kind and number of atoms that make up a compound. For example, the symbol for

*Commonly referred to as salt, this naturally-occurring compound is sodium chloride, NaCl.*

sodium is **Na**, and the symbol for chlorine is **Cl**. So you can write the formula for the compound sodium chloride like this: **NaCl**. This tells you that there is one chlorine atom for every sodium atom in sodium chloride.

Not all chemical formulas are as simple as **NaCl**. For instance, water is made up of the elements hydrogen (H) and oxygen (O), and its chemical formula is $H_2O$. (You say this "H-two-O.") That is because each water molecule is made up of two hydrogen atoms bonded to one oxygen atom. The number "2" below and to the right of the "H" shows that there are two hydrogen atoms in a water molecule. When there is no number written below and to the right of the element symbol, then there is only one of that type of atom.

---

## STOPPING TO THINK 6

The chemical formula for baking soda is $NaHCO_3$. What elements are in baking soda? How many of each kind of atom is represented by the formula for baking soda?

---

## Classifying Matter: Elements, Compounds, and Mixtures

Everything around you is an element, a compound, or a mixture of both. The oxygen in the air you breathe and the copper in pennies are examples of elements. The water you drink and the salt and sugars in the foods you eat are examples of compounds. So are the proteins, fats, and carbohydrates that make up the cells in your body. Everything that is not a pure element or compound is a mixture of elements, compounds, or both. Even air is a mixture of several elements and compounds, including the elements nitrogen and oxygen and the compounds carbon dioxide and water.

*Ocean water is a mixture of compounds, including water ($H_2O$), salt (NaCl), and others.*

## ANALYSIS

1. Make a copy of the table below in your science notebook. Use the Periodic Table of Elements to find out which atoms make up a molecule for each of the substances listed. The first row has been completed for you.

Chemical Formulas of Common Substances

| Substance | Chemical formula | Atoms that make up the molecule |
|---|---|---|
| Water | $H_2O$ | 2 hydrogen atoms, 1 oxygen atom |
| Hydrogen peroxide | $H_2O_2$ | |
| Carbon dioxide | $CO_2$ | |
| Sucrose (table sugar) | $C_{12}H_{22}O_{11}$ | |
| Alanine (an amino acid) | $C_3H_7O_2N$ | |
| Oleic acid (a fat) | $C_{12}H_{24}O_2$ | |

2. Sodium is a metallic solid, and chlorine is a poisonous yellow-green gas. Sodium and chlorine react to form sodium chloride, which is common table salt.

   a. Is table salt an element or a compound? Explain.

   b. Describe the physical properties of table salt.

   c. How do the properties of table salt compare with those of sodium and chlorine?

3. Is seawater an element, compound, or mixture? Explain your answer.

4. Explain the relationship between an atom and a molecule.

## EXTENSION

Visit the *Issues and Physical Science* page of the SEPUP website for links to learn more about Dmitri Mendeleev's work and the work of other chemists.

MODELING

**M**ost substances on earth are not pure elements made up of a single type of atom. "Energy connections" called **chemical bonds** can hold atoms together to form molecules. Molecules are composed of two or more atoms held together with chemical bonds. Atoms can combine with atoms of the same element, with atoms of another element, or even with atoms of several elements through chemical bonds. When the atoms of more than one element bond in specific, regular proportions they form a substance called a compound. Water, for example, is a compound because its molecules are made from atoms of hydrogen and oxygen in exact proportions. These proportions (2:1) are shown in its chemical formula, $H_2O$.

Compounds can be found everywhere. Many everyday materials—from wood to gasoline to aspirin—are made of compounds. In this activity, you will build molecules of several compounds.

**CHALLENGE** ⟹ **How do atoms combine to form molecules?**

*The Atomium, a building modeled after the crystal structure of metal, was built in Brussels, Belgium for the 1958 World's Fair.*

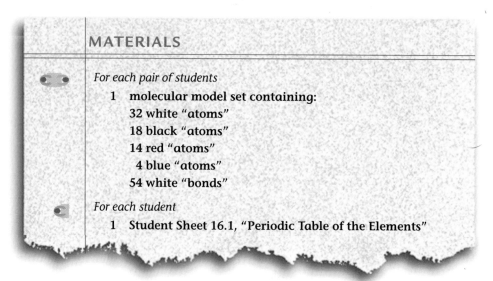

MATERIALS

*For each pair of students*

1 molecular model set containing:
32 white "atoms"
18 black "atoms"
14 red "atoms"
4 blue "atoms"
54 white "bonds"

*For each student*

1 **Student Sheet 16.1, "Periodic Table of the Elements"**

# PROCEDURE

## Part A: Making Simple Molecules

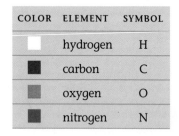

| COLOR | ELEMENT | SYMBOL |
|---|---|---|
| | hydrogen | H |
| | carbon | C |
| | oxygen | O |
| | nitrogen | N |

1. Build a model of a molecule of water with two hydrogen (white) atoms and one oxygen (red) atom. Use the white bonds (tubes) to make the connections that represent chemical bonds.

2. Follow your teacher's directions to draw a diagram of this molecule in your science notebook.

3. What do you think is the name and chemical formula of this molecule? Record these on your diagram.

4. Pull the model apart.

5. Every time you make a molecule, all of the bonding sites (the "sticks" on the atom models) must be connected to the sites on another atom.

   a. Using this rule, make two models: a molecule of hydrogen and carbon and a molecule of hydrogen and nitrogen.

   b. Draw each molecule that you construct.

   c. Record next to each drawing the chemical formula for the molecule.

6. Follow your teacher's demonstration to construct a molecule using two oxygen atoms. Remember, all the bonding sites must be connected.

7. Construct two molecules: one using 2 hydrogen atoms and one using 2 nitrogen atoms.

8. Draw a diagram of each of the molecules you made for Steps 6 and 7.

9. Next to each diagram record the chemical formula for the molecule.

10. Take apart all of the models, and return all of the pieces to the set.

### Part B : Making More Complex Molecules

11. Construct and draw at least four more molecules according to the following two rules:

    • Each molecule must contain between two and five atoms.

    • All the bonding sites (the protruding "sticks") of an atom must be connected to those of another atom.

    After drawing each molecule, pull it apart before constructing the next.

12. Construct and draw two more molecules following only one rule:

    • All the bonding sites must be connected to those of another atom.

13. Take all the molecules apart, and return all the pieces to the set.

14. Compare your drawings with those of the other pair in your group.

15. Construct and draw a model of a molecule with the formula $CO_2$.

## ANALYSIS

1. How many different elements were you working with?

2. What was the role of the "sticks" on each atom model?

3. Was it possible for an atom to make more than one bond? Explain and give an example.

4. How many bonds could each of the following make with hydrogen? Copy the table below into your science notebook. Use the atomic numbers to help you find the elements on the periodic table.

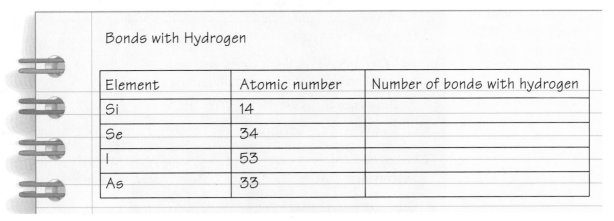

Bonds with Hydrogen

| Element | Atomic number | Number of bonds with hydrogen |
|---------|---------------|-------------------------------|
| Si | 14 | |
| Se | 34 | |
| I | 53 | |
| As | 33 | |

5. If you had two oxygen atoms and one hydrogen atom, could you form a molecule? Explain.

6. Make a drawing to show the difference between an atom and a molecule.

7. Which model provides more information—a chemical formula or a sketch of the molecule?

LABORATORY

In Activity 12, "Evaluating Materials," and Activity 13, "Product Life Cycle," you compared plastic and glass bottles and aluminum cans to evaluate which was the best material for drinks. However, within these categories, there are more choices. For example, not all plastics are the same. Even plastics that look alike can have different properties and they can be used for different purposes.

You may have noticed that two plastic cubes can be the same size, shape, and color, but one is heavier. This could be because they are made of two types of plastic with different chemical and physical properties. Knowing the properties of plastics is helpful when deciding which plastic to use to manufacture a product.

CHALLENGE

**How do the physical and chemical properties of plastics affect their uses?**

*Plastic is one of the most diverse synthetic materials in existence.*

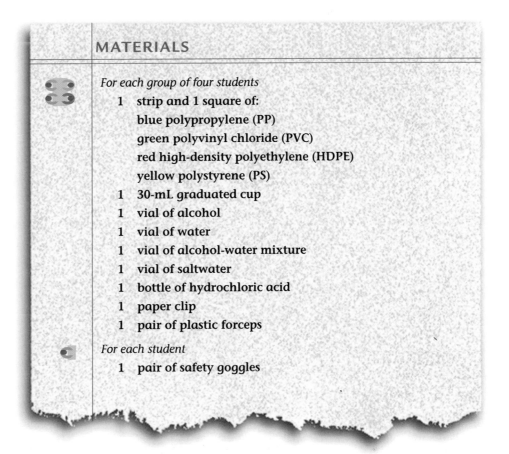

## MATERIALS

*For each group of four students*

1 strip and 1 square of:
   blue polypropylene (PP)
   green polyvinyl chloride (PVC)
   red high-density polyethylene (HDPE)
   yellow polystyrene (PS)

1 30-mL graduated cup
1 vial of alcohol
1 vial of water
1 vial of alcohol-water mixture
1 vial of saltwater
1 bottle of hydrochloric acid
1 paper clip
1 pair of plastic forceps

*For each student*

1 pair of safety goggles

### SAFETY

Wear safety goggles at all times during this lab. Do not allow solutions to touch your skin or clothing. Clean up any spills immediately. If accidental contact occurs, inform your teacher, and rinse exposed areas.

## PROCEDURE

### Part A: Investigating Plastics

1. Examine the four different types of plastic strips and squares. They have been coded by color so you can tell them apart. Your group will work together to determine the properties of each type of plastic.

2. Read the procedure for each test shown in the table, "Testing Properties of Plastics," on the next page.

3. In your notebook, construct a data table "Properties of Plastics" to record the results of the tests. Be sure to add a column for the heat and acetone tests your teacher will conduct.

4. With your group, determine the properties of each of the four types of plastics using the tests in the table.

| Testing Properties of Plastics | |
| --- | --- |
| **Property** | **Test** |
| **Flexibility** | 1. Gently bend the plastic strip back and forth.<br><br>2. Observe its flexibility (ability to bend).<br><br>3. Record your observations.<br><br>Hint: You may want to rank the relative flexibility of each plastic on a scale of 1–4, with 1 representing the least flexible. |
| **Crease color** | 1. Gently bend the strip of plastic in half.<br><br>2. Observe the color of the crease that is produced.<br><br>3. Record your observations. |
| **Hardness** | 1. Using the end of a paper clip, gently try to draw a line in the plastic strip.<br><br>2. Record your results.<br><br>Hint: You may want to rank the relative hardness of each plastic on a scale of 1–4, with 1 representing the piece that was scratched the least. |
| **Density relative to alcohol** | 1. Place a plastic square in the vial labeled "Alcohol," cap it, and gently shake the vial.<br><br>2. Observe whether the plastic floats or sinks.<br><br>3. Use forceps to remove the piece from the vial. |
| **Density relative to alcohol-water mixture** | 1. Shake the vial labeled "Alcohol-Water" well to create an alcohol-water mixture.<br><br>2. Place a plastic square in the vial, cap it, and gently shake the vial.<br><br>3. Observe whether the plastic floats or sinks.<br><br>4. Use forceps to remove the piece from the vial. |
| **Density relative to water** | 1. Place a plastic square in the vial labeled "Water," cap the vial, and shake it gently to wet the plastic.<br><br>2. Observe whether the plastic floats or sinks.<br><br>3. Use forceps to remove the piece from the vial. |
| **Density relative to saltwater** | 1. Gently shake the vial labeled "Saltwater" until no salt crystals are visible in the water.<br><br>2. Place a plastic square in the vial, cap the vial, and shake it gently to wet the plastic.<br><br>3. Observe whether the plastic floats or sinks.<br><br>4. Use forceps to remove the piece from the vial. |

5. Record the results of the tests in your data table.

6. Your teacher will demonstrate the effects of acetone and heat on each of the four types of plastic. As your teacher performs the tests, record your observations in your data table.

## Part B: Identifying a "Mystery" Plastic

7. Your teacher will give you samples of an unknown plastic. With your group, decide which tests you will conduct to determine what type of plastic it is.

8. In your notebook, design a data table to record the results of your testing. Title the table "Properties of Different Plastics."

9. Test the mystery plastic sample, and record the results in your data table.

## ANALYSIS

1. Using evidence from your table, "Properties of Plastics," identify the plastics which were scratched. How will this property affect their use?

2. Below is a scale showing the relative density of the four liquids you used to determine the density of the plastics.

   a. Which plastic sample was the most dense? Explain your evidence.

   b. Which plastic sample is the least dense? Explain your evidence.

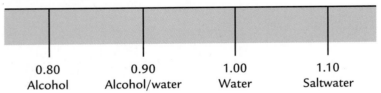

**Relative density**

| | | | |
|---|---|---|---|
| 0.80 | 0.90 | 1.00 | 1.10 |
| Alcohol | Alcohol/water | Water | Saltwater |

   c. In your science notebook, make a copy of the scale shown above. On it draw a labeled arrow that shows where each plastic falls on this scale of relative density.

3. What type of plastic is your mystery sample? Explain the evidence you used to come to this conclusion.

**4.** You are a materials scientist asked to recommend a type of plastic for manufacturing three products. Using the information in your table, "Properties of Plastics," choose the best plastic for each of the following products. Be sure to include evidence from the activity in your answer.

    **a.** nail polish (high in acetone) container

    **b.** dishwasher-safe food container

    **c.** sports drink container

## EXTENSION

Collect several different types of plastic products from home. Design your own investigation using the tests in this activity to determine the type of plastic the samples are made from. You may want to use additional tests or resources. Be sure to have your plan approved by your teacher before starting your investigation.

In the last activity, you observed that different types of plastics have specific properties. For example, the polyvinyl chloride (PVC) used to make food packaging softens and bends when exposed to heat or liquid acetone, but the high-density polyethylene (HDPE) used to make milk jugs does not. Their properties differ because they are made of different molecules. Materials engineers can use **chemical reactions** to create products with particular properties. A chemical reaction occurs when the atoms and molecules of two or more substances rearrange to form new substances.

In this activity you will mix two **reactants**, or inputs, which react chemically to create a new **product**, or output. Then you will compare the physical and chemical properties of the substances before and after they have reacted chemically.

**CHALLENGE** ⟹ **How are reactants changed by a chemical reaction? How are the products different?**

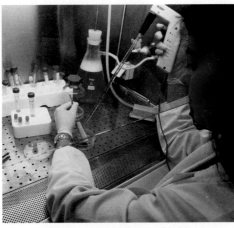

*These materials scientists study the creation of new materials. The scientist above is preparing a material used to repair bones. The scientist on the right is testing a new form of bullet-proof glass to see if it meets safety requirements.*

## MATERIALS

*For each group of four students*
- 1 bottle of polyvinyl alcohol (PVA) solution
- 1 bottle of sodium borate solution

*For each pair of students*
- 4 white "hydrogen atoms"
- 2 black "carbon atoms"
- 1 red "oxygen atom"
- 7 white "bonds"
- 2 30-mL graduated cups
- 1 plastic spoon
- 1 stir stick
-   paper towels
-   warm soapy water

*For each student*
- 1 pair of safety goggles

## SAFETY

Wear safety goggles at all times during this lab. Do not allow solutions to touch your skin or clothing. Clean up any spills immediately. If accidental contact occurs, inform your teacher, and rinse exposed areas.

## PROCEDURE

1. In your science notebook, create a table to record your observations of the reactants before the reaction and the results after the reaction is completed.

   Hint: Read through the entire procedure before making your table so you know what you will need to record.

2. Pour 10 mL of polyvinyl alcohol (PVA) into an empty 30–mL graduated cup. As you pour, be sure to observe the PVA and then record in your table its color, how well it pours, whether it can be stirred, and if it appears sticky.

3. Pour 2.5 mL of sodium borate into the other empty graduated cup. As you pour, be sure to observe its properties and record them in your table.

4. One partner should slowly add all of the sodium borate to the PVA while the other stirs constantly with the stir stick. Observe the changes, and keep stirring until nothing further happens. Record all changes that occurred as you stirred.

5. Observe the properties of the new substance that results. Record your observations in your data table.

6. Transfer your new product from the cup onto a paper towel using the spoon. Immediately wash the cups. Then investigate and describe additional properties, such as:

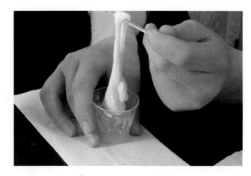

Stickiness: Does it stick to your hands? To the desk? To the paper towel?

Stretchiness: What happens when you pull it slowly? When you pull it quickly?

Bounciness: Try bouncing a small piece.

7. In your table summarize the properties of this new substance.

8. Follow your teacher's directions for cleanup.

## ANALYSIS

1. How do the physical properties of the final product compare to the properties of:

   a. polyvinyl alcohol (PVA), one of the reactants?

   b. sodium borate, the second reactant, which you added to the PVA?

2. What evidence can you provide that a new substance formed?

3. Plastics are a category of materials. Compare the plastics that you worked with in this activity to the properties of the plastics you tested in Activity 18, "Properties of Plastics." From these two investigations, what can you say about the properties of plastics?

MODELING

**P**lastics, including the substance you made in Activity 19, "Creating New Materials," have different properties, but they all belong to a group of materials called polymers. **Polymers** are compounds made of thousands of repeating smaller molecules. The molecules that repeat in a polymer are called monomers. Notice their names. Monomer starts with the prefix *mono* which means "one" (in Greek). Polymer starts with the prefix *poly* meaning "many." So, a polymer is made of many monomers.

In this activity you will construct paper-clip models to help you understand the properties of polymers. Scientists use models to help explain things we cannot see. But keep in mind that a scientific model like the molecular model you have worked with, does not have to look like the real thing—it just has to act like it in one or more important ways.

CHALLENGE

**How can you use models to represent changes that occur during a chemical reaction?**

*In what ways is this architectural model like the building it represents? In what ways does it differ?*

## MATERIALS

*For each group of four students*

  1   wide-mouthed plastic bottle
48   silver paper clips
  6   colored paper clips
  2   clear plastic cups
  1   plastic spoon

*For each student*

  1   Student Sheet 20.2, "Polymers in Daily Life"

# PROCEDURE

## Part A: Examining a Monomer

1. In your science notebook, create a table to record how well a monomer, a polymer, and a cross-linked polymer can be poured, stirred, and pulled, as shown by the models you will make. Read through the entire procedure before constructing the table so you will know what you will need to record.

2. Work with your group to investigate the properties of the model monomers. Put 24 unconnected silver paper clips in the wide-mouthed bottle. Each paper clip represents one monomer.

3. Slowly pour the monomers from the bottle into the plastic cup. (If necessary, gently shake the bottle.) Repeat this two or three times. Describe how quickly the clips come out of the bottle. Record your observations in your data table.

4. Use the plastic spoon to stir the monomers in the cup. Record your observations.

5. Reach into the cup and pull out a single monomer. Record in your table your observations about pulling out the monomer.

## Part B: Forming a Polymer

6. Each member of your group will now link six paper clips from the remaining 24 clips into a straight chain, as shown in the diagram at left. Each clip represents an individual monomer.

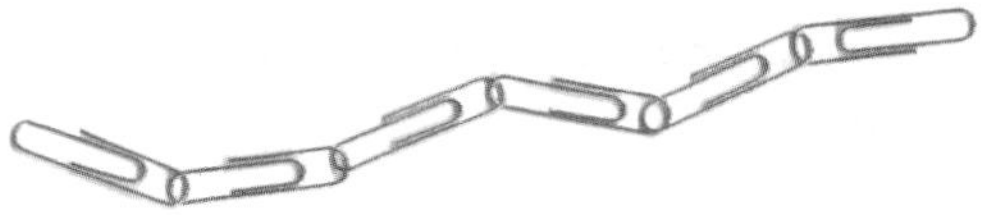

Model of a polymer

7. Link your four chains together to make one long chain of 24 paper clips. You have just made a model of a polymer like the polyvinyl alcohol (PVA) you used in Activity 19, "Designing New Materials." (You would need thousands of paper clip monomers to make a realistic paper clip polymer.)

Model of a longer polymer molecule

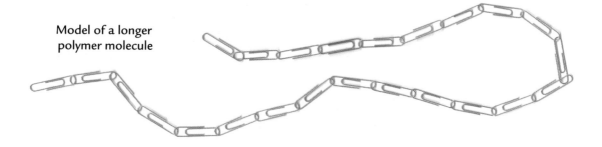

8. Put your polymer in the wide-mouthed bottle. Leave one or two paper clips hanging out of the top. Now pour the polymer into a plastic cup two or three times. Record your observations.

9. Use the plastic spoon to stir the polymer in the cup. Record your observations.

10. Reach into the cup, and pull out a single paper clip. Record your observations.

## Part C: Cross-Linking a Polymer

11. Separate the polymer back into four chains of six paper clips each. Each part represents individual polymer molecules. Place the chains in four parallel rows as shown in the diagram below.

12. Use two colored paper clips to connect, or cross-link, the first and second chain. Continue to do this with all four of the chains, as shown in the diagram below. You have just made a model of a cross-linked polymer, like cross-linked polyvinyl alcohol (PVA). You have constructed a model of a chemical reaction that chemically bonds polymers together into cross-linked polymers. The colored paper clips represent the sodium borate molecules that linked the polymer polyvinyl alcohol chains together in the chemical reaction in Activity 19, "Designing New Materials."

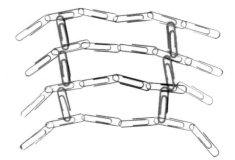

13. Test how well your cross-linked polymer can be stirred, pulled, and poured. Record your observations in your data table.

14. Separate all of the paper clips, and put the 24 silver paper clips back in the plastic cup.

## ANALYSIS

1. Models provide ways to represent complex systems. In Activity 19, "Creating New Materials," and this activity you made a total of three models of polymers. Analyze each of the models you built.

    a. In your science notebook, make a table like the one below.

    b. Fill in the table using observations from this activity.

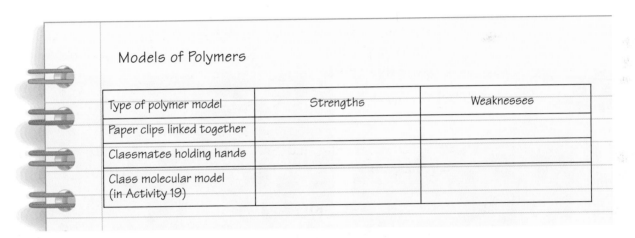

Models of Polymers

| Type of polymer model | Strengths | Weaknesses |
|---|---|---|
| Paper clips linked together | | |
| Classmates holding hands | | |
| Class molecular model (in Activity 19) | | |

2. Compare the models you built in this activity:

    a. Which was the most helpful when you analyzed the physical properties of a polymer?

    b. Which was the most helpful when you analyzed the chemical reaction that occurred?

3. Using examples from this and Activity 19, "Designing New Materials," explain the relationships between a monomer, a polymer, and a cross-linked polymer. Include a sketch to illustrate your explanation.

4. How does cross-linking affect the properties of a polymer?

5. All plastics are polymers. Based on what you observed with the models, what advantages do you think polymers have over monomers?

**READING**

**C**an you imagine a world without plastics? Plastic soft drink containers, bags, pens, DVDs, and computer and television parts are just a few things made of plastics that would be different. For thousands of years, however, people lived without plastics. But today, materials scientists and engineers have created plastics to make everyday products that in the past were made from glass, metal, and wood. In this activity, you will read how a plastic, a synthetic polymer, is made through a chemical reaction.

**CHALLENGE** ⟶ **What is the chemical structure of plastics?**

*Bakelite was the first synthetic plastic, invented by Belgian scientist Leo Beakeland in 1907. In the 1920s, the versatile Bakelite was manufactured to make all sorts of products from auditorium walls to radios.*

*For each student*

1  **Student Sheet 21.1, "Three-Level Reading Guide: Polymer Parts"**
1  **Student Sheet 19.1, "Comparing Properties of Polymers"**

# READING

*Use Student Sheet 21.1, "Three-Level Reading Guide: Polymer Parts," to guide you as you complete the following reading.*

## Plastics are Polymers

What makes plastics different from other materials such as glass and aluminum? The answer is found in the wide variety of plastic compounds that can be made from chains of carbon atoms. Scientists make new plastics by designing compounds with a wide variety of properties.

The majority of plastics used to make products are synthetic. This means that they are made in laboratories and factories, and do not exist in nature. The first plastic was developed in 1907. Some natural polymers include the cellulose that makes up wood and cotton, the protein that forms strands of human hair, and raw rubber that is collected from rubber trees.

Plastics are part of a larger category of compounds called polymers. A **polymer** is a substance made up of thousands of repeating small molecules. The prefix "poly-" means "many," and the word "polymer" means "many parts." The small molecules that repeat in a polymer are called monomers. The prefix "mono-" means "one," and so a monomer is "one part." You modeled the formation of a polymer from many monomers when you attached paper clips to make a long chain. Each paper clip represented the monomers that bond together to form a polymer. The long chain of paper clips represented the polymer.

Take polyethylene, for example. The plastic that was color-coded red in Activity 18, "Properties of Plastics," was polyethylene. Polyethylene means "many ethylenes," and it is a chain of ethylene molecules. The ethylene molecule is the monomer.

$$
\begin{array}{c}
\text{H} \quad \text{H} \\
| \qquad | \\
\text{C} = \text{C} \\
| \qquad | \\
\text{H} \quad \text{H}
\end{array}
$$

$$
\cdots
\left[
\begin{array}{c}
\text{H H H H H H H H H H H H} \\
| \ | \ | \ | \ | \ | \ | \ | \ | \ | \ | \ | \\
-\text{C}-\text{C}-\text{C}-\text{C}-\text{C}-\text{C}-\text{C}-\text{C}-\text{C}-\text{C}-\text{C}-\text{C}- \\
| \ | \ | \ | \ | \ | \ | \ | \ | \ | \ | \ | \\
\text{H H H H H H H H H H H H}
\end{array}
\right]
\cdots
$$

ethylene
· single molecule
· monomer

polyethelene
· thousands of the same molecule linked together
· polymer

Adding the prefix *poly-* to the name of a monomer forms the names of many synthetic polymers. Think about the other plastics you used in Activity 18: polystyrene—a chain of styrene molecules; polyvinyl chloride—a chain of vinyl chloride molecules; high-density polyethylene—a chemically bonded chain of ethylene molecules; and polypropylene—a chain of propylene molecules.

Synthetic plastics, like the four you investigated in Activity 18, have been in use for less than 100 years. However, people have been using natural polymers like wood, natural rubber, and wool for centuries.

## Investigating the Structure of Polymers

*Herman Staudinger*

Scientists began to investigate the atomic and molecule structure of natural polymers so they could learn how to make synthetic polymers. In 1920, the German chemist Herman Staudinger proposed that polymers were made of long chains of many small molecules. He thought that the length of the chain was related to the physical properties of the polymer. At the time, his ideas were considered radical, and many scientists did not take them seriously. But he continued to collect data that supported his ideas. From his work, and the work of other scientists, dozens of synthetic plastics were developed. Staudinger's research on the properties and structure of plastics was so important that he received the Nobel Prize in 1953.

Today, scientists know that changing the length of a polymer chain is not the only way to change its properties. Another way is to cross-link a polymer. You modeled this process in Activity 19, "Designing New Materials," when you mixed the polyvinyl alcohol with sodium borate. The sodium borate provided the cross-links. You also modeled cross-linking in Activity 20, "Modeling Polymers" when you cross-linked the paper clip chains with different-colored paper clips. Think about how the properties of polyvinyl alcohol and sodium borate were different from the properties of the cross-linked polymer.

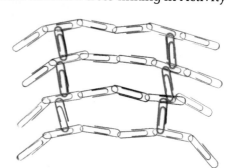

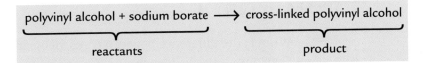

polyvinyl alcohol + sodium borate ⟶ cross-linked polyvinyl alcohol

reactants                                      product

Why does cross-linking a polymer change its properties? New chemical bonds form and change the structure of the molecules. The polyvinyl alcohol and sodium borate are reactants, and the result of their chemical reaction leads to the formation of a new product. The molecules and physical properties of the product are different than either of the reactants.

As Staudinger found, the number of cross-links is related to the physical properties of a cross-linked polymer, just as the length of the polymer chain was related to the physical properties of the polymer. If there are few cross-links, the cross-linked polymer has "memory." After it is stretched, it "remembers" to return to its original shape, like a rubber band. If a plastic has more cross-links, the result is a harder substance that cannot be stretched and does not return to its original shape.

One problem with cross-linking is that it is often difficult to reverse. In fact, the more cross-links there are in a polymer, the harder it is to break down the polymer chemically. This means that cross-linked polymers are usually difficult to recycle.

A polymer that is commonly cross-linked to improve its uses is rubber. Natural rubber gets sticky in hot weather and brittle in cold weather, and it falls apart very easily. But when rubber is cross-linked, its properties change. Cross-linking rubber makes it more stable and elastic. Most of the rubber products in the world around you, from food containers to car tires, are made of cross-linked rubber. While this makes better products, a trade-off is that it causes disposal problems.

Cross-linked rubber is so stable that it does not degrade. This can make recycling cross-linked polymers difficult. However, there are ways to reuse the material. For example, old tires can be shredded and made into chips. These chips are used on playgrounds, running tracks, and in road construction. Scientists and engineers have also developed ways to use old tires as a source of energy.

*It is estimated that two to three billion tires sit in landfills across the United States. Is this an environmental disaster or an opportunity to find new ways to deal with them?*

## ANALYSIS

1. What is the difference between a synthetic and a natural polymer? Give one example of each.

2. Why do two polymers, such as polystyrene and polyethylene, have different properties?

3. Explain why cross-linking a polymer like polyvinyl alcohol or rubber changes its properties. Include a diagram showing the relationships between a monomer, a polymer, and a cross-linked polymer.

In the beginning of this unit you considered materials used to make a single-material product, a drink container. But what about the materials that go into a more complex product—for example, a computer?

A computer contains many pieces that must be manufactured and put together. Think about all of the components—parts—in all of the computers in the world that make computers work. What raw materials are needed to make the components? How much waste is created? What impact does that waste have on our environment?

In this activity you will analyze the materials used and the amounts of waste produced to manufacture a computer.

**CHALLENGE** ➤ **What is the environmental impact of manufacturing a computer?**

*Manufacturing a computer requires assembling many parts, each made from unique materials.*

## MATERIALS

*For each pair of students*

    1   set of colored pencils

*For each student*

    1   sheet of graph paper or Student Sheet 22.1, "Pie-Chart Template"

    1   Science Skills Student Sheet 3a and 3b, "Bar Graphing Checklist"

## PROCEDURE

1. With your partner, read the information in Table 1, "Materials in a Desktop Computer," below. Discuss the information in the table.

### Table 1: Materials in a Desktop Computer
(weighing approximately 27 kg (60 lb)

|  | % of total weight | % recyclable |
| --- | --- | --- |
| Aluminum | 14 | 80 |
| Copper | 7 | 90 |
| Glass | 24 | 0 |
| Iron compounds | 20 | 80 |
| Lead | 6 | 5 |
| Plastic | 25 | 20 |
| Zinc | 2 | 60 |
| Other metals | 2 | ___ |

2. With your partner read the information in Table 2, "Waste Products from Manufacturing Selected Computer Components," below. Discuss the information in the table.

### Table 2: Waste Products from Manufacturing Selected Computer Components

| Component | Component weight (kg) | Total waste produced during manufacturing (kg) | Hazardous waste produced during manufacturing (kg) |
| --- | --- | --- | --- |
| Computer chip | < 0.5 | 40 | 3 |
| Circuit board | 2 | 21 | 18 |
| Monitor | 20 | 1 | 0.9 |

3. With your partner decide which of you will construct a pie chart for the data in Table 1, and who will construct a bar graph for Table 2. You might want to try sketching ways to represent the information before constructing your final chart or graph. Be sure to label your work and give it a title.

4. Show your work to your partner. Together write down the conclusions that can be drawn from the information shown in the pie chart and the bar graph.

## ANALYSIS

1. What are the top three materials by weight in a computer?

2. You are a materials scientist asked to present the information in Tables 1 and 2 to a group of computer manufacturers who want to reduce the effect of the computer life cycle on the environment. What information from your data would help them? Make a list of statements summarizing the information your graphs and charts show.

3. Based on your list from Analysis Question 2, what two statements do you think are the most important to discuss with the manufacturers? Explain why they are the most important.

READING

**A**s you saw in the last activity, a computer is made of many parts, each manufactured from one or more materials. One essential part of a computer, and of many other electronic devices, is a **circuit board.** It works like a wiring system to transfer electricity to each operating part of the computer. To do this a circuit board contains a network of copper paths. These paths conduct the flow of electricity within the computer. A chemical process called **etching** is used to create the copper paths on the circuit board. In this activity you will find out how this works by etching your own circuit board.

CHALLENGE

**How is a computer circuit board produced?**

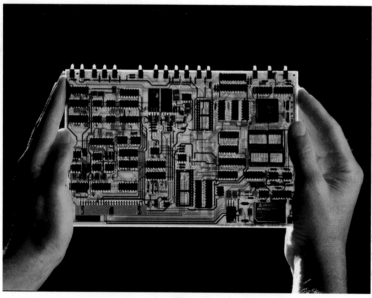

*The large circuit board (left) holds many smaller circuit boards, one of which is magnified on the right.*

## MATERIALS

*For each group of four students*

1   felt-tip permanent marker
1   piece of copper-coated plastic
1   piece of steel wool
1   pair of forceps
1   battery harness with light bulb
1   9-volt alkaline battery

*For each pair of students*

1   piece of paper

*For each student*

1   Student Sheet 23.1, "Three-Level Reading Guide: Etching Circuit Boards"

### SAFETY

Wear safety goggles at all times during this lab. Do not allow solutions to touch your skin or clothing. Clean up any spills immediately. If accidental contact occurs, inform your teacher, and rinse exposed areas.

## PROCEDURE

### Part A: Designing and Etching a Circuit Board

1.  Listen carefully as your teacher describes how a circuit board works.

2.  Outline the shape of the copper-coated plastic on a piece of paper.

3.  Using a pencil, work with your partner to create a circuit board design. It should be a pattern that will conduct electricity from one end of the board to the other. Create a sketch of your design, making sure to use thick lines.

4.  Share your design with your group. Decide which design will be etched on the piece of copper-coated plastic.

5.  Select someone in your group to clean the surface of the copper-coated plastic piece by rubbing the copper-coated side with steel wool. Cleaning will remove surface dirt and other impurities that might interfere with the etching reaction. Once you clean it, be careful not to touch the copper surface with your fingers. Oil from your fingers will interfere with the etching process.

6. Use the marker to draw your design on the copper-coated side of the circuit board and to write your initials on the plastic side. Be sure to make thick lines with the marker.

7. Let the ink dry for 1 minute.

8. Re-trace your design and your initials and again let the ink dry for 1 minute.

9. Look at the copper chloride etching solution your teacher has prepared and record your observations in your science notebook. Now place your circuit board in the tray. It will soak there overnight.

### Part B: Examining the Circuit Board

10. Observe the used copper chloride after the etching process is completed. Describe your observations in your science notebook.

11. Obtain your circuit board from your teacher after it has been rinsed off with water.

12. Rub your circuit board with steel wool to remove any remaining ink.

13. Examine your circuit board, and then test it with the battery-and-light-bulb circuit. Record the results of your test.

### Part C: Reading

*Use Student Sheet 23.1, "Three Level Reading Guide: Etching Circuit Boards" to guide you as you complete the following reading.*

# READING: MAKE PRODUCTS, MAKE WASTE

## Making Everyday Products

We buy and use products every day. These products include drinks and items we consume and dispose of right away. But we also buy products that serve us for longer periods of time, like sneakers, cell phones, or computers. What happens before you buy a product? It has to be made from materials, and the materials have to come from somewhere.

Take, for example, a computer. To manufacture a computer the parts must be made first. To make the parts raw materials or recycled materials must be obtained. As you saw in the demonstration, copper is one of the raw materials that end up in a circuit board. Mining companies dig out copper-containing rocks, known as copper ore, from deposits in the earth. Refining companies then physically crush the rock and chemically remove the copper from the ore. The copper that is removed and purified is then sold to companies that use copper in their products.

Copper-containing rock can be mined from open pit mines (left) on the earth's surface or from tunnel mines (right) that are blasted into the surface.

Hot liquid metal copper is poured into molds where it will cool.

## Making Circuit Boards

During the production of a circuit board, a chemical reaction etches a copper circuit on a piece of plastic. To etch means to use a corrosive solution to make a design in a material by dissolving the material not wanted. The copper that was protected from the etching solution is left on the board and creates a metal path. The metal path determines how electricity flows throughout the computer. This is a process that removes much of the copper on the board, leaving it in the etching solution.

## Making Waste

Each step in the process from raw materials to finished circuit board creates some form of waste. After ore is mined to obtain copper, the copper-containing rock is extracted to be used in products. However, more than 98% of the ore does not contain any form of copper, so a lot of waste remains.

As you observed in this activity, after a circuit board is etched the used etching solution and rinse water contain copper. Other steps in the computer manufacturing process create yet more wastes that have copper in them. Solutions containing copper above a certain concentration are considered toxic. In fact, the U.S. Environmental Protection Agency (EPA) reported that in the year 2000, of all the toxic chemicals released by companies in the United States, the most common toxic substance was copper-containing waste. About 1.5 billion pounds of these chemicals were released into the environment that year.

*A technician works with a machine (left) that etches copper circuit boards. Mining and manufacturing copper-containing substances can result in waterways that are polluted with copper waste.*

## Copper Isn't Always Bad

Like other living organisms, the human body needs small amounts of copper and other metals for it to work properly. That's why they are often among the ingredients of vitamin and mineral supplements. The U.S. Food and Drug Administration's (FDA) recommended daily intake of copper for adults is about 2 milligrams (mg). But in much larger amounts, copper, like many other metals, can be toxic. Drinking water that has high levels of copper can cause vomiting, diarrhea, stomach cramps, and nausea. Eating or drinking very high amounts of copper can cause liver and kidney damage. Inhaling copper dust over long periods of time can cause dizziness, headaches, diarrhea, and irritation of the nose, mouth, and eyes. Since high levels of copper can be toxic, proper disposal is crucial.

Today, the United States has laws that prevent companies and individuals from dumping toxic waste directly into the soil, waterways, and sewer systems. This helps keep our environment cleaner and safer. But manufacturing products that we have come to depend on, like circuit boards, still produces toxic waste. Figuring out how to handle this waste in ways that will not harm the environment is a problem many companies and government agencies face every day. If you consider the amount of waste produced by manufacturing products every year, that's a lot of toxic waste that is built up in the course of one year. It often costs companies a great deal of money to dispose of toxic waste safely.

## ANALYSIS

1. Describe the changes that occurred during the etching process in:

   a. your circuit board.

   b. the copper chloride etching solution.

2. What do you think should be done with the used copper chloride etching solution?

3. Etching circuit boards creates large amounts of copper-containing toxic waste. What ways can you think of to reduce the amount of copper-containing waste produced in the United States?

   Hint: You may want to look at Student Sheet 13.1, "Green Chemistry Guidelines," to help you think of ways to improve methods of manufacturing.

LABORATORY

**M**anufacturing circuit boards produces water that contains copper compounds. The concentration of copper in the waste is one factor that will determine how the waste can be disposed. **Concentration** is the amount of one substance in another substance. In this activity you will determine the amount of copper compounds in the used copper chloride solution from Activity 23, "Producing Circuit Boards." It is important to know the concentration of copper in the solution because there are local, state and federal laws that set limits on what types of wastes can be released and at what concentrations. For this reason, manufacturers need to dispose of the used copper chloride solution in ways that do not put high concentrations of copper in rivers or waterways.

One way to dispose of the waste is to reduce the concentration of copper in the waste by diluting it, and then releasing it into a waterway. When waste is **diluted**, it is combined with water. This does not change the waste chemically, but decreases the concentration of waste per volume of water. Once the waste is diluted to below the limit set by law, it can be disposed of in a waterway. Depending on where the manufacturer is located, limits for the maximum concentration of copper that can be released in a single day from a single place may range from 1 to 10 parts per million (ppm). **Parts per million** is a way of expressing the concentration of a substance in one million parts of another substance.

In this activity you will determine the concentration of the used copper chloride solution in parts per million. Knowing the concentration will help you decide if dilution is a way to dispose of the waste.

CHALLENGE

**How much copper is in the used copper chloride solution?**

## MATERIALS

*For each group of four students*

1   30-mL dropper bottle of each of the following:

100,000 ppm copper chloride solution

water

5% ammonia solution

used copper chloride solution from Activity 23, "Producing Circuit Boards"

1   cup of water

*For each pair of students*

1   SEPUP tray

1   dropper

1   stir stick

1   sheet of white paper

paper towels

1   copy of Transparency 24.1, "Diluting and Testing Copper Chloride"

*For each student*

1   pair of safety goggles

1   Student Sheet 24.1, "Determining Concentration"

1   Student Sheet 24.2, "Treating Waste"

**SAFETY**

Wear safety goggles at all times during this lab. Do not allow solutions to touch your skin or clothing. Clean up any spills immediately. If accidental contact occurs, inform your teacher, and rinse exposed areas.

## PROCEDURE

### Part A: Preparing a Dilution of 100,000 ppm Copper Chloride

1. Place the copy of Transparency 24.1, "Diluting and Testing Copper Chloride" underneath your SEPUP tray. This will help you see the colors of the solutions as you perform the dilutions.

2. Put 10 drops of 100,000-ppm copper chloride solution in Cup 1 of the SEPUP tray.

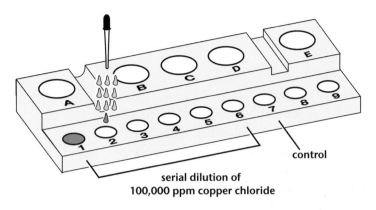

serial dilution of
100,000 ppm copper chloride

control

3. Use a clear dropper to transfer one drop of 100,000-ppm copper chloride solution from Cup 1 to Cup 2. Return any excess in the dropper to Cup 1, and rinse the inside of the dropper in the cup of water.

4. Add 9 drops of water to Cup 2. Stir the solution with the stir stick. Clean the stir stick.

5. Use the dropper to transfer one drop from Cup 2 to Cup 3. Return any excess in the dropper to Cup 2, and rinse the inside of the dropper.

6. Add 9 drops of water to Cup 3, and stir.

7. Continue this dilution process through Cup 6 by moving a drop of solution from the previous cup to the next cup, adding 9 drops of water, and stirring. Be sure to return any excess solution in the dropper to the previous cup, and rinse the dropper.

8. Add 10 drops of water to Cup 7. This cup will act as a control to ensure that the water you added to Cups 1–6 does not contain copper.

9. Record the color of the solutions in Cups 1–7 in the first column of the data table on Student Sheet 24.1, "Determining Concentration."

10. You will use ammonia solution to indicate if copper is present in the solution in each of the cups. Add 5 drops of ammonia to each of the seven cups, and stir. Be sure to clean the stir stick after mixing each cup to avoid contamination.

11. If after adding ammonia, the solution is green, blue-green, or blue, copper is present in the solution. Record your observations in the second column of your data table.

## Part B: Concentration of Copper in Used Copper Chloride Solution

12. Place 10 drops of the used copper chloride solution into Cup 9. Add 5 drops of ammonia, and stir. Record your observations.

13. Determine the concentration of copper in the used copper chloride solution. To do this, compare the color of the solution in Cup 9 to the colors in Cups 1–7. Record the concentration for the cup that has the closest concentration to Cup 9 on Student Sheet 24.1, "Determining Concentration."

14. Dispose of the solutions in your SEPUP tray as directed by your teacher.

## ANALYSIS

1. Which contains a more dilute solution, Cup 1 or Cup 2? Explain.

2. Was there copper in Cups 1–6? How did you know it was or was not there? Explain, using evidence from this activity.

3. What is the concentration of copper in the used copper chloride solution from Activity 23, "Producing Circuit Boards"? Use the evidence from this activity to support your answer.

4. How many liters of water would you need to dilute 1 liter of used copper chloride solution from 100,000 ppm of copper to less than 1 ppm?

5. Based on your answers to Analysis Questions 3 and 4, how many liters of water would it take to dilute your waste from Activity 23 to 1 ppm, an acceptable concentration to pour down the drain?

6. Is dilution an acceptable way to dispose of the used copper chloride solution? Explain.

## EXTENSION

Towns, cities, and states in the United States set limits on the amount of copper that can be disposed of down drains. Find out what the local limit is in your area.

LABORATORY

So far in this unit you have performed two chemical reactions. In Activity 19, "Creating New Materials," you cross-linked polyvinyl alcohol in a chemical reaction that produced a new polymer. In Activity 23, "Producing Circuit Boards," you observed a chemical reaction that etched copper. These are two examples of chemical reactions. You may be amazed to know that there are chemical reactions going on around you and inside of you every day. Whether you are cooking your dinner in a pan or releasing energy from food in your cells, chemical reactions are changing reactants into products. Understanding chemical reactions is helpful when creating materials and in deciding how to reduce the waste created at the same time.

In this activity you will conduct two chemical reactions in closed containers. Scientists call a container a **closed system** if none of the reactants or products can escape from the reaction container. If a chemical reaction takes place in a container that allows any reactants or products to escape, it is called an **open system.** You will investigate what changes and what stays the same when a chemical reaction takes place in a closed system.

CHALLENGE

**How does the total mass of the reactants compare to the total mass of the products in a chemical reaction?**

*Two liquid reactants mix and undergo a chemical reaction that results in the creation of a yellow product.*

## MATERIALS

*For each group of four students*
1    balance
1    SEPUP tray to hold copper chloride bottles

*For each pair of students*
1    10-mL graduated cylinder
1    aluminum washer
2    reaction bottles

*For each student*
1    Student Sheet 25.1, "Mass of Reactants and Products"
1    pair of safety goggles

## SAFETY

Wear safety goggles at all times during this lab. Do not allow solutions to touch your skin or clothing. Clean up any spills immediately. If accidental contact occurs, inform your teacher, and rinse exposed areas.

## PROCEDURE

### Part A: Chemical Reaction in an Closed System

1. With your partner, place an aluminum washer in the bottom of one of the reaction bottles.

2. Fill the dropper with 1-mL of 100,000-ppm copper chloride solution.

3. Being careful not to squeeze the dropper and mix the two reactants, place the top on the bottle and twist the lid securely.

4. Use the balance to measure the total mass of the bottle, dropper, and reactants to the nearest $\frac{1}{10}$ of a gram. Record this initial total mass on Student Sheet 25.1, "Mass of Reactants and Products."

5. Observe the two reactants and record your observations on Student Sheet 25.1.

6. While holding the reaction bottle securely with one hand, use the other hand to squeeze the dropper, releasing the copper chloride solution into the bottle. Swirl the bottle to mix the copper chloride solution with the aluminum washer.

7. Set the bottle on the table, and observe. On Student Sheet 25.1, record your observations both as the reaction happens and after there are no more signs of a reaction.

8. Determine the total final mass of the reaction bottle to the nearest $\frac{1}{10}$ gram. Record this final mass on your student sheet.

9. Calculate the change in total mass.

## Part B: Another Chemical Reaction in a Closed Chamber

10. Now conduct a second chemical reaction in a closed system. With your partner, pour 4mL of 0.8 M sodium hydrogen phosphate into the bottom of the second reaction bottle.

11. Fill the dropper with 1-mL of 100,000-ppm copper chloride solution.

12. Being careful not to bump or drop any of the copper chloride into the bottle, carefully twist the dropper top securely onto the bottle.

13. Use the balance to measure the total mass of the bottle, dropper, and reactants to the nearest $\frac{1}{10}$ of a gram. Record this initial total mass on Student Sheet 25.1, "Mass of Reactants and Products."

14. Observe the two reactants and record your observations on Student Sheet 25.1.

15. While holding the reaction bottle securely with one hand, use the other hand to squeeze the dropper, releasing the copper chloride solution into the bottle. Swirl the bottle to mix the copper chloride solution with the sodium hydrogen phosphate solution.

16. Set the bottle on the table, and observe. On Student Sheet 25.1, record your observations both as the reaction happens and after there are no more signs of a reaction.

17. Determine the total mass of the reaction bottle to the nearest $\frac{1}{10}$ gram. Record this final mass on your student sheet.

18. Calculate the change in total mass.

19. Clean up according to your teacher's directions.

# ANALYSIS

1. What evidence do you have that a chemical reaction took place between:

   **a.** copper chloride solution and aluminum?

   **b.** copper chloride solution and sodium hydrogen phosphate?

2. What can you conclude about the effect of a chemical reaction on the mass of reactants in a closed system? Support your answer with evidence from this activity.

 3. Using what you now know about the Law of Conservation of Mass, how would you respond if a company said it had developed a way to make hazardous materials and wastes "disappear"?

LABORATORY

When the wastebasket is full, what do you do with the waste? Take it out to the garbage can? Most likely this is the easiest option. In Activity 23, "Producing Circuit Boards," you saw that the chemical reaction that produces a circuit board also produces copper chloride waste. What do large manufacturing companies do with waste? What is the best choice for the environment? For years, people have gotten rid of waste through incineration. **Incineration** is the burning of wastes at very high temperatures—greater than 650°C (1,200°F). In this activity, you will explore how well incineration works to eliminate the copper-containing toxic waste.

CHALLENGE ⟹ **When waste is incinerated, what happens to potentially toxic heavy metals?**

*A toxic waste incineration facility.*

## MATERIALS

*For each group of four students*
- 1    dropper bottle of water
- 1    dropper bottle of ammonia

*For each pair of students*
- 1    sample of ash from metal paper
- 1    sample of ash from nonmetal paper
- 1    SEPUP tray
- 1    stir stick
- 1    dropper
- 1    piece of white paper
- 1    paper towel

*For each student*
- 1    pair of safety goggles
- 1    Student Sheet 24.2, "Treating Waste"

## SAFETY

Wear safety goggles at all times during this lab. Do not allow solutions to touch your skin or clothing. Clean up any spills immediately. If accidental contact occurs, inform your teacher, and rinse exposed areas.

## PROCEDURE

### Part A: Observing Incineration

1. In your science notebook, make a table like the one shown below.

Testing for Copper

| Substance | Color after adding ammonia | |
|---|---|---|
| | Metal paper | Nonmetal paper (control) |
| Unburned paper | | |
| Smoke | | |
| Ash | | |

2. Watch as your teacher uses ammonia to test two pieces of paper—one metal and one nonmetal—for copper. Record your observations in your table. The nonmetal paper is being tested as a control.

3. To simulate incineration, your teacher will burn both pieces of paper. Observe as your teacher uses ammonia to test the smoke, one of the products of incineration, for the presence of copper. Record your observations in your table.

### Part B: Testing Ash for Copper

4. Place your SEPUP tray on a piece of white paper.

5. Use your stir stick to put one scoop of ash from the metal paper into Cup 1.

6. With your stir stick, break the ash into smaller pieces.

7. Add 20 drops of water to Cup 1, and stir. Clean the stir stick.

8. Use your stir stick to put one scoop of ash from the nonmetal paper into Cup 2.

9. Add 20 drops of water to Cup 2, and stir. Clean the stir stick.

10. Add 5 drops of ammonia to Cups 1 and 2 to test for the presence of copper. Stir Cup 1, clean the stir stick, and stir Cup 2. Record your observations in your table.

11. Dispose of the substances in your SEPUP tray as directed by your teacher.

## ANALYSIS

1. Which of the three items in your table, "Testing for Copper,"—paper, smoke, or ash—are products of incineration?

2. Which of the products of incineration contained copper? Explain your evidence.

3. How did incineration change the metal paper?

4. What are the advantages and disadvantages of using incineration to dispose of heavy metal wastes?

5. Look at the information on Transparency 26.1, "Municipal Waste Disposal in the U.S. and Japan," and Transparency 26.2, "Relative Land-masses of the U.S. and Japan." Based on what you know about incineration and the information shown, why do you think these two countries handle waste disposal differently?

**LABORATORY**

**D**eciding how to handle waste produced from manufacturing is challenging. It can be diluted or incinerated, as you saw in previous activities. In some cases, it contains valuable materials that can be **reclaimed** and then reused. To reclaim metal means to get it back so it can be used again. Reclaiming metal from waste reduces the amount of new metal needed for manufacturing.

One way to reclaim copper from used copper chloride is to combine the waste with a solution that **precipitates** the copper. The metal copper precipitates, or falls out of solution because of a chemical reaction. Reclaiming the copper can be a useful way to deal with waste because it reduces the amount of toxic waste that is discarded, and provides copper that can be used again to make new products. Chemists have found that other types of metal are particularly effective in removing copper from waste products. In this activity you will test three metals to find out which one is best at reclaiming copper from waste.

CHALLENGE ➡ **Which metal is best at reclaiming copper from the used copper chloride solution?**

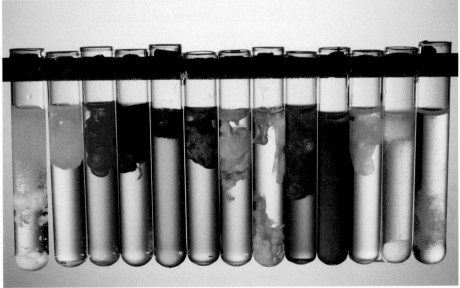

*Mixing two chemicals (left) results in a chemical reaction that creates an orange precipitate. Test tubes (right) hold the results of several metal precipitation reactions.*

## MATERIALS

*For each group of four students*

1   dropper bottle of used copper chloride solution from Activity 23, "Producing Circuit Boards"

1   dropper bottle of 5% ammonia solution

1   cup of water

*For each pair of students*

1   SEPUP tray

1   aluminum washer

1   iron washer

1   zinc washer

1   plastic spoon

1   dropper

paper towels

*For each student*

1   pair of safety goggles

1   Student Sheet 24.2, "Treating Waste"

## SAFETY

Wear safety goggles at all times during this lab. Do not allow solutions to touch your skin or clothing. Clean up any spills immediately. If accidental contact occurs, inform your teacher, and rinse exposed areas.

## PROCEDURE

Read through the entire procedure before you begin, and in your science notebook prepare a data table for recording your observations and results.

1. With your partner carefully examine each of the three metal washers: aluminum, zinc, and iron. Record your observations in your data table.

2. Add 10 drops of used copper chloride solution to Cups 1–4 of the SEPUP tray.

3. Using forceps, place the aluminum washer in Cup 1, the iron washer in Cup 2, and the zinc washer in Cup 3. Cup 4 will serve as a control for comparison purposes.

4. Observe the reaction in each cup for 5–10 minutes. Record your observations of each reaction in your data table. Be sure to include a comparison of the results obtained with each of the different metals.

5. Using the plastic spoon, remove the pieces of metal from the cups, and place them on a paper towel. Clean the spoon with a paper towel after each piece is removed.

6. In your data table, record your final observations of each metal.

7. Record your observations of the solutions left in each cup.

8. Using a dropper, put 5 drops of each of the solutions into a clean cup in the SEPUP tray. Do this by transferring 5 drops from Cup 1 to Cup A, from Cup 2 to Cup B, from Cup 3 to Cup C, and from Cup 4 to Cup D. Be sure to clean the dropper with water after each transfer so the solutions do not mix.

9. Test for copper in each solution by adding 2 drops of ammonia solution to Cups A–D. If copper is present in the solution, a deep blue color or a blue-green precipitate will form when ammonia is added.

10. Record your observations of the ammonia test in your data table. Dispose of the metals and solutions in your SEPUP tray as directed by your teacher.

## ANALYSIS

1. Explain the purpose of including Cup 4 and Cup D in your investigation.

2. Prepare a written report summarizing your investigation. Put your report on a clean sheet of paper. Include your name, the date, and a title for your report. Your report should have the following three components:

   a. A statement of the problem you were trying to resolve.

   b. A description of the materials and procedure you used to solve the problem.

   c. An analysis of the results, which should include:

      • a copy of your data table.

      • a summary of the results shown by the data in your data table.

      • an answer to this question: Which metal seemed to work best at removing the copper from solution? (Describe your evidence completely in your answer.)

      • any problems you may have had with the investigation.

      • any additional questions related to the problem that you would like to investigate.

**3.** Companies that make circuit boards often reclaim copper from copper-containing solutions. This allows them to reuse the copper, or sell it. Based on your results from this investigation and the information below, which metal would you recommend a company use to reclaim copper? Support your answer with evidence, and identify the trade-offs of your decision.

## More Information on Metals

| Metal | Cost per pound in 2007 (U.S. dollars) | Maximum wastewater concentration (ppm) | Health Benefits | Health Hazards |
|---|---|---|---|---|
| Aluminum | $1.30 | Not Restricted | Trace amounts may help enzymes function. | High levels may cause bone disease. |
| Copper | $2.60 | 5 | Essential for nervous system functions and energy metabolism, the recommended daily intake for an average adult is 2 mg. | Large amounts ingested over time cause liver and kidney damage. |
| Iron | $0.02 | 100 | Essential for formation of red blood cells, the recommended daily intake is 18 mg for an average adult. | Large amounts ingested over time may cause inflammation and damage to organs. |
| Zinc | $1.75 | 2.7 | Small amounts are needed for functioning of enzymes and forming proteins. The recommended daily intake for an average adult is 15 mg. | Large amounts ingested over time may cause inflammation and damage to organs. |

## EXTENSION

What other metals can precipitate copper from the used copper chloride solution? Design an experiment to find out. After your teacher approves your investigation, conduct the experiment, and present the results to the class.

LABORATORY

In the last activity, you conducted a chemical reaction with solid metals to precipitate copper metal from the used copper chloride solution. The brown deposit that formed was solid copper. Reclaiming copper from waste solutions has two advantages. First, it reduces the volume of toxic copper compounds that are thrown away as copper is replaced in solution with another, less toxic metal. Second, copper is a valuable metal that can be reused or sold.

Solid metals are not the only reactants that precipitate copper. Certain solutions can also form copper precipitates when they react with the used copper chloride solution. As you work to determine the best way to treat the waste from circuit-board manufacturing, you will evaluate two more chemical reactions that reclaim copper from the used copper chloride solution.

CHALLENGE

**Which compound in solution is best for reclaiming copper metal from the used copper chloride solution?**

*A goldsmith sorts printed computer circuit boards to reclaim the precious metal before the boards are recycled.*

## MATERIALS

*For each group of four students*

5 dropper bottles, each containing one of the following:

used copper chloride solution from Activity 23, "Producing Circuit Boards"

sodium carbonate solution

sodium hydrogen phosphate solution

5% ammonia solution

water

1 cup of water

*For each pair of students*

1 SEPUP tray

1 SEPUP funnel

2 pieces of filter paper

1 dropper

1 stir stick

1 pair of forceps

*For each student*

1 pair of safety goggles

1 Student Sheet 24.2, "Treating Waste"

Answer to Analysis Question 2 from Activity 23, "Producing Circuit Boards"

## SAFETY

**Wear safety goggles at all times during this lab. Do not allow solutions to touch your skin or clothing. Clean up any spills immediately. If accidental contact occurs, inform your teacher, and rinse exposed areas.**

# PROCEDURE

## Part A: Precipitation of Metals

1. In your science notebook, prepare a data table like the one shown on the next page.

2. Add 15 drops of used copper chloride solution to Cups 1 and 2 of the SEPUP tray.

Precipitating Copper

| Cup | Reactants | Observation of products | | |
|-----|-----------|-------------------------|-----------|----------------------------|
| | | Precipitate in filter | Filtrate | Color after adding ammonia |
| A | Used copper chloride + sodium carbonate solution | | | |
| B | Used copper chloride + sodium hydrogen phosphate solution | | | |

3. Add 20 drops of sodium carbonate solution to Cup 1, and stir. Rinse the stir stick.

4. Add 20 drops of sodium phosphate solution to Cup 2, and stir.

5. Examine the results of the reaction in Cups 1 and 2.

## Part B: Filtration

6. Now you will filter out the copper precipitate. Use the illustration below as a guide to fold the filter paper and set up the funnel.

7. Place the funnel over large Cups A and B of the SEPUP tray.

8. The solid that formed when you mixed the liquids in Steps 3 and 4 is a

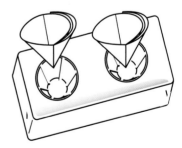

**Step 1**
Fold filter paper in half.

**Step 2**
Fold filter paper in half again.

**Step 3**
Open with three thicknesses of paper on one side of the cone and one thickness on the other.

**Step 4**
Place in funnel and add 3–5 drops of water from the dropper bottle to hold it in place.

precipitate. It can be removed by filtering. Use a clean dropper to transfer both the precipitate and the solution from Cup 1 to the filter paper above Cup A. Rinse the dropper thoroughly.

Hint: If the solid is difficult to remove, add a few drops of water to Cup 1. Use the dropper to remove the water and the precipitate, and transfer it to the filter paper.

9. Use a clean dropper to transfer the precipitate and solution from Cup 2 to the filter paper above Cup B.

10. Wait a few minutes as the solutions pass through the filter paper. After most of the liquid has filtered through, move the funnel so that it rests over Cups C and D.

11. Use forceps to gently pick up the filter paper in Cups A and B, and inspect the precipitate. Record your observations of the precipitate.

12. The filtered liquids left in Cups A and B are now called the filtrates. In your data table, record your observations of the filtrates.

13. Add 5 drops of ammonia to Cups A and B, and stir. Record your observations and the results of the ammonia test in your table.

14. Dispose of the filter papers and solutions in your SEPUP tray as directed by your teacher.

## ANALYSIS

1. Which solution was most effective at removing copper from the used copper chloride solution—sodium carbonate or sodium phosphate? Explain your evidence.

2. The table, "Summary of Precipitation Reactions," on the next page, shows information about each of the substances you used to precipitate copper. Based on your answer to Analysis Question 1, your results from Activity 27, and the information on the next page, which precipitation reaction would you recommend a company use to reclaim copper?

   Be sure to support your answer with evidence, and discuss the trade-offs.

## Summary of Precipitation Reactions

| Metal | Cost per pound (U.S. dollars in 2007) | What are the products of the reaction? | What can be done with these products? |
|---|---|---|---|
| Aluminum | $1.30 | Copper<br><br>Aluminum chloride | Reuse copper<br><br>Easy disposal of aluminum chloride through release into environment |
| Iron | $0.02 | Copper<br><br>Iron chloride | Reuse copper<br><br>Restricted disposal of iron chloride— must be treated, stored, or diluted |
| Zinc | $1.75 | Copper<br><br>Zinc chloride | Reuse copper<br><br>Highly restricted disposal of zinc chloride— must be treated or stored |
| Sodium Carbonate | $0.07 | Copper carbonate<br><br>Dissolved salt | Reuse copper carbonate<br><br>Easy disposal of dissolved salt through release into environment |
| Sodium Phosphate | $0.09 | Copper phosphate,<br><br>Dissolved salt | Reuse copper phosphate<br><br>Easy disposal of dissolved salt through release into environment |

3. Making 1,000 circuit boards can produce more than 18,500 liters (5,000 gallons) of copper-containing wastes. How do you think this toxic waste should be handled? Review your results from Activities 24–28, and the information you have collected on Student Sheet 24.2, "Treating Waste," and support your answer with evidence. Be sure to consider dilution, incineration, precipitation, and any other option that would reduce the environmental harm from the production of circuit boards.

4. **Reflection:** Look back at your answer to Analysis Question 2 from Activity 23, "Producing Circuit Boards." Now that you've completed the unit, has your idea of what to do with the waste changed? Explain.

TALKING IT OVER

**T**he Sunnyvale school district has been awarded a Green Computer Grant. To use the grant money, the school district must purchase "green" computers. The term "green" describes activities or products that disturb our environment less than current activities or products do. "Green" houses, for example, would have solar panels for energy, and be made from recycled building materials. "Green" electronics have been engineered in ways that produce less waste and thus reduce the environmental impact of their product life cycle. The Sunnyvale school district must show how the computers they decide to purchase have "green" features.

You are a materials scientist asked by the Sunnyvale school district to analyze proposals from computer companies about their products. You will recommend which computers to purchase based on the computer's green features and your knowledge of the products' life cycles.

CHALLENGE ⟹ **Which "green" computers should the school district purchase?**

*Deciding which computer to buy can be based not only on the computer's features, but also the environmental impact of the entire computer life cycle.*

## MATERIALS

*For each group of four students*

   1   transparency of Student Sheet 29.1, "Life Cycle of a Computer"

   1   poster board or chart paper

       assorted markers

       tape

       transparency marker

*For each student*

   1   Student Sheet 29.2, "Analyzing a Computer Proposal"

   1   Student Sheet 29.3, "Comparing Computer Proposals"

   1   Student Sheet 13.2, "Principles of Green Chemistry"

## PROCEDURE

1. With your group, review Transparency 29.1, "Life Cycle of a Computer" and identify each of the life cycle stages listed below. Use a transparency marker to label each stage on the transparency:

   - raw materials
   - manufacturing
   - useful life
   - end of life
   - recycling

2. With your group, you will perform a life cycle analysis for a hypothetical new material. To analyze this proposed change, you will predict how using the new material will affect each stage of the life cycle. To do this:

   - Read the news flash that follows.

**NEWS FLASH**

# New Polymer to Revolutionize Computer Manufacturing

Scientists and engineers have announced the creation of a new plastic made from plant-based polymers. It is hoped that this material will replace the synthetic polymers currently used to make computer monitors. Since the new plastic is made from plant-based materials, this would reduce the need for the raw material, petroleum. When recycled, the polymer can be broken down into a material that can be used to make computer monitors a second and third time, much like the process used to recycle glass bottles. This is an improvement over plastics currently used to make computer monitors since the current plastics cannot be reused to manufacture new monitors.

- With your group use a transparency of Student Sheet 29.1, "Life Cycle of a Computer," to think about which step(s) would change using the new material. Share your ideas with the class.

3. Now you will perform a life-cycle analysis for "green" computers. Your teacher will assign your group one of the four computer proposals described on the pages that follow.

4. With your group, read your assigned proposal. Fill out Student Sheet 29.2, "Analyzing a Computer Proposal," to help you identify how each feature of the proposal will change the life cycle of the computer.

5. Your group will work together to present a life-cycle analysis to the class. In your presentation you should be prepared to:

   - Describe each feature of the computer proposal.

   - Point out on your transparency of Student Sheet 29.1, "Life Cycle of a Computer," how your proposal would modify the life cycle of a computer.

   - Explain how each feature changes the life cycle and reduces the environmental impact of the computer.

   - Explain which "Principles of Green Chemistry." are incorporated in the proposal.

     Hint: Refer to Student Sheet 13.1

6. Make your presentation to the class, and listen to those of the other groups. As you listen to each presentation, record information on Student Sheet 29.3, "Comparing Computer Proposals." You will use this information to choose a proposal.

   Note: For each of the four computer plans presented below, the system specifications are the same. That means that the memory, processing speed, and software programs are identical.

## Proposal A Features

- Each computer has a cathode ray tube (CRT) monitor.

- The glass used in the monitor is from recycled glass products.

- Company reuses copper from circuit-board etching to produce more circuit boards.

- Computers are shipped in bulk. This reduces the amount of packing material needed to individually ship each computer.

## Proposal B Features

- Each computer has a cathode ray tube (CRT) monitor.

- Old computers are shipped back to the computer company. The company takes apart the old computers and reclaims metal components, such as the copper from the circuit board and the wires, to reuse in new computers.

- Nontoxic manufacturing wastes are sent to landfills. Hazardous materials are labeled, packaged, and sent to hazardous-materials facilities.

- The plastic cases that hold the monitors are made from a plant-based plastic.

## *Proposal C Features*

- Each computer has a flat screen liquid-crystal display (LCD) monitor that uses about 50% less electricity and 30% less materials than the standard CRT monitor.

- Reclaimable metals are precipitated from waste solutions and are reused in the manufacturing process.

- 15% of the plastic components of the computer are made of recycled plastic.

- The company will take back the computers once they are no longer being used, dismantle them, and use the metal components for further computer manufacture.

## *Proposal D Features*

- Each computer has a flat screen liquid-crystal display (LCD) monitor that uses about 50% less electricity and 30% less materials than the standard CRT monitor.

- Computers are shipped in bulk, reducing the amount of packing material needed to individually ship each computer.

- 15% of the metal components of the computer are made of recycled metal.

- The company offers a coupon for 50% off a new computer if the current computer is kept and upgraded for at least eight years (instead of buying new computers).

## ANALYSIS

1. Which proposal would you recommend the district choose for its Green Computer Grant? State your opinion, citing evidence from Student Sheet 29.3, "Comparing Computer Proposals," and previous activities. Include a discussion of the trade-offs involved in your decision.

2. With your group, explain how the science you learned in this unit helped you analyze your proposal. To do this, choose one feature of your proposal and explain which concept you learned helped you to understand that this feature would improve the life cycle of a computer.

3. The proposals your group analyzed did not include the cost of each computer. The school board members did not provide this information earlier because they wanted you to evaluate the plans based only on the chemistry of the materials and the products' life cycles.

   • Read the list price for each computer proposal below.

   • Knowing the price of each computer, does your answer to Analysis Question 1 change? Explain.

| Proposal Costs | | |
| --- | --- | --- |
| **Proposal** | **Cost per computer** | **Purchase plan** |
| A | $1,250 | Year one—120 computers purchased |
| B | $1,650 | Year one—60 computers purchased<br>Year two—30 computers purchased<br>Year three—30 computers purchased<br>The price is locked in for all three years. |
| C | $2,450 | Year one—120 computers purchased |
| D | $1,800 | Year one—120 computers purchased |

4. **Reflection:** Do you think that there should be green guidelines for families and individuals when they buy products, such as computers?

# Index

# Credits

Abbreviations: t (top), m (middle), b (bottom), l (left), r (right), c (center)

All illustrations by Seventeenth Street Studios / Valerie Winemiller.

Cover (front): wind power generators: Digital Vision / Getty Images; cart: Lab-Aids®, Inc.; (back): student hands: Lab-Aids®, Inc.

"Problem Solving" icon photo: ©Thom Lang / Corbis

"Talking It Over" icon photo: ©Michael Keller / Corbis

Unit title (B1) ©Wolfgang Kaehler / Corbis; Unit Opener (B2, B3): tl: Bob Krist / Corbis; tr: Peter Bowater / Photo Researchers, Inc.; br: ©Free Agents Limited /Corbis; bl: ©Amet Jean Pierre /Corbis Sygma; cl: John-Francis Bourke / Getty Images; B7 John-Francis Bourke / Getty Images; B8 ©DK Limited / Corbis; B9 Chris Knapton / Photo Researchers, Inc.; B10: cr: Beh Johnson / Photo Researchers, Inc.; br: Juan Silva / Getty Images; B11: cr: ©Bob Krist / Corbis; br: ©Amet Jean Pierre /Corbis Sygma; B12 David Nunuk / Photo Researchers, Inc.; B14: bl: © image100 / Corbis; br: PhotoDisc; B19 Andrew Lambert Photograph / Photo Researchers, Inc.; B22 Tom Morrison / Getty Images; B23 SPL / Photo Researchers, Inc.; B24: tl: Hulton Archive / Getty Images; tr: Wikipedia; B29: tl: ©Tom Grill / Corbis; br: Photodisc; B31: © Free Agents Limited / Corbis; B34: ©Wolfgang Kaehler / Corbis; B39: br: Volker Steger / Photo Researchers, Inc.; bl: Mauro Fermariello / Photo Researchers, Inc.; B42 Spencer Grant / Photo Researchers, Inc.; B43 Lab-Aids©, Inc.; B44: tc: Lab-Aids©, Inc.; br: Lab-Aids©, Inc.; B46: br: ©Alen MacWeeney / Corbis; bl: © Underwood & Underwood / Corbis; B48; bl: Keystone / Getty Images: br: Lab-Aids©, Inc.; B49: Doug Menuez / Getty Images; B51: bl: © Comstock / Corbis; br: © Bisson Bernard / Corbis Sygma; B54: cl: Maximiliam Stock / Photo Researchers, Inc.; cr: Maximiliam Stock / Photo Researchers, Inc.; B57: tl: Per-Anders Pettersson / Getty Images: tr: Peter Bowater / Photo Researchers, Inc.; bl: © Farrell Grehan / Corbis; B58: tl: © Ed Young / Corbis; tr: © Lowell Georgia / Corbis; B64: Lawrence Migdale / Photo Researchers, Inc.; B68 ©Vince Streano / Corbis; B71: bl: David Taylor / Photo Researchers, Inc.; br: Andrew Lambert Photography / Photo Researchers, Inc.; B75 © Philippe Eranian / Corbis; B80 TWPhoto / Corbis; B83: tl: © Karen Kasmauski / Corbis; cr: © SW Productions / Brand X / Corbis; B84: cl: © Tom Grill / Corbis: cr: © Colorblind / Corbis.

Kit item:

Element Card Photos: © 2007 Theodore Gray/www.periodictable.com

# SEPUP

# Issues & Life Science

## GENETICS

SCIENCE
EDUCATION FOR
PUBLIC
UNDERSTANDING
PROGRAM

SEPUP

UNIVERSITY OF CALIFORNIA AT BERKELEY

LAWRENCE HALL OF SCIENCE **LHS***

INCORPORATED

RONKONKOMA, NEW YORK

**This book is part of SEPUP's middle school science course sequence:**

## Issues and Earth Science

Studying Soils Scientifically
Rocks and Minerals
Erosion and Deposition
Plate Tectonics
Weather and Atmosphere
The Earth in Space
Exploring the Solar System

## Issues and Life Science

Experimental Design: Studying People Scientifically
Body Works
Cell Biology and Disease
Genetics
Ecology
Evolution
Bioengineering

## Issues and Physical Science

Studying Materials Scientifically
The Chemistry of Materials
Water
Energy
Force and Motion

Additional SEPUP instructional materials include:
CHEM-2 (Chemicals, Health, Environment and Me): Grades 4–6
SEPUP Modules: Grades 7–12
Science and Sustainability: Course for Grades 9–12

Science and Global Issues Biology: Course for Grades 9–12

 This material is based upon work supported by the National Science Foundation under Grant No. 9554163. Any opinions, findings, and conclusions or recommendations expressed in this material are those of the authors and do not necessarily reflect the views of the National Science Foundation.

*For photo and illustration credits, see page D-90, which constitutes an extension of this copyright page.*

The preferred citation format for this book is
SEPUP. (2009). Issues and Life Science. Lawrence Hall of Science, University of California at Berkeley. Published by Lab-Aids®, Inc., Ronkonkoma, NY

**SEPUP**
Lawrence Hall of Science
University of California at Berkeley
Berkeley CA 94720-5200

e-mail: sepup@berkeley.edu
Website: www.sepuplhs.org

Published by:

17 Colt Court
Ronkonkoma NY 11779
Website: www.lab-aids.com

## A Letter to *Issues and Life Science* Students

As you examine the activities in this book, you may wonder, "Why does this book look so different from other science books I've seen?" The reason is simple: it is a different kind of science program, and only some of what you will learn can be seen by leafing through this book!

*Issues and Life Science,* or *IALS,* uses several kinds of activities to teach science. For example, you will design and conduct an experiment to investigate human responses. You will explore a model of how species compete for food. And you will play the roles of scientists learning about the causes of infectious disease. A combination of experiments, readings, models, debates, role plays, and projects will help you uncover the nature of science and the relevance of science to your interests.

You will find that important scientific ideas come up again and again in different activities. You will be expected to do more than just memorize these concepts: you will be asked to explain and apply them. In particular, you will improve your decision-making skills, using evidence and weighing outcomes to decide what you think should be done about scientific issues facing society.

How do we know that this is a good way for you to learn? In general, research on science education supports it. In particular, the activities in this book were tested by hundreds of students and their teachers, and they were modified on the basis of their feedback. In a sense, this entire book is the result of an investigation: we had people test our ideas, we interpreted the results, and we revised our ideas! We believe the result will show you that learning more about science is important, enjoyable, and relevant to your life.

*IALS Staff*

*ISSUES & LIFE SCIENCE* **PROJECT**

Director (2003–2008): Barbara Nagle

Director (1995–2002): Herbert D. Thier

**AUTHORS**

Barbara Nagle

Manisha Hariani

Donna Markey

Herbert D. Thier

Asher Davison

Susan K. Boudreau

Daniel Seaver

Laura Baumgartner

**OTHER CONTRIBUTORS**

Kathaleen Burke

Richard Duquin

**CONTENT AND SCIENTIFIC REVIEW**

Peter J. Kelly, Emeritus Professor of Education and Senior Visiting Fellow, School of Education, University of Southampton, Southampton, England

Deborah Penry, Assistant Professor, Department of Integrative Biology, University of California at Berkeley, Berkeley, California

**RESEARCH ASSISTANCE**

Marcelle Siegel, Leif Asper

**PRODUCTION**

*Design and composition:* Seventeenth Street Studios

*Administrative assistance:* Roberta Smith and Anna Vorster

We would also like to thank Miriam Shein and Sylvia Parisotto for their contributions to this publication.

## FIELD TEST CENTERS

This course is a revision of *Science and Life Issues*. The following centers participated in field testing the original course or the revised materials. We are extremely grateful to the center directors and teachers who taught the program. These teachers and their students contributed significantly to improving the course.

### REGIONAL CENTER, SOUTHERN CALIFORNIA

Donna Markey, *Center Director*
   Kim Blumeyer, Helen Copeland, Pat McLoughlin, Donna Markey, Philip Poniktera, Samantha Swann, Miles Vandegrift

### REGIONAL CENTER, IOWA

Dr. Robert Yager and Jeanne Bancroft, *Center Directors*
   Rebecca Andresen, Lore Baur, Dan Dvorak, Dan Hill, Mark Kluber, Amy Lauer, Lisa Martin, Stephanie Phillips

### REGIONAL CENTER, WESTERN NEW YORK

Dr. Robert Horvat, *Center Director*
   Kathaleen Burke, Dick Duquin, Eleanor Falsone, Lillian Gondree, Jason Mayle, James Morgan, Valerie Tundo

### JEFFERSON COUNTY, KENTUCKY

Pamela Boykin, *Center Director*
   Charlotte Brown, Tara Endris, Sharon Kremer, Karen Niemann, Susan Stinebruner, Joan Thieman

### LIVERMORE, CALIFORNIA

Scott Vernoy, *Center Director*
   Rick Boster, Ann Ewing, Kathy Gabel, Sharon Schmidt, Denia Segrest, Bruce Wolfe

### QUEENS, NEW YORK

Pam Wasserman, *Center Director*
   Gina Clemente, Cheryl Dodes, Karen Horowitz, Tricia Hutter, Jean Rogers, Mark Schmucker, Christine Wilk

### TUCSON, ARIZONA

Jonathan Becker, *Center Director*
   Peggy Herron, Debbie Hobbs, Carol Newhouse, Nancy Webster

### INDEPENDENT

*Berkeley, California:* Robyn McArdle
*Fresno, California:* Al Brofman
*Orinda, California:* Sue Boudreau, Janine Orr, Karen Snelson
*Tucson, Arizona:* Patricia Cadigan, Kevin Finegan

# Contents

# Genetics

**D**

# Unit D

# Genetics

**G**race thought her new brother would look more like her than her adopted sister does. But as she looked down at the new baby, she just couldn't see a resemblance.

"Look at his light eyes and red hair! No one else in our family has red hair," Grace remarked.

Her mother smiled. "Well, Dad's sister had red hair when she was young. Then it got darker."

Grace was surprised to hear that. But she still didn't understand why her baby brother looked so different from her.

• • •

Have you ever wondered why some children look very much like their biological parents while others look completely different? Why doesn't a child look like a simple blend of his or her parents? Why do some siblings look so different?

In this unit, you will begin to find answers to these questions. Because many of the same principles apply to all organisms, you will study humans and other organisms as well.

INVESTIGATION

**S**ome children look very similar to one of their biological parents. Some appear to be more of a blend of both parents, while others don't look very much like either parent. What are the reasons for this variation in family resemblance? What causes variation among people in general? You will look at six different human **characteristics**, such as eye color, to study human variation. Each of these characteristics can occur in different versions, or **traits** (TRATES).

CHALLENGE

How much variation is shown by the students in your class?

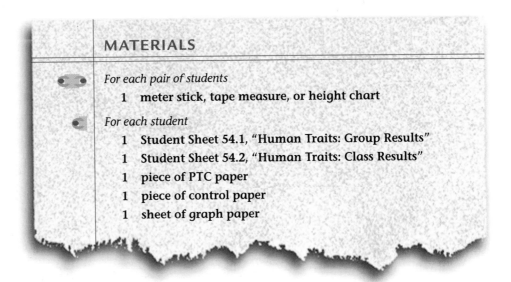

MATERIALS

*For each pair of students*
    1   meter stick, tape measure, or height chart

*For each student*
    1   Student Sheet 54.1, "Human Traits: Group Results"
    1   Student Sheet 54.2, "Human Traits: Class Results"
    1   piece of PTC paper
    1   piece of control paper
    1   sheet of graph paper

# PROCEDURE

**TONGUE ROLLING**

1. Working with your group, decide whether each person's eyes are blue, gray, green, brown, or hazel (hazel eyes are a very light brown with yellow or green tones). If a person's eyes are difficult to classify, choose the color that is closest. Record your results on Student Sheet 54.1, "Human Traits: Group Results."

2. Try to roll your own tongue into a U-shape similar to that shown at left. On the student sheet, record who can and who cannot roll his or her tongue.

3. Try to cross all the fingers of the hand you normally write with as shown below. You may use your other hand to help position the fingers. You should begin by crossing your pointer finger over your thumb, then try to cross your middle finger over your pointer finger. Continue trying to cross each finger, one by one, on top of the next finger. On the student sheet, record who can and who cannot cross his or her fingers like this.

4. Working with a partner, use a meter stick or height chart to measure each other's height in centimeters (cm). Round to the nearest 5 cm and record the results on the student sheet.

**FINGER CROSSING**

5. Working with a partner, use a meter stick or measuring tape to measure each other's arm span in centimeters (cm). Obtain the arm span by spreading your arms out sideways as far as possible, and having your partner measure from the tips of the fingers on one hand to the tips of the fingers on the other hand, as shown below. You may have to ask another student to help you hold the meter stick or measuring tape. Round to the nearest 5 cm and record the results on the student sheet.

MEASURING ARM SPAN

6. Obtain one piece of plain paper and one piece of PTC paper from your teacher.

   a. Place the piece of plain paper on your tongue and move it around to be sure it mixes with your saliva. Then remove and discard the piece of paper as directed by your teacher.

   b. Do the same thing with the PTC paper. Record whether the PTC paper tastes different from the plain paper. If it tastes different, also record whether the taste is mild or strong.

7. Complete Table 1, "Group Results Summary," on Student Sheet 54.1. Note that you do not have to record totals for the height and armspan.

8. Have one person report your group's results to your teacher.

9. Record the class totals on Student Sheet 54.2, "Human Traits: Class Results."

10. Prepare a bar graph of the class data of one of the traits, as assigned by your teacher. Be sure to label your axes and title your graph.

## ANALYSIS

1. For each of the six characteristics you studied, how many versions, or traits, are observed in your class? Copy a table like the one below into your science notebook. (For example, if your class has people with brown and blue eyes only, then you would fill in the first column with "eye color," the second column with "brown and blue," and the third column with the number "2" to represent the two colors observed.)

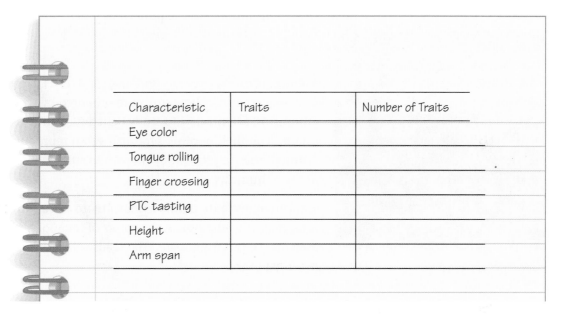

| Characteristic | Traits | Number of Traits |
|---|---|---|
| Eye color | | |
| Tongue rolling | | |
| Finger crossing | | |
| PTC tasting | | |
| Height | | |
| Arm span | | |

 2. Which of the traits you investigated—for eye color, tongue rolling, PTC tasting, crossing all your fingers, height, and arm span—do you think people inherit from their biological parents? Explain.

 3. If a trait is not inherited, what else might cause it? Explain or give some examples.

 4. If you studied more people in your community, would you expect to find more traits for each characteristic? Explain your answer.

5. **Reflection:** Who do you most look like in your family? Explain.

## EXTENSION

Gather data on ten more people who are not in your class and bring the results to class to add to the totals.

LABORATORY

Some traits appear to be passed from parents to their children. These are called **inherited** traits. The inherited bits of information that are passed directly from the parents' cells to the child's cells are called **genes**.

How do scientists find out whether a specific trait is inherited? If a trait is inherited, what information can the pattern of inheritance provide? Can anything else affect an inherited trait, or do genes determine everything about you?

*Flowering* Nicotiana *plants*

All organisms have genes and inherited traits. Scientists have learned a lot about how traits are inherited by studying other organisms. Scientists who study genetics often investigate yeast, plants, fruit flies, or other organisms that reproduce quickly. Through these studies, they have made discoveries that also apply to humans.

You will investigate plants to learn more about how traits are inherited. You will look at the colors of the plants right after they first sprout from seeds. The seeds will be from *Nicotiana*, a garden plant.

CHALLENGE

**What color leaves will you observe on the offspring of two green parent plants?**

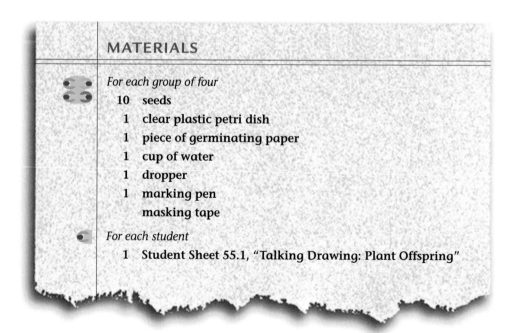

## MATERIALS

*For each group of four*
10 seeds
1 clear plastic petri dish
1 piece of germinating paper
1 cup of water
1 dropper
1 marking pen
masking tape

*For each student*
1 Student Sheet 55.1, "Talking Drawing: Plant Offspring"

# PROCEDURE

1. Observe the pictures of plant seedlings shown below. The pictures show seedlings of the parent and grandparent plants that produced the seeds you will plant. In other words, the seeds you will sprout are offspring of the parent plants displayed in the figure. Think about the possible colors of the offspring that may grow from the seeds you plant.

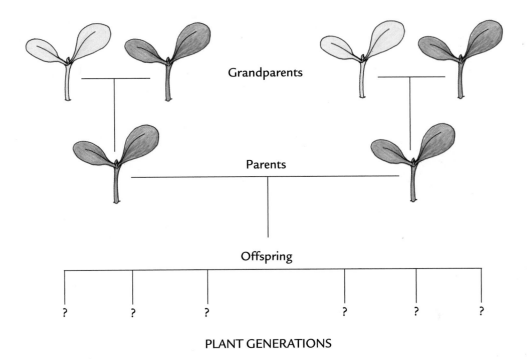

PLANT GENERATIONS

2. Place a piece of germinating paper into the bottom of your petri dish.

3. Fill the dropper with water and add drops to the paper until the paper is wet. Pour off any excess water, so that the seeds will not drown.

4. Arrange 10 seeds in the dish. Try to leave plenty of room between each seed so they will have room to grow.

5. Put the cover on the dish and use tape and a marking pen to label the dish with your group members' names. Place the label near the side of the dish.

6. Following your teacher's directions, place the dish where the seeds will receive plenty of light.

7. Check your seeds every day or two. Carefully add a few drops of water to each piece of germinating paper as needed to keep the papers moist. Avoid having any excess water in the dishes. In about ten days, your seeds will have sprouted and grown enough for you to observe their appearance. At that time, you will complete Activity 62, "Analyzing Genetic Data."

## ANALYSIS

1. Use Student Sheet 55.1, "Talking Drawing: Plant Offspring," to record your prediction for the color or colors of the plants that will grow from seeds. You may make more than one prediction, but be sure to indicate which one you think is most likely to happen.

2. What are your reasons for each prediction you proposed for Question 1? Explain.

VIEW AND REFLECT

**A**bout 100 years ago, a French doctor named Antoine Marfan described the symptoms of a young patient. Today, those symptoms are recognized as a genetic disease known as the Marfan syndrome. A syndrome is a condition that causes a pattern of physical changes. The physical changes observed in the Marfan syndrome are a result of changes in the body's connective tissue.

Connective tissue provides the connections between tissues in the body. It is found in all your organs. For example, if you ever looked closely at uncooked chicken, you may have noticed the connective tissue that attaches the skin to the muscle of the chicken.

Today, genetic counselors advise people who suspect they may have a genetic condition. If one member of this couple has the Marfan syndrome, what are the chances that any child they have will have the Marfan syndrome?

CHALLENGE

**Would you want to find out if you could have a genetic disease? Why or why not?**

## PROCEDURE

1. In your science notebook, list five diseases that can be "caught" from another person and five diseases that are inherited.

2. Read the e-mail below from Joe to his friend Megan.

3. Make a table in your science notebook to record the advantages and disadvantages of being tested, based on what you know so far about the Marfan syndrome. Leave room to add more rows to your table later.

4. Prepare a list in your science notebook of the questions you think Joe should ask Dr. Foster before he decides whether to be tested.

5. In order to prepare to watch the story on the video, first read Analysis Questions 1–4.

6. Find out more about the Marfan syndrome by watching the video "How Do Your Genes Fit?" Look for answers to Analysis Questions 1–4 and to your own questions from Step 4 as you watch the video.

To: meganR@talk.com
From: joeF@email.com

Hey Megan—

I'm trying to act cheerful because Dad says you feel the way you act, but I'm feeling kind of down. I miss my mom. It's been exactly three years since she died of that strange heart condition. The doctor didn't even know about the condition until she died.

Now Dr. Foster is saying he thinks it might have been genetic, and that means I could have inherited it. He went to a medical convention where he learned more about a condition called the Marfan syndrome. He began to suspect it caused Mom's heart problem. Now Dr. Foster's saying I should be tested even though I'm totally healthy. He says the test will tell if I inherited this Marfan gene from my mom.

He says some of the symptoms of this syndrome are being very tall and having a long face and loose joints. I'm tall and have a long face, like my mom, but I'm not double-jointed as she was. She could bend her fingers in the strangest positions—my sister and I always thought it was so cool!

They say there's a way to tell if I've got the gene my mom had, but it's complicated. Lots of our relatives would have to give blood to be tested too. Dad doesn't want me to have the test. He doesn't know if our health insurance will cover the costs. He says that doctors are making too much of a fuss about genetic diseases, and says we're better off just taking what comes and not knowing too much. Then he says if I have the gene, we might lose my health insurance and people will find out and won't hire me when I'm older.

But I keep thinking about some things Dr. Foster told me. He told me about a volleyball player named Flo Hyman who was in great shape, but then died suddenly in the middle of a game because she had this Marfan syndrome. Then I saw in the newspaper they think that the guy who wrote the musical *Rent* might also have had it. Dr. F. says if I know, I can be careful and maybe have surgery to prevent heart problems. But what if I had to give up playing soccer?

I sure wish your mom hadn't gotten that new job and moved you halfway across the state. What do you think I should do? Should I talk Dad into letting me have the test? Or should I try to forget the whole thing?

Miss ya,
Joe

## ANALYSIS

1. What are the signs that suggest a person may have the Marfan syndrome?

2. What causes the Marfan syndrome?

3. Can you "catch" the Marfan syndrome from another person, the way you can catch the flu? Explain.

4. What effect can the Marfan syndrome have on a person's life?

5. Look back at the questions you wrote in your science notebook for Step 4 of the Procedure.

   a. Were any of your questions answered? Record the new information you learned from the video.

   b. What new questions would you want to ask a doctor or genetic counselor?

6. Copy the lists of words shown below:

| List 1 | List 2 | List 3 |
|--------|--------|--------|
| hair dyed blonde | cold | environmental and genetic |
| PTC taster | mononucleosis | |
| suntan | genetic disease | arm span |
| environmental trait | athlete's foot | height |
| blue eyes due to contacts | chicken pox | natural eye color |
| long hair | infectious disease | skin color |
| | | susceptibility to disease |

a. In each list, look for a relationship among the words. Cross out the word or phrase that does not belong.

b. In each list, circle the word or phrase that includes the others.

c. Explain how the word or phrase you circled is related to the other words on the list.

7. **Reflection:** How would you behave toward a fellow student whom everyone suspects has the Marfan syndrome?

## EXTENSION

Go to the *Issues and Life Science* page of the SEPUP website for links to websites on the Marfan syndrome and other genetic conditions.

READING

**E**very human is the child of two biological parents. Most organisms that you are familiar with, like the kittens in the photo, are also the offspring of two parents. They have certain features of both parents, but are not exactly like either parent. Some organisms however, are the offspring of only one parent. They reproduce by making an exact copy of themselves. In this activity, you will read about how different organisms reproduce.

CHALLENGE **What is the difference between sexual and asexual reproduction?**

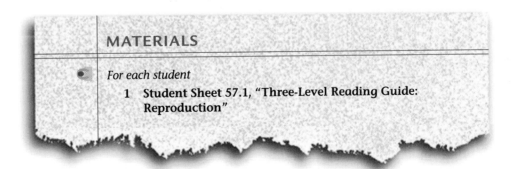

**MATERIALS**

*For each student*

1 Student Sheet 57.1, "Three-Level Reading Guide: Reproduction"

# READING

*Use Student Sheet 57.1, "Three-Level Reading Guide: Reproduction," to guide you as you complete the following reading.*

## Asexual Reproduction

If you go to an art gallery, you might see an art historian inspecting a work of art, trying to determine whether it is the original or a "reproduction." A reproduction may not be a perfect copy of the original, but it's close.

Organisms reproduce in two ways. Some organisms can use **asexual reproduction** (in which they make exact copies of themselves). If you completed the Cell Biology and Disease unit of *Issues and Life Science*, you learned about bacteria and other microorganisms. These organisms reproduce themselves asexually. A single-celled organism, such as a bacterium or an amoeba, reproduces by dividing in two (see figure below). Each new organism produced (offspring) is identical to the parent cell.

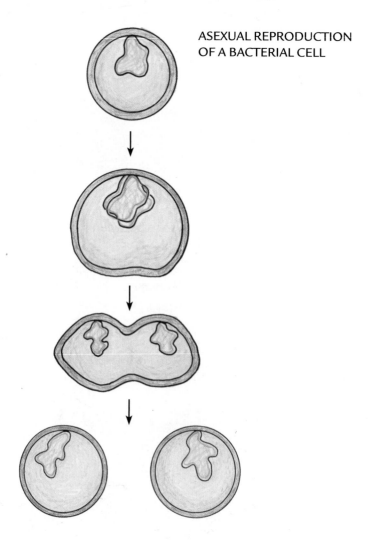

ASEXUAL REPRODUCTION
OF A BACTERIAL CELL

## STOPPING TO THINK 1

In asexual reproduction of a bacterial cell, is it clear which cell is the parent and which is the offspring? Explain.

These two identical offspring are both called clones of the single parent organism. A clone inherits all of its traits from its one parent. If you completed the Cell Biology and Disease unit, you may remember the clumps of bacteria that grew in the petri dishes in Activity 47, "Reducing Risk." Each clump was formed by many divisions over time, starting from one bacterial cell. In other words, each bacterium in the clump is a clone reproduced from that one original cell (see figure below). Each of these clones has identical traits, except in rare cases when a random change occurs. Imagine copying a sentence and making a small mistake. In the same way, a gene can be reproduced slightly differently from the original gene. This change can cause the offspring cell to have a different trait from the parent cell. This type of random change is known as a **mutation** (myoo-TAY-shun).

**BACTERIAL CLONES**

*Each clump of bacteria on this petri dish contains many cells, each identical to an original parent cell.*

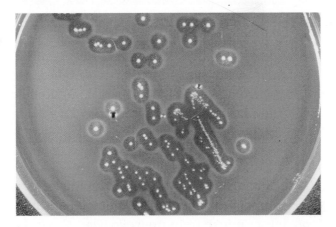

Even some multicellular organisms can reproduce asexually. Budding is the name given to a process in which a small new organism grows directly out from the parent's body. One animal that reproduces this way is the *Hydra* (see figure below).

**BUDDING HYDRA**

*One way the* Hydra *reproduces itself is by asexual budding. The "buds" will soon break off from the parent to become identical offspring organisms.*

The strawberry plant (see photo below) can also reproduce asexually, by generating tiny new plants on a rootlike runner. Each of these little plants can eventually separate from the parent and become a new individual identical to its parent. Any organism that is produced through asexual reproduction can be considered a clone, since it inherits all its traits from one parent.

runners

new plant

parent plant

**ASEXUAL REPRODUCTION OF A STRAWBERRY PLANT**

*A strawberry plant can produce a new copy of itself by using runners.*

## STOPPING TO THINK 2

Your friend tells you, "Only single-celled organisms reproduce asexually. After all, how could a multicellular organism do that?" How do you respond to your friend?

## Sexual Reproduction

Most animals and plants can also reproduce by **sexual reproduction**. In fact, humans and many other animals can only reproduce sexually. Such organisms inherit traits from two parents, not one. You are not a perfect copy of either of your parents. You also are not a perfect blend of your parents' traits. What determines which traits you get from each parent?

Sexual reproduction occurs when a tiny **sperm cell** produced by a male unites with an **egg cell** produced by a female, as shown on the next page. The union of the sperm and the egg is called **fertilization** (fur-tul-uh-ZAY-shun).

The cell that results will have genes from both the egg and the sperm. Because genes help to determine traits, sexual reproduction produces a new cell that develops into an individual with traits inherited from both parents. This new individual will be different from each of its biological parents. Also, because no two sperm or egg cells contain exactly the same information, no two offspring produced by the same parents are identical. A unique set of inherited genes means a unique set of inherited traits.

SPERM AND EGG:
FERTILIZATION

*The tiny sperm cell is about to fertilize a large egg cell.*

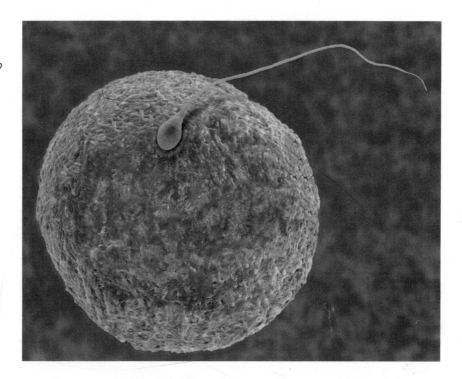

There is an exception to the last statement: identical twins. Identical twins result when one fertilized egg splits before beginning to grow and develop—the two eggs then become two genetically identical offspring or children. Only one fertilization occurs, but two organisms are produced.

Asexual and sexual reproduction are summed up in the table below.

| Reproduction | |
| --- | --- |
| **Asexual** | **Sexual** |
| One parent | Two parents |
| Offspring (clones) identical to parent | Offspring inherit traits from both parents |

## STOPPING TO THINK 3

"Fraternal twins" result when two eggs are both fertilized by sperm cells, and both develop into offspring. (This is very common in dogs and cats.) Why are identical twins much more similar than fraternal twins? Explain.

## Cloning

In nature, a **clone** is an offspring produced by asexual reproduction. Yet you've probably heard the term cloning used to describe a process that produces a sheep (or other animal) identical to its one parent. How can this be possible given that sheep (like humans) always have two parents? (Remember, mammals never reproduce asexually.)

Scientists have now produced certain organisms artificially through a type of asexual reproduction. Consider the cloning of a sheep, illustrated in the figure below. The part of the cell that contains the genes (the nucleus) is removed from one of the cells of the sheep's body. This nucleus is placed into an egg cell whose nucleus has already been removed. If this artificially fertilized egg develops in a womb, it grows into a sheep that is genetically identical to the sheep that its nucleus came from. It is therefore a clone of that sheep.

*adult sheep to be cloned*

*body cell from sheep*

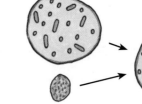

*egg cell from another sheep with nucleus removed*

*nucleus from body cell*

*nucleus is injected into egg cell*

**CLONING A SHEEP**

*artificially fertilized egg develops into a (younger) clone of first sheep*

## STOPPING TO THINK 4

How is a clone different from an identical twin?

For example, if Ocean's coin toss results in heads (**T**), and Lucy's coin toss results in tails (**t**), your first entry will be:

| Gene Combo Results | | | | |
|---|---|---|---|---|
| Offspring | Ocean's Contribution (**T** or **t**?) | Lucy's Contribution (**T** or **t**?) | Offspring's Genes (**TT**, **Tt**, **tT**, or **tt**?) | Offspring's Tail Color (blue or orange?) |
| 1 | **T** | **t** | **Tt** | blue |

---

**Remember:**
**TT** = *blue tail*
**Tt**, **tT** = *blue tail*
**tt** = *orange tail*

---

5. Repeat Steps 2–4 until you have filled in every row of the table.

6. Get together with the other pair in your group to prepare a simple table summarizing your results. Include the total number of times you got each gene combo (**TT**, **Tt**, **tT**, or **tt**) and the number of times you got each tail color (blue or orange).

7. Report the summary of your results to your teacher.

8. Add another row to your table to record the class data.

## ANALYSIS

1. What is the ratio of blue-tailed to orange-tailed critter pups? Use the class data to answer this question:

   a. Divide the number of blue-tailed offspring by the number of orange-tailed offspring.

   $$ratio\ of\ tail\ colors\ = \frac{number\ of\ blue\text{-}tailed\ offspring}{number\ of\ orange\text{-}tailed\ offspring}$$

   b. Round this value to the nearest whole number. Then express it as a ratio by writing it like this:

   $$\frac{\quad\quad\quad\quad\quad}{(whole\ number)} : 1$$

   c. Express this ratio as a pair of fractions, so that you can use them to complete the following sentence:

   "About _____ of the offspring have blue tails, and about _____ of the offspring have orange tails."

   d. Explain why the class obtained such a large ratio. For example, why isn't the ratio of blue to orange tails 1:1, that is, ½ blue and ½ orange?

2. You and your partner are about to toss two coins 100 times. Predict about how many times the outcome would be:

   **a.** heads–heads

   **b.** heads–tails

   **c.** tails–heads

   **d.** tails–tails

 3. How sure are you that you will get exactly the results you predicted for Question 2? Explain your answer.

4. Look back at Activity 58, "Creature Features." Do the results of the coin-tossing model match the Generation Three critter data? Explain.

5. What are the advantages and disadvantages of using coin tosses in a model for how genes are passed from parents to offspring? Explain.

6. Review the rules of genetics that the class developed in the last activity. Which ones make this model work?

7. Write your own definition of the phrase *dominant trait* as it is used in genetics. **Hint:** Does it mean that every time any pair of critters mates, most of the offspring will have blue tails? Why or why not?

## EXTENSION

For a larger sample size, view the data gathered by fellow students from other locations. Go to the *Issues and Life Science* page of the SEPUP website for instructions.

READING

I n Activity 59, "Gene Combo," you investigated a model for how inheritance works. This model is based on the work of Gregor Mendel. He discovered the behavior of genes 40 years before scientists learned where genes are located in the cell and almost 100 years before scientists discovered what the genes are made of!

CHALLENGE ▷ **Who was Gregor Mendel, and how did he discover the basis of heredity by breeding pea plants?**

## READING

### Part A: Mendel's Life

GREGOR MENDEL 1866

In 1865 an Austrian monk named Gregor Mendel published his work on the behavior of genes. Mendel lived in a monastery that was devoted to teaching and science, as well as religious matters. Mendel had prepared to be a science teacher and had studied math, botany, and plant breeding for several years. The monastery had an experimental garden for agricultural research. Research then, as now, included breeding varieties of plants and animals in order to produce superior food and other products. Mendel became interested in the pea plants he was working on. He wondered how the colors, shapes, and heights of offspring pea plants were related to those of the parent plants. He began a careful study of how characteristics are inherited in pea plants. Mendel's discoveries depended upon research about breeding plants, careful experiments, and creative thinking. He understood that plant seeds are produced by sexual reproduction. He also understood the mathematics of probability.

His experiments were planned so carefully and recorded so thoroughly that anyone could repeat his procedure and confirm his findings. The patterns he discovered apply to all sexually reproducing organisms, from petunias to peas, from earthworms to humans. His discoveries have helped people answer questions ranging from how to produce disease-resistant food crops to explaining human diseases such as cystic fibrosis and sickle-cell disease.

### STOPPING TO THINK 1

What personal qualities do you think Mendel must have had that helped him in his work?

## Part B: Mendel's Experiments with Pea Plants

Plants in general, and pea plants in particular, were excellent organisms for Mendel to study, for the following reasons:

- They grow into mature plants very quickly; in about 60–80 days their seeds grow and develop into mature plants.

- They produce numerous seeds rapidly.

- They have many observable characteristics that come in just two alternatives (such as purple or white flowers, yellow or green pods), with no blending of these traits (no lavender flowers, no yellowish green pods).

| Mendel's Results | Flower color | Seed color | Seed surface | Pod color |
|---|---|---|---|---|
| Original cross (generation one) | purple x white | green x yellow | wrinkled x smooth | green x yellow |
| Generation two offspring | all purple | all yellow | all smooth | all green |
| Generation three offspring | 705 : 224 (purple:white) | 6,022 : 2,001 (yellow:green) | 5,474 : 1,850 (smooth:wrinkled) | 428 : 152 (green:yellow) |

Mendel decided to breed extremely large numbers of pea plants and search for simple patterns in the offspring. The table above shows the results he obtained for four of the characteristics he studied.

Notice that Mendel did hundreds of crosses, and observed and counted the offsprings' traits for thousands of pea seeds, pods, and flowers. He then analyzed all these results and applied his knowledge of statistics and probability to infer the behavior of individual genes.

### STOPPING TO THINK 2

a. What were the advantages for Mendel in using pea plants for his breeding investigations?

b. Why did Mendel perform so many crosses for the same characteristics?

As he looked at the data, Mendel noticed an interesting relationship. If he calculated the ratio of the two traits in the third generation, he obtained a ratio very near to 3:1.

For example, for seed color the ratio of yellow to green seeds can be calculated as

$$\frac{6{,}022 \ yellow}{2{,}001 \ green} = \frac{3.01 \ yellow}{1 \ green}$$

This is almost exactly a 3:1 ratio of yellow:green. This means that for every 1 green-seeded plant, there were almost exactly 3 yellow-seeded plants in the third generation.

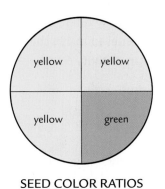

**SEED COLOR RATIOS**

You can also express this in terms of the fractions ¾ yellow and ¼ green, as shown in the pie graph at left.

Mendel concluded that not only did the green-seeded trait reappear in the third generation, but the probability of a third-generation plant having that trait was ¼—that is, about one green-seeded plant for every four plants produced overall.

He found the same ratio with other characteristics also. The 3:1 ratio he found for all of these different characteristics was the clue to how the parents' genes combine in their offspring. Based on his analysis, he proposed that:

- Each trait that appears in the second generation is the dominant version of the characteristic. The trait that is "hidden" is called **recessive**.

- Every plant has two copies of the gene for each characteristic. These two copies are called **alleles**. (The evidence suggested there was more than one copy of the gene for each characteristic in each plant, so the simplest assumption that would work was to have two alleles, or copies, per characteristic.)

- Each pea plant receives only one allele for each characteristic from each parent and ends up with two alleles of its own.

He then used these ideas to argue that the 3:1 ratio is exactly what is expected in the third generation for every plant characteristic. In the last two activities, you have explored this proposal, using disks and coins as models for genes.

## STOPPING TO THINK 3

Explain how the model in Activity 59, "Gene Combo," works exactly like Mendel's explanation for his results with pea plants.

Mendel published his results in a paper that was mostly ignored at the time. Scientists and breeders failed to understand what he had done. Never before had someone used mathematics to tackle a complex biological problem. Mendel's work was rediscovered and understood only after scientists realized that genes must be located on the chromosomes found in the nucleus of the cell. You will learn about chromosomes in Activity 63, "Show Me the Genes!"

## ANALYSIS

1. Based on Mendel's results, which trait for each pea characteristic is dominant? In your science notebook make a table like the one below. In your table, list the dominant and recessive traits for each characteristic.

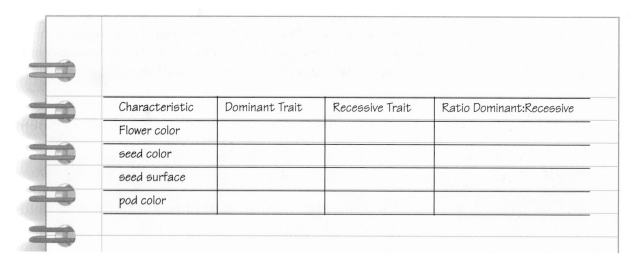

| Characteristic | Dominant Trait | Recessive Trait | Ratio Dominant:Recessive |
|---|---|---|---|
| Flower color | | | |
| seed color | | | |
| seed surface | | | |
| pod color | | | |

2. **a.** Calculate to the hundredths place the ratio of dominant to recessive for each characteristic in the third generation. Record the ratio for each characteristic in the table you prepared for Question 1.

   **b.** Why are the ratios not exactly 3:1?

3. Look at the pie chart on the previous page, which shows the ratio of green-seeded and yellow-seeded offspring. Explain why a 1:3 ratio of green-seeded plants to yellow-seeded plants is the same as a fraction of ¼ green-seeded plants.

4. Mendel performed his experiments on more characteristics than the four shown in the circle graph, "Seed color ratios," on the previous page. Why was it important for him to look at more than one characteristic?

5. **Reflection:** People often think of mathematics as important to physics and chemistry, but not to life science (biology). What is your opinion?

PROBLEM SOLVING

In previous activities you learned that each offspring receives half of its genes from one parent and half from the other parent. You also learned that different versions of a gene are called alleles. You used coin tosses to model the way alleles are passed from parents to offspring. You observed that each offspring received two alleles, one from each parent. In the simulation to determine tail color, if one parent contributed a blue tail-color allele (**T**), and the other parent contributed an orange tail-color allele (**t**), the allele combination was **Tt**. This is a critter's **genotype** (GEEN-oh-type) for that characteristic. Because the allele for the blue tail color was dominant, the physical appearance of the tail was blue. We call this the critter's **phenotype** (FEEN-oh-type) for the characteristic. In this activity you will learn how a table, called a Punnett (PUN-it) square, can help you predict the genotypes and phenotypes in a breeding experiment.

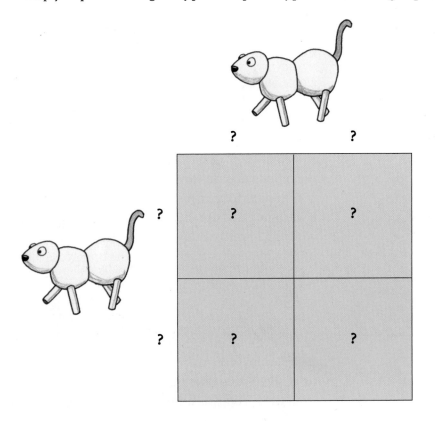

CHALLENGE  **How can Punnett squares help you predict patterns of inheritance?**

MATERIALS

*For each student*
  1   Student Sheet 61.1, "Punnett Squares—Step by Step"

## PROCEDURE

Read "How to Use Punnett Squares," and then complete the Punnett squares on Student Sheet 61.1.

## HOW TO USE PUNNETT SQUARES

A **Punnett square** is a diagram you can use to show the likelihood of each outcome of a breeding experiment . It is used when each parent's genes for a trait are known. By filling in the squares, you can find the possible genotypes of the two parents. You can also predict the chances that each phenotype will occur.

Consider the cross between Skye and Poppy as an example. The two phenotypes for tail color are blue and orange. As you modeled in Activity 58, "Creature Features," there are two versions of the tail-color gene, one for blue and one for orange. These two versions are called alleles. As you saw in Activity 59, "Gene Combo," the blue allele is written as uppercase **T** and the orange allele as lowercase **t**. This is because we know that blue tail color is dominant to orange. (You might also use **B** for blue and **b** for orange, since blue is the dominant trait. But you need to use the same letter, uppercase and lowercase, for the two alleles of any one gene. To avoid confusion, always remember to underline the uppercase letter.)

Because Skye is from an island where there are no orange-tailed critters, we can assume he has only blue tail-color alleles. So, his genotype for tail color is **TT**. Because Poppy is from an island where there are no blue-tailed critters, we can assume she has only orange tail-color alleles. So, her genotype for tail color is **tt**. An organism that has only one kind of allele for a characteristic is called **homozygous**. Skye is homozygous for the blue tail-color trait, while Poppy is homozygous for the orange tail-color trait.

## STEP 1:
## *Starting a Punnett Square*

*Every Punnett square should have a title, four boxes, the genotypes of the parents' traits listed at the left side and the top of the square, and a key.*

Write the possible alleles donated by each parent along the top of the table and left side of the table—it doesn't matter which parent you use for each position. In the table below, Skye's alleles are placed along the top and Poppy's at the left.

Each **T** along the top represents an allele in the sperm cell produced by Skye. Each **t** on the left represents an allele in the egg cell from Poppy.

## STEP 2:
## *Completing a Punnett Square*

Complete each box of the table by combining one allele from the top and one allele from the left, as shown to the right.

When you combine one allele from each parent into a box, you are representing a sperm cell fertilizing an egg.

## STEP 3:
## *Making Conclusions Using a Punnett Square*

Now you can use the Punnett square to make some conclusions. All of the offspring of Skye and Poppy will have one allele for blue tail color and one allele for orange tail color. Their genotypes will be T̲t. An organism that has alleles for two different traits is called **heterozygous.** Because blue tail color is dominant over orange, the phenotype of all offspring is blue tails, as found in the breeding experiment between Skye and Poppy.

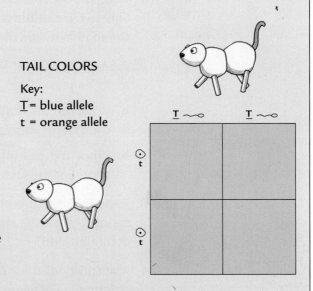

TAIL COLORS

Key:
T̲ = blue allele
t = orange allele

STARTING A PUNNETT SQUARE

*Remember: an underlined uppercase letter is used for the allele for the dominant trait. A lowercase letter is used for the allele for the recessive trait.*

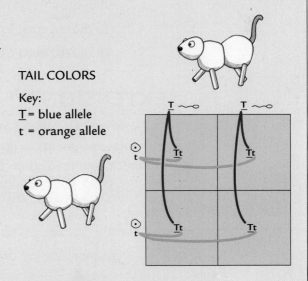

TAIL COLORS

Key:
T̲ = blue allele
t = orange allele

COMPLETING A PUNNETT SQUARE

## ANALYSIS

1. Compare the results of your Punnett square for Problem 1 on Student Sheet 61.1 with the results of the Ocean/Lucy cross in Activity 59, "Gene Combo." Why are they similar?

2. Refer to the table of Mendel's results in Activity 60, "Mendel, First Geneticist," on page D-32.

   a. What are the traits for pea flower color? Suggest letters you might use to represent the alleles for flower color.

   b. What are the traits for seed surface? Suggest letters you might use to represent the alleles for seed surface.

3. Review your results on Student Sheet 61.1. Why is it impossible for offspring to show the recessive trait if one parent is homozygous for the dominant trait?

4. A scientist has some red-eyed fruit flies. She knows that red eyes are dominant over white eyes in fruit flies. She wants to find out if the fruit flies she has are homozygous for the red eye color.

   a. What cross will be best to find out if the red-eyed fruit flies are homozygous?

   b. Use Punnett Squares to show what will happen if the red-eyed fruit flies are crossed with white-eyed fruit flies when:

      i. the red-eyed fruit flies are homozygous.

      ii. the red-eyed fruit flies are heterozygous.

## EXTENSION

Draw Punnett Squares for Generation 1 and Generation 2 of Mendel's pea plant experiments as listed in Table 1 of Activity 60. Did Mendel's results match your predictions from the Punnett Squares?

LABORATORY

**I**n this activity, you will obtain data from the seeds you germinated in Activity 55, "Plants Have Genes, Too!" and investigate whether your own data agree with Mendel's model for inheritance.

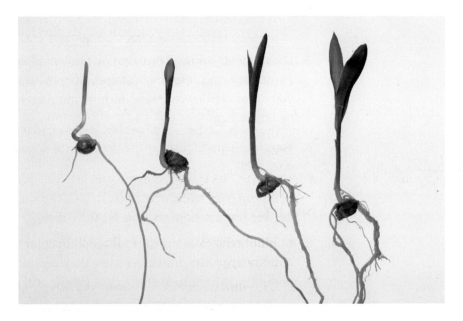

CHALLENGE

**Do your results agree with Mendel's model for inheritance?**

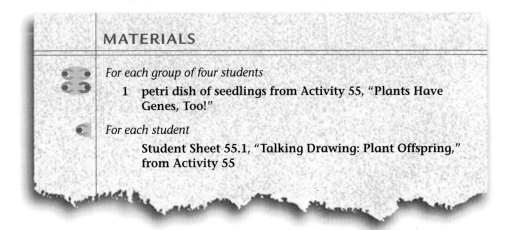

## MATERIALS

*For each group of four students*

1   petri dish of seedlings from Activity 55, "Plants Have Genes, Too!"

*For each student*

Student Sheet 55.1, "Talking Drawing: Plant Offspring," from Activity 55

## PROCEDURE

1. Get your dish of sprouted seedlings.

2. With the lid off, examine each seedling plant carefully. With your partner, count the number of green seedlings and the number of yellow seedlings.

3. Prepare a data table in your science notebook to summarize your results. Add an extra line for the class total results.

4. Report your results to your teacher, as directed.

5. Look at your original drawing on Student Sheet 55.1, "Talking Drawing: Plant Offspring." On the bottom half of the sheet, draw the results that you observe from your seedlings. Explain any differences between the two drawings.

6. Your teacher will display the class's total data. Record the data in your data table.

## ANALYSIS

1. Compare the class's results for seedling color to Mendel's results for various pea plant traits. Why are they similar? What do they suggest about the inheritance of the pale yellow and green *Nicotiana* traits?

2. Do each group's results fit Mendel's model? Explain.

3. When you first set out these seeds to germinate, you were told that they were all the offspring of two green parent plants. You were also told that each of the green parents had one green parent and one yellow parent.

   a. Based on the class's results, what can you conclude about the color alleles of each of the green parents of your seedlings?

   b. How is this breeding cross similar to the one you modeled in Activity 59, "Gene Combo"? Explain.

4. What were the genotype and phenotype of the parent plants of your seedlings?

5. Construct a Punnett square to show what will happen if one of the green parent-generation *Nicotiana* plants is crossed with a pale yellow plant. Explain the results.

## EXTENSION

For a larger sample size, view the data gathered by fellow students from other locations. Go to the *Issues and Life Science* page of the SEPUP website for instructions.

READING

**E**ven before he began his experiments on pea plants in the 1860s, Mendel knew that the genes had to be in the male and female sex cells—the sperm (or pollen) and the egg. However, no one knew *where in the cell* the genes were located until fifty years later. An individual gene is too small to be seen with a light microscope. So how did the microscope enable scientists to figure out where in the cell the genes are located? Scientists studying dividing cells, like the one shown in the photo below, provided evidence to support Mendel's ideas.

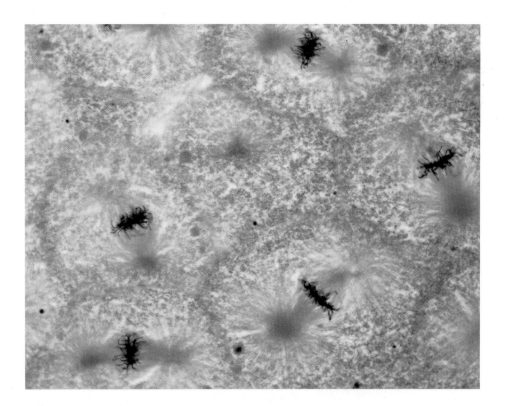

CHALLENGE **What role do chromosomes play in the inheritance of genes?**

# READING

## Part A: Chromosomes and Cell Division

Every organism must make new cells. Single-celled organisms, such as bacteria, yeast, paramecia, and amoebas, use cell division to reproduce asexually. In multicellular organisms, cell division (shown below) is necessary for the organism to grow to adulthood and to replace injured and worn out cells. When you get a cut and lose some blood, additional new blood cells and new skin cells are produced from the division of cells in your body.

CELL DIVISION

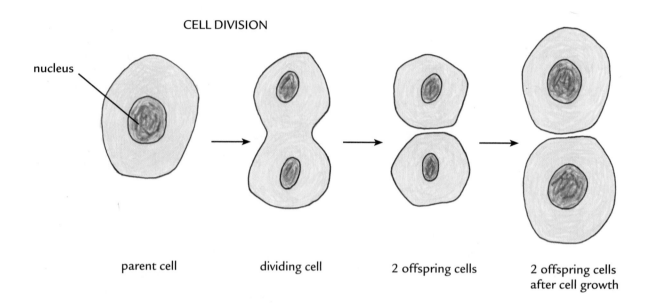

nucleus

| parent cell | dividing cell | 2 offspring cells | 2 offspring cells after cell growth |

## STOPPING TO THINK 1

How is the function of cell division in single-celled organisms different from cell division in multicellular organisms?

CHROMOSOMES IN
DIVIDING PLANT CELLS

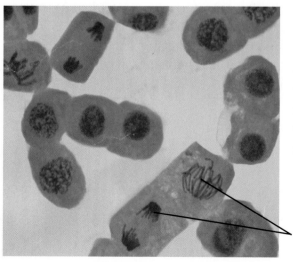

chromosomes

In the early 1900s, scientists studying cells in rapidly growing parts of plants made an interesting observation. They saw that just before cell division, the membrane around the nucleus was no longer visible and little dark structures, which they called **chromosomes**, appeared, as shown at left. When the cells split apart, the chromosomes were divided evenly between the two new cells.

When a cell is not dividing, the chromosomes are long, fine strands, like very thin spaghetti, packed into the nucleus of the cell. Before the cell divides, it makes copies of all its chromosomes so that its two offspring cells can each get a complete set. Then the chromosomes become coiled, which makes them visible when observed under a microscope. Finally, the cell divides, as shown below.

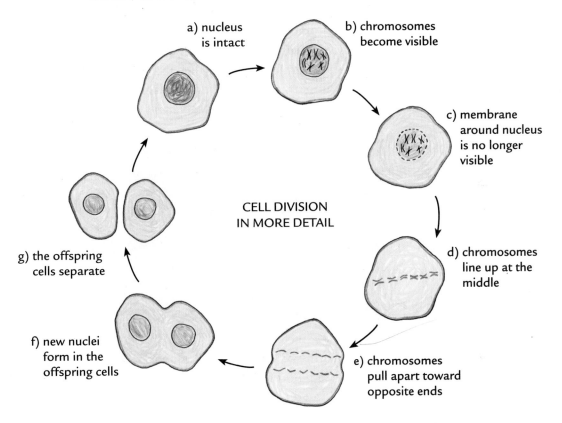

a) nucleus is intact

b) chromosomes become visible

c) membrane around nucleus is no longer visible

CELL DIVISION IN MORE DETAIL

d) chromosomes line up at the middle

e) chromosomes pull apart toward opposite ends

f) new nuclei form in the offspring cells

g) the offspring cells separate

Each cell in a human body contains 46 chromosomes. When a human cell divides, the two cells that result each contain 46 chromosomes. How can 46 chromosomes become two sets of 46? It's not magic: each crisscrossed chromosome is two identical copies that are attached to each other. As you can see below, each doubled chromosome then splits during division to become two identical, but now separate, chromosomes.

A CHROMOSOME DURING CELL DIVISION

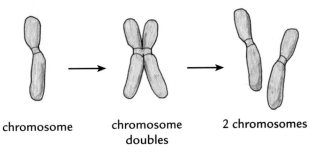

chromosome

chromosome doubles

2 chromosomes

....................................................................................................................

## STOPPING TO THINK 2

What would happen to the number of chromosomes in each cell if copies of them were not made before cell division?

....................................................................................................................

## Part B: Chromosomes and Sexual Reproduction

The 46 chromosomes in a human cell can be sorted into 23 matching pairs, as shown below. Each chromosome looks identical to its partner, with one exception: pair number 23, which are also called the sex chromosomes. Female humans have two X-chromosomes, while males have one X-chromosome and one Y-chromosome.

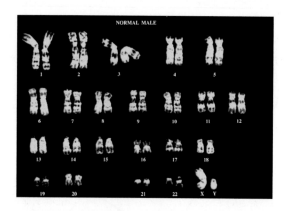

**THE 46 CHROMOSOMES IN EVERY CELL OF A MALE HUMAN**

*These chromosomes were photographed in a flattened cell; the images of each chromosome were cut out and sorted by size.*

Soon after the 23 pairs of chromosomes were observed, scientists declared that the 23 pairs of chromosomes behaved just like the genes in Mendel's model. What did they mean by that?

Sex cells (sperm and egg) are formed by a special kind of cell division, in which each cell receives copies of exactly half of the chromosomes. In humans, the body's cells contain 46 chromosomes, but the egg and sperm contain only 23 chromosomes. When a sperm fertilizes an egg cell to form the first cell of a new organism, the new cell has 46 chromosomes, as illustrated below. Half come from the mother and half come from the father.

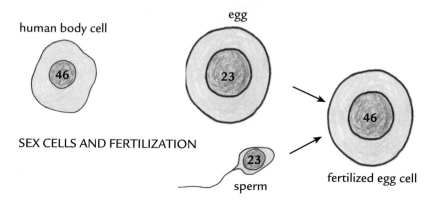

human body cell

egg

SEX CELLS AND FERTILIZATION

sperm

fertilized egg cell

## STOPPING TO THINK 3

Why must the number of chromosomes in the sperm and egg be half the number of chromosomes in the other cells of an organism?

When sex cells are produced, exactly one member of each chromosome pair moves into each offspring cell. Thus, when an egg and a sperm cell come together in fertilization, the new cell has 23 complete pairs of chromosomes, or 46 total chromosomes. Think of the 23 pairs of chromosomes as 23 pairs of socks. An egg cell has one of each kind of sock, and a sperm cell has the matching sock for each of the egg's socks. Only when they come together, when the sperm fertilizes the egg, does the resulting cell contain 23 complete pairs of socks. One member of each pair has come from the female parent, and the other from the male parent. The chromosomes of each pair carry genes for the same characteristics (see below), but the two alleles of any one gene can be different, as you've learned before.

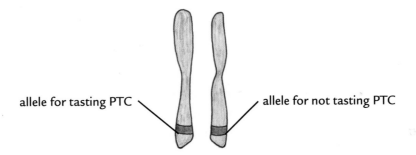

allele for tasting PTC — allele for not tasting PTC

ALLELES IN HUMANS FOR THE ABILITY TO TASTE PTC

*A matching pair of chromosomes contains two different alleles for PTC tasting, since this PTC-tasting person is heterozygous. The two alleles of the gene might differ in a single bit of genetic information.*

By comparing the microscope evidence to the work of Gregor Mendel, scientists realized that the chromosomes must carry the genes. Once scientists understood the location of the genes and the way they were passed to offspring, they realized the importance of Mendel's work.

## STOPPING TO THINK 4

Consider two children with the same two parents. Would you expect them to have the same sets of chromosomes? Explain why or why not.

### Part C: So Many Genes . . .

Human cells contain approximately 30,000 pairs of different genes. However, the human nucleus contains only 23 pairs of chromosomes. Each gene is a small portion of a chromosome. Only by careful study can scientists determine which gene (or group of genes) is responsible for a specific trait, such as eye color or blood type in humans or seed color in pea plants.

Furthermore, the more complex the trait being studied, the greater the number of different genes which contribute to it. Even diseases such as cancer are proving to result from the combined effects of many genes.

The genes are part of a long molecule called **DNA**, which stands for deoxyribonucleic acid. Each chromosome contains a long DNA molecule. Sometimes, before a cell divides, a mistake is made in a gene when the DNA is copied to make a new set of chromosomes. These mistakes are called **mutations**. If the mutation occurs during the formation of a sex cell, an offspring that results from that sex cell will be affected by the mutation. Genes give instructions to the body. Even though some mutations don't make much difference and some are even helpful, most mutations are harmful.

A mutation in a gene is like a change in a word in a sentence. For example, consider the sentence, "I hear that noise." The four letters in the word "hear" communicate a meaning. What if we change one of the letters? The results might include

I heer that noise.

I fear that noise.

The first change makes the word look a little funny, but it still sounds the same, and the meaning of the sentence would be unchanged if you heard it spoken aloud. But the second change completely changes the meaning of the sentence. Like this change in the sentence, some mutations change the information provided by the genes in which they occur.

......................................................................................................

### STOPPING TO THINK 5

How exactly does a mutation change the form of an organism? When do such mutations occur?

......................................................................................................

## ANALYSIS

1. Draw a flow diagram (a series of pictures) such as the one below that shows the locations and relative sizes of DNA, genes, chromosomes, and cells in a human body. Write a paragraph to explain your diagram.

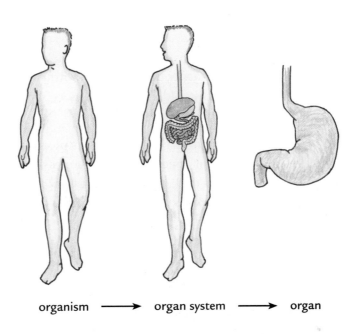

organism   ⟶   organ system   ⟶   organ

**LABORATORY**

**G**enes help determine everything about you. But how big a role do they play? Magazine and newspaper articles often describe the impact of genes and the environment on the development of human traits. Sometimes these articles refer to this as the "Heredity vs. Environment" or "Nature vs. Nurture" debate. In fact, this is not a debate that one side will "win." Your genes and your environment *both* make you a unique person. Researchers would like to know more about how genes and the environment affect human traits.

Investigations of other organisms provide examples of how genes and the environment affect traits. The shapes of trees, the colors of hydrangea flowers, and the dark coloring at the tips of a Siamese cat's ears are all traits determined by both heredity and the environment. In this activity, you will use *Nicotiana* seeds to investigate how genes and the environment affect plant growth and development.

*The cooler temperature at the tips of the cat's ears, face, paws, and tail is necessary for the dark color to develop, even though the gene for dark color is in every cell of the cat.*

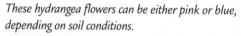
*These hydrangea flowers can be either pink or blue, depending on soil conditions.*

CHALLENGE

How does the environment affect the inherited green color trait in *Nicotiana?*

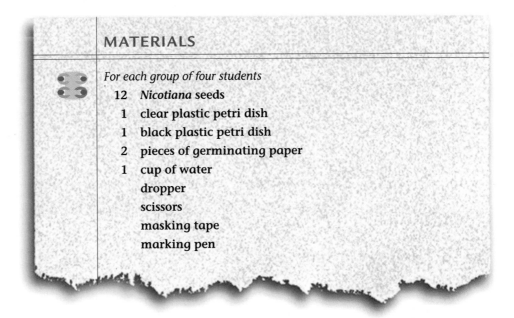

**MATERIALS**

*For each group of four students*

12 *Nicotiana* seeds
1 clear plastic petri dish
1 black plastic petri dish
2 pieces of germinating paper
1 cup of water
  dropper
  scissors
  masking tape
  marking pen

# PROCEDURE

## Part A: Planting the Seeds

1. Review the Materials list. With your group, design an experiment to test the effect of light on the inherited green color trait in *Nicotiana*.

   When designing your experiment, think about the following questions:

   • What is the purpose of your experiment?

   • What variable are you testing?

   • What is your hypothesis?

   • What variables will you keep the same?

   • What is your control?

   • How many trials will you conduct?

   • Will you collect qualitative and/or quantitative data? How will these data help you form a conclusion?

   • How will you record these data?

2. Record your hypothesis and your planned experimental procedure in your science notebook.

3. Make a data table that has space for all the data you need to record. You will fill it in during your experiment.

4. Obtain your teacher's approval of your experiment.

5. Conduct your experiment and check your seedlings every day. As with your earlier experiment, wait until the seedlings are old enough for you to be able to see which color trait they have developed.

### Part B: Analyzing Results

6. Collect your seedlings.

7. Observe your seedlings carefully to see if there are any differences. Record your observations in the data table you prepared when you set up your experiment.

8. Report your results to your teacher, as directed.

9. After analyzing your results, respond to the questions below.

## ANALYSIS

1. Was your hypothesis correct? Explain.

2. What effect did heredity have in determining the color of the seedlings?

3. What effect did the environment have in determining the color of the seedlings?

4. Can heredity alone ensure that an organism will grow well and be healthy? Explain.

5. Can the environment alone ensure that an organism will grow well and be healthy? Explain.

6. **Reflection:** What role do you think genes and the environment play in human development and health? Explain your thinking and give some examples.

## EXTENSION

For a larger sample size, view the data gathered by fellow students from other locations. Go to the *Issues and Life Science* page of the SEPUP website for instructions.

INVESTIGATION

**W**hen you considered Skye and Poppy's breeding, you focused on their tail colors. The tail-color inheritance followed the same pattern described by Mendel in his pea plant inheritance experiments. One gene, for which there are two alleles, determines each characteristic. Each characteristic has two versions, or traits. For the characteristic of tail color, the traits are blue and orange, and the alleles of the tail-color gene are referred to as **T** and **t**. One trait is completely dominant over the other, recessive, trait. In this case, blue tail color (**T**) is dominant over orange (**t**).

In fact, Skye and Poppy have a variety of traits. Some of them follow the pattern of inheritance that was described by Mendel. Others are inherited in a slightly different pattern. In this activity, you will look at some other traits and investigate how they are inherited.

Skye

Poppy

Lucy

Ocean

CHALLENGE **What are some patterns of inheritance other than the one discovered by Mendel?**

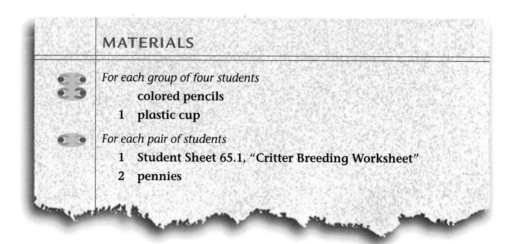

## THE MODEL

The table below shows Skye's and Poppy's traits. It also shows the traits of all their offspring. In this activity, you will look at more traits in the Generation Three offspring, which are produced when Generation Two offspring mate with each other. Lucy, a female, and Ocean, a male, are the Generation Two critters who will mate.

| Table 1: Generation One and Generation Two Traits | | | |
|---|---|---|---|
| **Characteristic** | **Skye** | **Poppy** | **100 Offspring (such as Lucy and Ocean)** |
| Body segments (number) | 2 | 3 | 3 |
| Leg color | blue | red | blue |
| Eyes (number) | 2 | 3 | 2 |
| Nose length | short | long | medium |
| Tail color | blue | orange | blue |
| Tail style | straight | curly | 48 curly, 52 straight |
| Antennas (number) | 1 | 2 | 2 |
| Spikes (color and number) | 1 short blue | 2 long green | 1 short blue + 2 long green |
| Sex | male | female | 53 female, 47 male |

## PROCEDURE

1. Work in pairs. Place Student Sheet 65.1, "Critter Breeding Worksheet," between you and your partner. The person sitting on the left side will toss a penny for Ocean, while the person on the right will toss a penny for Lucy.

2. For each toss, each partner should:

   • Hold a penny in cupped hands.

   • Shake it to the count of ten.

   • Allow it to drop from a height of about 20–40 cm (8–16 inches) onto the desk.

| Table 2: Critter Code | | |
|---|---|---|
| **Characteristic** | **Alleles** | **Trait** |
| Body segments (number) | **BB** <br> **Bb** <br> bb | 3 <br> 3 <br> 2 |
| Leg color | **LL** <br> **Ll** <br> ll | blue <br> blue <br> red |
| Eyes (number) | **EE** <br> **Ee** <br> ee | 2 <br> 2 <br> 3 |
| Nose length | **NN** <br> **Nn** <br> nn | long <br> medium <br> short |
| Tail color | **TT** <br> **Tt** <br> tt | blue <br> blue <br> orange |
| Tail style | **SS** <br> **Ss** <br> ss | curly <br> *curly or straight <br> straight |
| Antennas (number) | **AA** <br> **Aa** <br> aa | 2 <br> 2 <br> 1 |
| Spikes (color and number) | **GG** <br> **HH** <br> **GH** | 1 short blue <br> 2 long green <br> 1 short blue + <br> 2 long green |

*To find out if an **Ss** critter's tail is curly or straight, toss a coin. If it shows heads, the critter's diet contains "crittric" acid, and it develops a curly tail. If the coin shows tails, the critter's diet does not contain "crittric" acid, and it develops a straight tail.

3. The partner on the left tosses a penny to determine which allele for number of body segments Ocean gives to his offspring. If the penny shows heads, write <u>B</u> in the column titled "From Ocean" on Student Sheet 65.1. If the penny shows tails, write *b*. The other partner tosses a penny to determine the allele which Lucy gives. Write the letter for that allele in the column titled "From Lucy."

4. Determine the offspring's phenotype for number of body segments. Look at the alleles you wrote under "From Ocean" and "From Lucy." Compare these alleles with the Critter Code in Table 2 (or with the information in the first column of Student Sheet 65.1). Then write the appropriate trait in the next column. For example, if you wrote <u>B</u>b for the alleles, the trait is "3 segments."

5. Continue tossing coins and filling in Student Sheet 65.1 until you have completed the table. Use the Critter Code to determine the phenotype for each characteristic, based on the genotype of the offspring. Note the special instructions for tail style.

6. Find out if your critter is male or female by determining its sex chromosomes as follows:

   a. Ocean is an XY male. The partner representing Ocean tosses a penny. If it shows heads, Ocean donates an X chromosome to the offspring. If the penny shows tails, Ocean donates a Y chromosome to the offspring.

   b. Lucy is an XX female. The partner representing Lucy does not need to toss a penny. Lucy can donate only an X chromosome to the offspring.

   Write the sex (male or female) of the offspring in the appropriate space.

7. Use the following materials provided by your teacher to make your critter.

| Table 3: Critter Parts | |
|---|---|
| Body segments | Large foam balls connected by toothpicks |
| Heads | Small foam balls |
| Legs | Pieces of red or blue drinking straws |
| Eyes | Blue thumbtacks |
| Nose | Brass fastener, adjust length |
| Tail | Blue or orange pipe cleaner |
| Antennas | Yellow paper clip |
| Spikes | Pieces of blue or green drinking straws |

8. Draw your critter and color in the body parts.

## ANALYSIS

1. Look at the other critters made by your classmates. They are all siblings (brothers and sisters). What are their similarities and differences?

2. Which characteristics show a simple dominant/recessive pattern like tail color? List them in a table and indicate which version is dominant and which is recessive for each trait.

   Hint: Look at Table 1 to see which traits have this pattern.

   *Some traits do not show a simple dominant vs. recessive pattern. Look at Table 1 to help you answer Questions 3–5.*

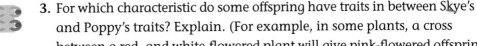

3. For which characteristic do some offspring have traits in between Skye's and Poppy's traits? Explain. (For example, in some plants, a cross between a red- and white-flowered plant will give pink-flowered offspring. This is called incomplete dominance.)

4. For which characteristic do some offspring have both Skye's and Poppy's traits? Explain. (For example, in humans, a person with type A blood and a person with type B blood can have a child with type AB blood. This is called co-dominance, as both traits appear in the offspring.)

5. Which critter trait is affected by an environmental factor, such as light, temperature, or diet? Explain.

6. Consider the pattern for sex determination.

   a. How is a critter's sex determined?

   b. Whose genetic contribution—Ocean's or Lucy's—determines the sex of the offspring?

7. Who does your critter most look like—Skye, Poppy, Ocean, or Lucy? On which traits did you base your choice?

8. Draw a critter with all recessive traits. Since there is not a recessive trait for spikes, do not include spikes in the drawing.

PROBLEM SOLVING

**A**s you now know, genes are inherited and affect the characteristics of an organism. By growing *Nicotiana* seedlings, you've seen how a trait is inherited. You have also seen how Punnett squares can help make predictions about inherited traits in large numbers of offspring.

Studying human inheritance is more difficult. Scientists cannot perform breeding experiments on people. They must use other approaches when studying human genetics. Family histories, such as the one shown below, provide one way to gather evidence about inherited traits in humans.

### A PARTIAL PEDIGREE OF HEMOPHILIA IN THE ROYAL FAMILIES OF EUROPE

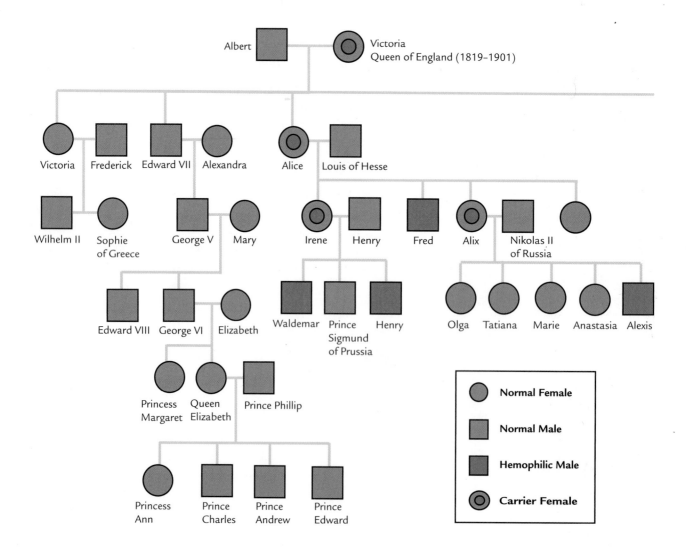

CHALLENGE  How can you use pedigrees to study human traits?

MATERIALS

*For each student*
1   Student Sheet 66.1, "Pedigree Puzzles"

# PROCEDURE

*Work with your group to read and discuss pedigrees.*

## What is a Pedigree?

One approach to studying genes in humans and other organisms is to collect data on a single trait within a family. These data can be used to construct a family tree used for genetic analysis. Such a tree is called a **pedigree**. Researchers use a pedigree to look for patterns of inheritance from one generation to the next. These patterns can provide clues to the way the trait is passed from parents to their offspring (or children).

The figure on the next page shows the pedigree for tail color in the breeding family of Skye and Poppy. Squares are used to represent males and circles are used to represent females. The zoo breeders were concerned that the orange tail color trait might be lost when it did not appear in the second generation, but it reappeared in the third generation.

CRITTER TAIL-COLOR PEDIGREE

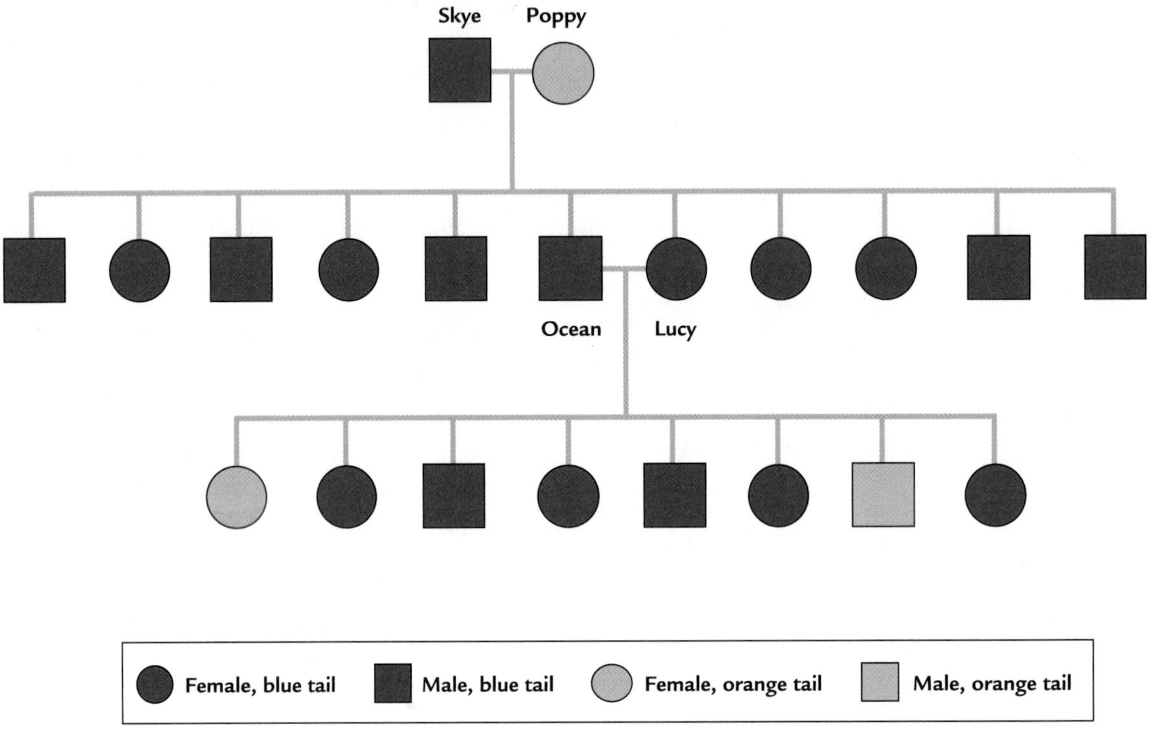

You have used Punnett squares and your knowledge of which trait is dominant to predict what fraction of the offspring of a particular pair of parents are likely to have each trait. But how do scientists find out which trait is dominant when they can't do breeding experiments? They analyze data provided by pedigrees.

## STOPPING TO THINK 1

a. Look carefully at at the figure above. Explain how the information in the pedigree tells you whether orange tail color is dominant or recessive.

b. You have used the symbols **T** and **t** for the alleles of the critter tail-color gene. On Student Sheet 66.1, "Pedigree Puzzles," label each critter in the diagram with the gene combination you think it must have.

c. Why don't you know whether each blue-tailed critter in Generation Three is homozygous or heterozygous?

## Learning from Data on Human Conditions

Most human traits, such as height, for example, are the results of interactions between many genes and environmental factors. But some hereditary diseases in humans, such as the Marfan syndrome (see Activity 56, "Joe's Dilemma"), are caused by a single gene. Pedigrees from several generations of a family enable scientists to figure out whether such a condition is dominant or recessive. Once doctors know this, they can predict how likely it is that a child of particular parents will have the condition.

For example, individuals with a condition called PKU, or phenylketonuria (feh-null-key-tun-YUR-ee-uh), cannot break down protein normally. This leads to the build-up of a chemical that causes mental retardation. If PKU is diagnosed shortly after birth, the child can be given a special diet. Children given this special diet for at least the first 10 years of life do not develop the symptoms of the condition. In most of the United States, newborns are routinely tested for PKU within a few days after birth.

Analysis of pedigrees indicates that PKU almost always appears in children of people who do *not* have the condition. The figure below shows a family in which two grandchildren inherited PKU and five did not. These numbers vary from family to family.

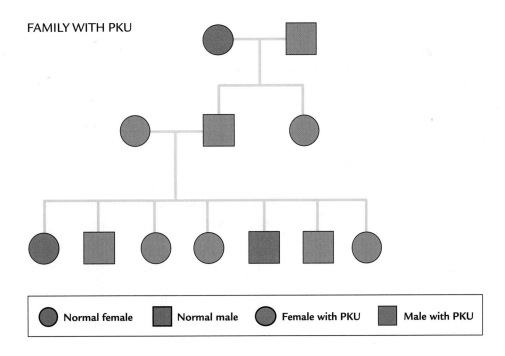

FAMILY WITH PKU

|  | Normal female |  | Normal male |  | Female with PKU |  | Male with PKU |

### STOPPING TO THINK 2

Is PKU likely to be a dominant or a recessive trait? How was it inherited by the individuals as shown in the pedigree? On Student Sheet 66.1, label each individual with the genotype(s) he or she might have.

Hint: Remember that if the condition is dominant, an affected individual could be homozygous or heterozygous. But if it's recessive, an affected individual must be homozygous for the trait.

In the study of genetic diseases, a person who is heterozygous for a recessive genetic condition is called a **carrier**. Such a person does not have the condition, but can pass on an allele for it to his or her children. The recessive allele is hidden, or masked—until it shows up in a homozygous individual who has the condition. A person who has a recessive condition is not called a carrier.

**Note:** In the Cell Biology and Disease unit of *Issues and Life Science,* you learned a very different use of the term *carrier.* When describing infectious diseases, a carrier is someone who does not show symptoms of an infectious disease but can infect other people with the microbe responsible for that disease.

### STOPPING TO THINK 3

Why is it impossible for an individual to inherit a recessive condition if only one parent is a carrier for that condition?

## Are All Hereditary Conditions Recessive?

PKU is a recessive trait; both parents must be carriers for a person to inherit it. Is this true for all other hereditary diseases, such as the Marfan syndrome? Consider polydactyly (paw-lee-DAK-tul-ee), which causes individuals to have an extra finger or toe on each hand or foot. This is not a dangerous condition, but it does run in families. The figure on the next page shows a typical pedigree of a family with polydactyly. One grandchild in this family has polydactyly, but her three siblings do not. These numbers vary from family to family.

FAMILY WITH POLYDACTYLY

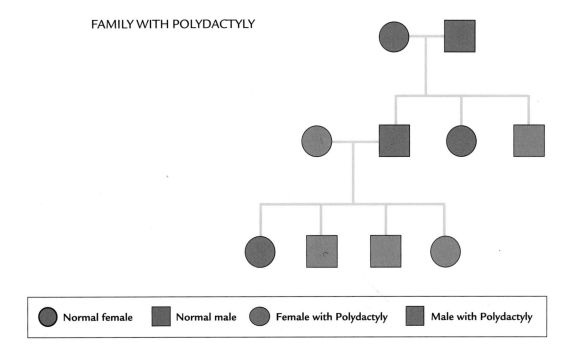

| ⬤ Normal female | ⬛ Normal male | ⬤ Female with Polydactyly | ⬛ Male with Polydactyly |

## STOPPING TO THINK 4

Is polydactyly likely to be a dominant or a recessive trait? How did the individuals in the pedigree above inherit it? On Student Sheet 66.1, label each individual with the allele combination(s) he or she might have.

Hint: Remember that if the condition is dominant, an affected individual could be homozygous or heterozygous. But if it's recessive, an affected individual must be homozygous for the trait.

Based on such pedigrees, scientists have concluded that polydactyly is a dominant trait. The condition does not skip a generation the way recessive traits can (see the pedigree for the family with PKU).

## The Genes for ABO Blood Groups

In certain plants, when purebred red flowers are crossed with purebred white flowers, the offspring are not red or white, but pink. These pink heterozygous flowers show both alleles they possess—the overall effect is an intermediate appearance. Red and white flowers are not dominant or recessive traits, but show **incomplete dominance**.

Recall the chemical PTC, which you tasted (or did not taste!) in Activity 54, "Investigating Human Traits." The ability to taste PTC is a dominant trait. However, there can be some incomplete dominance as well: heterozygous individuals may taste PTC less strongly than people with two copies of the tasting allele.

For some other characteristics, two traits both appear at the same time. Since both traits can be observed distinctly in a heterozygous individual, this is known as **co-dominance** (equal dominance).

### STOPPING TO THINK 5

Look back at Activity 65, "Breeding Critters—More Traits." Which characteristic modeled incomplete dominance? Which characteristic modeled co-dominance?

If you completed Activity 46, "Disease Fighters," in Unit C, "Cell Biology and Disease," you learned about the ABO blood groups. You saw that people with some blood types have an immune reaction to blood of certain other types; they cannot be given transfusions of these incompatible blood types. In Activity 68, "Searching for the Lost Children," you will see how blood typing can help solve real-life problems. There are *four* different blood types, A, B, O, and AB. How are blood groups inherited?

After investigating pedigrees from many families, scientists obtained the results listed in the table below.

| ABO Blood Types | | |
| --- | --- | --- |
| **Parents' Blood Types** | | **Children's Possible Blood Types** |
| O | O | O |
| A | O | A or O |
| B | O | B or O |
| A | A | A or O |
| B | B | B or O |
| A | B | AB, A, B, or O |

Based on these results, figure out the possible genotypes for each of the four blood types. Use Student Sheet 66.1 (page 2) to record your work.

| Blood Type | Possible Allele Pairs | | |
|---|---|---|---|
| O | _____ | | |
| A | _____ | or | _____ |
| B | _____ | or | _____ |
| AB | _____ | | |

## STOPPING TO THINK 6

Which two blood types are co-dominant? Which blood type is recessive?

# ANALYSIS

1. The following pedigrees represent the blood types in four unrelated families. In each case, the parents have Type A and Type B blood.

FOUR BLOOD TYPE PEDIGREES

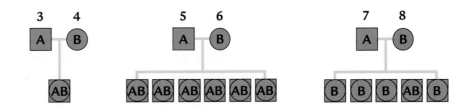

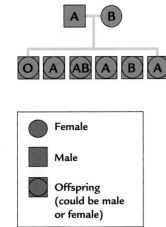

a. Which of the eight parents are definitely heterozygous for the Type O allele? Explain.

b. Which of the eight parents are probably not heterozygous for the Type O allele? Explain.

c. Can you be certain that the parents you named in response to Question 1b do not have a Type O allele? Explain.

RED represents the presence of a genetic condition in all the pedigrees for Analysis Questions 2–4.

2. The pedigree shown below represents Genetic Condition One. Use your understanding of pedigrees and this pedigree to answer the following questions. Use Student Sheet 66.1 (page 3) to try out allele combinations for related individuals.

   a. Is Genetic Condition One most likely a dominant or a recessive trait? Explain your reasoning.

   b. Is Jan most likely to be homozygous dominant, heterozygous, or homozygous recessive?

GENETIC CONDITION ONE

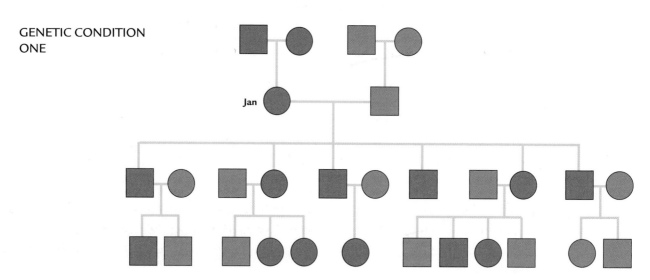

3. The pedigree shown below represents Genetic Condition Two.

   a. Is Genetic Condition Two most likely a dominant or a recessive trait? Explain your reasoning.

   b. Is Marcus most likely to be homozygous dominant, heterozygous, or homozygous recessive?

GENETIC CONDITION TWO

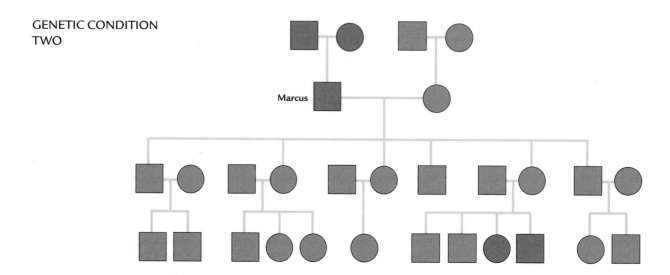

**4.** The pedigree shown below represents Genetic Condition Three.

   **a.** Is Genetic Condition Three most likely a dominant or a recessive trait? Explain your reasoning.

   **b.** Is Sophia most likely to be homozygous dominant, heterozygous, or homozygous recessive?

GENETIC CONDITION
THREE

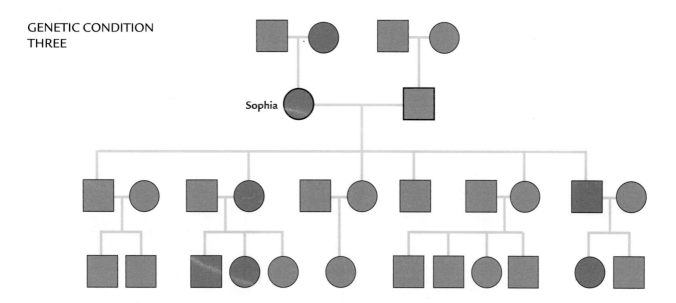

**5.** The term *carrier* is used very differently in genetics than in the study of diseases.

   **a.** What is being "carried" by a genetic carrier? What is being "carried" by a disease carrier?

   **b.** How does transmission occur for genetic conditions? How does transmission occur for infectious diseases?

TALKING IT OVER

**N**ew tests are being developed for genetic conditions as scientists learn more about the genes that cause them. These tests will help people plan their lives, as well as lead to actions that help prevent some conditions from having serious effects. But these new tests also raise issues for individuals and for society.

CHALLENGE

**How do individuals and society react to the issues raised by genetic testing?**

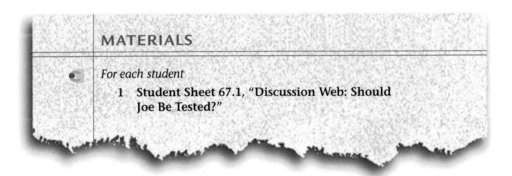

MATERIALS

*For each student*

1 Student Sheet 67.1, "Discussion Web: Should Joe Be Tested?"

# PROCEDURE

1. Review the table of advantages and disadvantages you recorded in your science notebook for Activity 56, "Joe's Dilemma."

2. Read the e-mail below from Joe to his friend Megan.

3. Add to your table from Activity 56, "Joe's Dilemma," any advantages and disadvantages of being tested that you learn from the reading.

# READING

to: meganR@talk.com

from: joeF@email.com

Megan—

I've learned more from the doctor and genetic counselor about this condition I might have. The Marfan syndrome is dominant—it's caused by a single mutated allele of a gene that affects connective tissue. Connective tissue is found in joints, the lens of the eye, the aorta—in other words, all over your body.

But having the Marfan syndrome doesn't mean that all those parts will be affected. I might still have the condition even though I have only some of the symptoms. The doctors started to figure this out after my mom died and my cousin Amber developed some problems with her eyes. Now they suspect that my grandfather, my uncle, and my cousin might have the Marfan syndrome. My grandfather and uncle are healthy so far, like me. The only way they can be sure if we have the Marfan syndrome is to test our genes. Dr. Foster says it's important to know if I have it so we know how closely to monitor my heart.

Because the Marfan syndrome can be caused by many different mutations in this gene, scientists can't test for just one Marfan mutation. They have to check to see if I inherited the mutated allele that runs in my family. They will compare my DNA to DNA from my grandfather, uncle, cousin, and other family members who do not have the Marfan syndrome. This test will let me know for sure if I have the Marfan gene that my mother had.

My dad still doesn't want me to be tested. He's worried people will treat me differently, or that he won't be able to get health insurance for me. Dr. Chee, my genetic counselor, said that can be a problem. She thinks more laws will be passed to prevent genetic discrimination. But, right now, we aren't sure if the legal system will protect me.

If the test is positive, I will probably have to quit playing soccer. We were hoping I'd get a soccer scholarship to college—Coach thinks there's a good chance I could. But I've been doing some reading. If you have the Marfan syndrome they keep a close watch on your heart. They can even do surgery if you develop serious heart problems. The doctor says I can probably live to a healthy old age, even if I do have this condition, as long as I take the right precautions.

What do you think I should do, Megan?

Joe

## ANALYSIS

1. Joe's family pedigree is shown below. How would a genetic counselor answer the following questions?

   a. If Joe has the Marfan syndrome, is he likely to be homozygous or heterozygous? Explain your answer.

   b. If Joe has the Marfan syndrome and has a child someday, what is the probability that his child will have the Marfan syndrome? (Assume that the child's mother does not have the Marfan syndrome.) Make a Punnett square and explain your answer.

PEDIGREE FOR JOE'S FAMLY

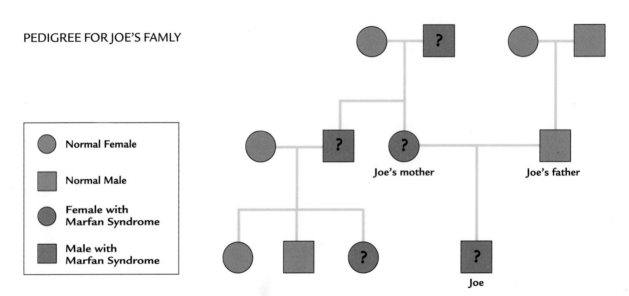

2. The Marfan syndrome is a dominant trait. Write your own definition of *dominant trait* as it is used in genetics. Use evidence to explain whether the dominant trait is always the most common trait in a human population.

3. Pretend that you are Joe's friend. Write a letter to Joe telling him whether you think he should be tested.

   Hint: To write a complete answer, first state your opinion. Provide two or more pieces of evidence that support your opinion. Then consider all sides of the issue and identify the trade-offs of your decision.

## EXTENSION

For links to more information on genetic conditions, go to the *Issues and Life Science* page of the SEPUP website. Use the website as a starting point to research issues related to genetic conditions and genetic testing.

INVESTIGATION

**T**he study of genetics provides scientists with answers to many questions and provides people with some practical solutions to problems. You learned about some of the practical outcomes of genetics when you studied Joe's dilemma. Genetic testing can help people take action about genetic conditions, but there are concerns involved as well.

Another practical outcome of genetics research is the ability to identify people. For example, wars and political actions sometimes lead to young children being taken from their families. When many years have passed, how can families ever find their children again?

**CHALLENGE** ➡ Can you use blood types to help identify lost children?

## MATERIALS

*For each student*
1   Student Sheet 68.1, "Guide to the Lost Children"
1   Student Sheet 68.2, "Finding the Lost Children"

## *Searching Scientifically*

Belinda and John and their good friends, Mai and Paul, almost never talk about their lost children. Five years ago, they were separated from their young children when enemy troops invaded their village of Namelia. Belinda and John escaped with their oldest son, but their two younger children, Serena and Noah, were captured. Mai and Paul lost both of their two young children. Many other young children and some of the elder people in the village were also captured.

When peace returned, the villagers searched for their lost children. After months of searching and waiting, there was no sign of them. But recently, the local authorities helped one family find one of their children in the village of Samarra, 100 miles away. He had been 6 years old when he was taken, so he remembered his parents and his name. Belinda and John decide to travel to Samarra with Mai and Paul.

When they reach Samarra, the authorities tell them they have found some children who were adopted during the war five years ago. These children were adopted shortly after the attack on Namelia, and evidence suggests they were originally from that village. The citizens of Samarra had fought the enemy troops and were able to save some of the children. The families who adopted the children have taken good care of them and they do not want to give them up. Nevertheless, the authorities hire some genetics experts, including you, to help identify the lost children.

One way to begin the process of identifying children of specific parents is to look at their blood groups. The ABO blood group and Rh factor will be used to determine which children cannot be matches. Rh factor is another kind of blood type. Rh positive is dominant over Rh negative.

## PROCEDURE

1. You have been chosen to join the genetics team going to Samarra. Before you leave you must review what you have learned about the genetics of the ABO blood group. Meet in your group of four to do this.

2. To help you with your assignment, look at your copy of Student Sheet 68.1, "Guide to the Lost Children." Fill in the possible alleles for each person in Tables 1 and 2.

3. Examine the information in Tables 1 and 2 about Belinda and John, Mai and Paul, and the eight children who are the right ages to be their children. Use this information to complete the steps below to decide which children might belong to each of the two couples.

   a. First determine which of the girls might be Belinda and John's lost daughter Serena. Use the table provided on Student Sheet 68.2, "Finding the Lost Children," to explain your reasoning for each of the four girls.

   b. Determine which of the boys might be Belinda and John's lost son Noah. Use the table provided to explain your reasoning for each of the four boys.

   c. Determine which of the boys might be Mai and Paul's lost son Ben. Use the table provided on Student Sheet 68.2, "Finding the Lost Children," to explain your reasoning.

   d. Determine which of the girls might be Mai and Paul's lost daughter Jade. Use the table provided to explain your reasoning.

## ANALYSIS

1. How certain are you that some of the eight children belong to Belinda and John or to Mai and Paul?

2. What additional evidence would help you identify the lost children?

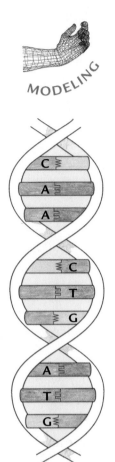

MODELING

**B**lood type results show that some of the lost children *might* be Belinda and John's or Mai and Paul's, but how can the investigators know for sure? DNA typing can be used to check for exact DNA matches. This is sometimes called **DNA fingerprinting** because it gives a unique result that helps identify people, but it is actually very different from regular fingerprinting. Since DNA fingerprints of relatives are much more alike than those of unrelated people, they can be used to find out if people are related.

Each person, except for identical twins, has unique genetic information. This information is encoded in long molecules of DNA in the chromosomes. DNA can be extracted from cells, cut into pieces, sorted, and stained. The pattern of these DNA fragments looks almost like a complicated bar code. DNA fingerprinting reveals your own unique pattern, which is almost as unique as your DNA itself.

The genetic code is made up of four "letters" (A, T, C, and G), each of which stands for one of four related chemicals that are strung together in the DNA. The order of these letters provides information. Since the sequences of the genes do not vary much among people, fingerprinting genes would not easily give information that could be used to tell people apart. (Two different alleles of the same gene might vary in only 1 of hundreds of letters.) However, long regions of DNA between the genes vary a lot more among people and can be used to tell people apart. That is why we "fingerprint" these regions between the genes.

*DNA is double-stranded. One strand provides the information in the gene. Both strands are needed when the gene is copied.*

CHALLENGE ➡ **What makes your DNA fingerprint unique?**

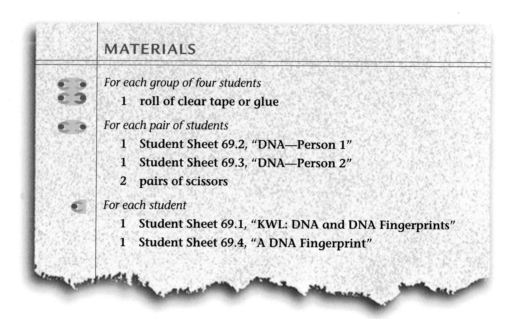

## MATERIALS

*For each group of four students*
1   roll of clear tape or glue

*For each pair of students*
1   Student Sheet 69.2, "DNA—Person 1"
1   Student Sheet 69.3, "DNA—Person 2"
2   pairs of scissors

*For each student*
1   Student Sheet 69.1, "KWL: DNA and DNA Fingerprints"
1   Student Sheet 69.4, "A DNA Fingerprint"

## PROCEDURE

*Use Student Sheet 69.1, "KWL: DNA and DNA Fingerprints," to guide you as you complete the following activity.*

### Part A: How are DNA fingerprints used?

1.  Compare the DNA fingerprints in the illustration. Blood found on a broken window pane at the scene of a burglary provided the first fingerprint. The other two fingerprints are from two suspects. In your science notebook, record your conclusion about whose blood was on the window.

Blood at crime scene          Suspect 1          Suspect 2

Different lengths of DNA are in different positions on the "fingerprint." That's because the fragments of a person's DNA are sorted by length. Note that some of the bands are darker than others. Pieces that are the same length are piled in one spot. Therefore, the dark bands represent the more common lengths of DNA in each person.

### Part B: Why is every person's DNA fingerprint so different?

2. Take one of the Student Sheets showing DNA sequences and give the other to your partner. Keep the Person 1 DNA separate from the Person 2 DNA.

3. Assemble the DNA strand: Cut out the strips of DNA. Tape them together in order, forming a single long strand. (Real DNA extracted from cells has several billions of these letters—and they're already strung together!)

4. Hold the DNA from Person 1 above the DNA from Person 2. Compare the DNA sequences, looking for similarities and differences. Record your observations in your science notebook.

5. Cut the DNA strand by making cuts only AFTER the sequence of letters AAG. For example, the following sequence would be cut like this:

A A T G C T A G T T C G G T G A T A A G ✂ C G G T G T T T A G G C T T A G

6. Sort your DNA pieces, with the longest piece at the left end of Student Sheet 69.4, "A DNA Fingerprint," and the shortest piece at the right end. See the example below.

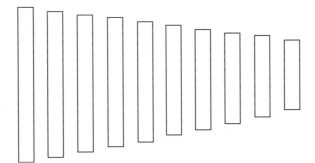

7. Tape or glue your DNA pieces onto Student Sheet 69.4, "A DNA Fingerprint."

8. Compare your DNA fingerprint to one prepared by another student who had the same person as you did. Do the DNA fingerprints match? Should they?

9. Read "How DNA Fingerprinting Is Performed in the Lab" on next page.

## How DNA Fingerprinting Is Performed in the Lab

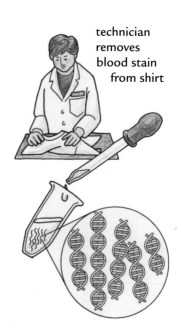

technician removes blood stain from shirt

1. Technicians put the cell sample into a tiny test tube. They break open the cells and use chemicals to extract, or take out, the DNA.

2. The DNA is cut into pieces with special chemicals called enzymes.

3. The pieces of DNA are separated based on their length:

   • The pieces are put into a hole in a flat, rectangular agar gel.

   • The technician then runs an electrical current across the gel, which makes the pieces of DNA move toward the positive end.

   • The smaller pieces of DNA move faster than the bigger pieces.

4. Special techniques are used to make the bands of differently sized DNA visible.

cut up DNA

short pieces of DNA

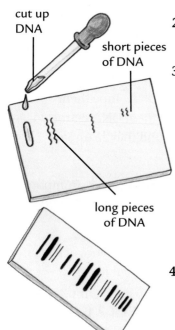

long pieces of DNA

## ANALYSIS

1. In your science notebook, create a table like the one below. In the table, match the steps you did in the simulation to the steps scientists use to make DNA fingerprints.

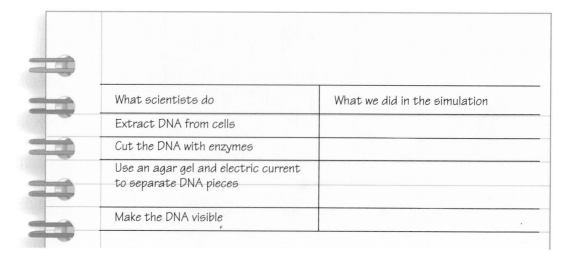

| What scientists do | What we did in the simulation |
|---|---|
| Extract DNA from cells | |
| Cut the DNA with enzymes | |
| Use an agar gel and electric current to separate DNA pieces | |
| Make the DNA visible | |

2. Look at this DNA fingerprint.

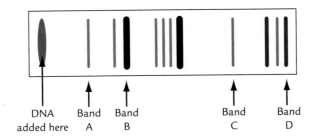

DNA added here    Band A    Band B      Band C    Band D

     **a.** Which single band represents the smallest pieces of DNA? Explain how you can tell.

     **b.** Which single band represents the most common length of DNA for this fingerprint? Explain how you can tell.

3. Why are DNA fingerprints unique to each person? In your explanation, refer to the way that DNA is cut up and sorted, and refer to the DNA of Person 1 and Person 2 from the activity.

## EXTENSION

Go to the *Issues and Life Science* page of the SEPUP website for links to web-sites about the Human Genome Project. Here you can explore some of the latest research on human genes.

**D**NA testing is more time-consuming and expensive than blood typing; that's why the investigators of the lost children used blood typing first. But DNA fingerprints are so reliable and show so much about a person's genetic information that they provide very strong evidence in cases involving identification.

DNA fingerprinting is used to verify biological relatives, to identify bodies, and to figure out who was present at the scene of a crime. Special techniques have recently been developed to increase the DNA found in very tiny specimens: DNA can now be collected from microscopic specks of blood, fragments of old teeth, or even the root of a single hair!

Many scientists use DNA fingerprinting and similar techniques in their work. Anthropologists use it to study ancient remains such as Egyptian mummies. Biologists use DNA fingerprinting to compare the DNA of various living organisms in order to investigate evolutionary relationships. Paleontologists have even used the technique on dinosaur blood found in insects preserved in amber. (But dinosaur cloning is still far from being possible!)

**CHALLENGE** ➡ **How can DNA fingerprinting help find the lost children?**

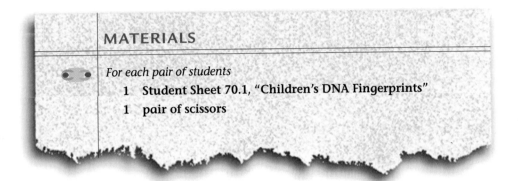

MATERIALS

*For each pair of students*
  1   Student Sheet 70.1, "Children's DNA Fingerprints"
  1   pair of scissors

## PROCEDURE

1.  The figure below shows the DNA fingerprints of a child, his or her biological parents, and an unrelated child. Examine and compare the DNA fingerprints. Record your observations in your science notebook.

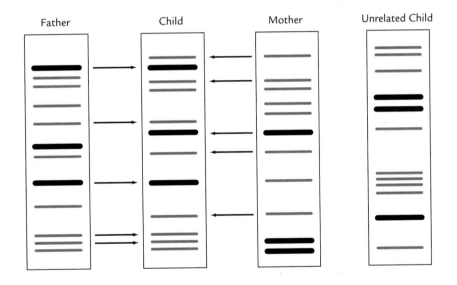

2.  To try to identify their missing children, Mai, Paul, Belinda, and John each give blood and have their DNA fingerprints made. They obtain a court order to test the blood of the children in Samarra.

Student Sheet 70.1, "Children's DNA Fingerprints," has the DNA fingerprints for the eight children you considered in Activity 68, "Searching
for the Lost Children." Cut out the DNA fingerprints and compare them
one by one to the parents' DNA fingerprints, shown below. Be sure to
include the label with the fingerprint (for example, "Girl 1").

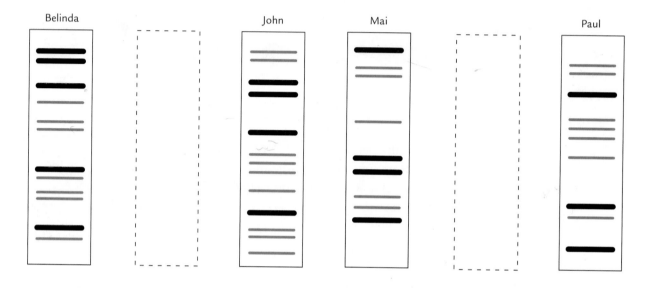

3. Record your observations and conclusions in your science notebook.

4. Luckily, Belinda remembers that she has a tooth that her daughter, Serena,
   lost when she was two years old. The root of the tooth is used to extract
   some DNA. Compare the daughter's DNA fingerprint to the DNA fingerprints of the girls in Samarra. Record your observations.

## ANALYSIS

1. Use DNA fingerprint evidence and the blood type evidence from Activity
   68, "Searching for the Lost Children," to explain each of the following:

   **a.** Which child or children are not likely to be those of Belinda and
   John?

   **b.** Which child or children are likely to be those of Belinda and John?

   **c.** Which child or children are not likely to be those of Mai and Paul?

   **d.** Which child or children are likely to be those of Mai and Paul?

2. Write a convincing statement about which of the eight children (if any) are
   the children of Belinda and John, and which of the children (if any) are the
   children of Mai and Paul. In your statement, provide as much evidence
   as you can to convince a judge that the biological children of these parents
   have been found. Be sure to include evidence from previous activities.

*Serena's DNA fingerprint*

# 71 Should We?

TALKING IT OVER

**D**NA fingerprinting can be used to identify children who are lost or kidnapped at a young age. Dr. Mary-Claire King helped develop and apply genetic techniques to identify over 50 lost children in Argentina. The methods she developed continue to help parents and grandparents find children in other countries torn by war and political conflict.

*These people in Argentina are demanding to know what happened to the children who disappeared.*

CHALLENGE ⟹ **What are the ethical issues involved in using genetic information?**

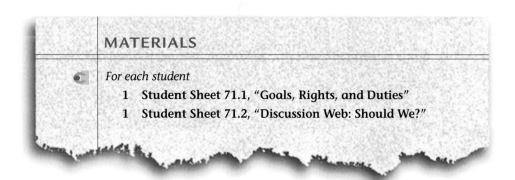

**MATERIALS**

*For each student*

1  **Student Sheet 71.1, "Goals, Rights, and Duties"**
1  **Student Sheet 71.2, "Discussion Web: Should We?"**

# A TRUE STORY

From 1976 to 1983, a military dictatorship controlled the country of Argentina. During that time, at least 15,000 citizens who were opposed to the dictatorship "disappeared." Most of the adults were killed. Witnesses reported that most of their children who were too young to talk or remember what happened were taken away to live with other families. At the end of the dictatorship, about 200 of these children were thought to still be alive.

The grandmothers of the lost babies formed a group and collected stories about the missing children. As the children entered kindergarten, school secretaries would secretly phone the grandmothers to report suspicious-looking birth certificates from newly registered students. Other evidence was also available: some of the mothers arrested during the dictatorship had managed to write the names of their children and themselves on prison walls before they died. In 1983, a new government replaced the dictatorship and a presidential commission was formed to study the problem. Thousands of people were interviewed. All these strands of evidence were collected and woven together. By 1984 the grandmothers thought they knew where many of their grandchildren were, but more evidence was needed before disrupting the lives of the children and their adoptive families. A genetics expert named Dr. Mary-Claire King was consulted.

Dr. King had perfected an advanced DNA fingerprinting technique to help make identification of biological relationships more reliable. She also helped set up a collection of blood samples and DNA fingerprints.

Using several types of evidence (including genetic evidence), some of the children were identified. Even with sophisticated genetic techniques, not all families were reunited: of the 200 missing children, only 50 were found by their grandmothers. Yet Dr. King's work continues to help people in Argentina and in other areas of the world.

Cases like this raise an important ethical question. Scientists can find ways to identify lost children, but how should society use this information? The decision to return the children to their biological parents affects adoptive parents, biological parents, and children. Sometimes the answers to these questions are difficult.

## Making a Decision

Consider the story of the lost children of Namelia. The court is convinced that Belinda and John have found both of their children. Mai and Paul have found their son. But the families who adopted the children were guilty of no wrong. They adopted the orphaned children, have taken good care of them, and want to keep them just as strongly as their biological parents want them back. A group of ethics experts has been asked to recommend what should be done.

You will use methods of ethical analysis to analyze the case of the lost children of Namelia. An analysis of goals, rights, and duties will help you explore the ethics of this case.

## PROCEDURE

Think about the goals, rights, and duties of each group of people involved in the decision of whether to return the children to their biological parents. Record your ideas on Student Sheet 71.1, "Goals, Rights, and Duties."

## Analyzing Goals, Rights, and Duties

**Goals:** *What is the action intended to accomplish?*

In this case, what goals would be accomplished by returning the children to their biological parents or grandparents? Goals may differ depending on whom you ask.

For example, the goals of a member of a sports team participating in a game might include having fun, making friends, and/or winning. The goals of the coaches may be the same, or may include other goals, such as teaching good sportsmanship. The goal of the umpire may be to be certain the game is played fairly and according to the rules. The goal of a parent may be for the team member to get exercise.

**Rights:** *What are the rights of the people involved?*

For example, in the United States, the right to an education, the right to freedom, and the right to a trial if one is accused of a crime are just a few of the rights to which everyone is entitled by law.

**Duties:** *What are the duties of the people involved?*

For example, parents have a duty to provide food and a home for their young children. A judge in a courtroom has a duty to ensure that the rules of the court and the law are followed.

## ANALYSIS

1. What are the pros and cons of reuniting the children with their biological parents or grandparents seven years later?

2. Imagine you are a judge trying to make a fair and final decision about whether to reunite the children from Samarra with their biological families from Namelia. Write your ruling and your explanation. Be sure to discuss any difficult ethical trade-offs you have had to make.

   Hint: To write a complete answer, first state your opinion. Provide two or more pieces of evidence to support your opinion. Then consider all sides of the issue and identify the trade-offs of your decision.

3. **Reflection:** How does the goals, rights, and duties method help you think about ethical issues?

## EXTENSION

Research an issue in genetics that interests you. To get started with links to more information on recent research and issues in genetics, go to the *Issues and Life Science* page of the SEPUP website.

# Index

A **bold** page number identifies the page on which the term is defined.

## Credits

# SEPUP

# Issues

# & Life Science

## EVOLUTION

SCIENCE
EDUCATION FOR
PUBLIC
UNDERSTANDING
PROGRAM

S E P U P

UNIVERSITY OF CALIFORNIA AT BERKELEY

LAWRENCE HALL OF SCIENCE **LHS***

**LaB-aiDS®**

**INCORPORATED**

RONKONKOMA, NEW YORK

**This book is part of SEPUP's middle school science course sequence:**

## Issues and Earth Science

Studying Soils Scientifically
Rocks and Minerals
Erosion and Deposition
Plate Tectonics
Weather and Atmosphere
The Earth in Space
Exploring the Solar System

## Issues and Life Science

Experimental Design: Studying People Scientifically
Body Works
Cell Biology and Disease
Genetics
Ecology
Evolution
Bioengineering

## Issues and Physical Science

Studying Materials Scientifically
The Chemistry of Materials
Water
Energy
Force and Motion

Additional SEPUP instructional materials include:
CHEM-2 (Chemicals, Health, Environment and Me): Grades 4–6
SEPUP Modules: Grades 7–12
Science and Sustainability: Course for Grades 9–12

Science and Global Issues Biology: Course for Grades 9–12

 This material is based upon work supported by the National Science Foundation under Grant No. 9554163. Any opinions, findings, and conclusions or recommendations expressed in this material are those of the authors and do not necessarily reflect the views of the National Science Foundation.

*For photo and illustration credits, see page F-64, which constitutes an extension of this copyright page.*

The preferred citation format for this book is
SEPUP. (2009). Issues and Life Science. Lawrence Hall of Science, University of California at Berkeley. Published by Lab-Aids®, Inc., Ronkonkoma, NY

**SEPUP**
Lawrence Hall of Science
University of California at Berkeley
Berkeley CA 94720-5200

e-mail: sepup@berkeley.edu
Website: www.sepuplhs.org

Published by:

17 Colt Court
Ronkonkoma NY 11779
Website: www.lab-aids.com

## A Letter to *Issues and Life Science* Students

As you examine the activities in this book, you may wonder, "Why does this book look so different from other science books I've seen?" The reason is simple: it is a different kind of science program, and only some of what you will learn can be seen by leafing through this book!

*Issues and Life Science,* or *IALS,* uses several kinds of activities to teach science. For example, you will design and conduct an experiment to investigate human responses. You will explore a model of how species compete for food. And you will play the roles of scientists learning about the causes of infectious disease. A combination of experiments, readings, models, debates, role plays, and projects will help you uncover the nature of science and the relevance of science to your interests.

You will find that important scientific ideas come up again and again in different activities. You will be expected to do more than just memorize these concepts: you will be asked to explain and apply them. In particular, you will improve your decision-making skills, using evidence and weighing outcomes to decide what you think should be done about scientific issues facing society.

How do we know that this is a good way for you to learn? In general, research on science education supports it. In particular, the activities in this book were tested by hundreds of students and their teachers, and they were modified on the basis of their feedback. In a sense, this entire book is the result of an investigation: we had people test our ideas, we interpreted the results, and we revised our ideas! We believe the result will show you that learning more about science is important, enjoyable, and relevant to your life.

*IALS Staff*

*ISSUES & LIFE SCIENCE* PROJECT

Director (2003–2008): Barbara Nagle

Director (1995–2002): Herbert D. Thier

**AUTHORS**

Barbara Nagle

Manisha Hariani

Donna Markey

Herbert D. Thier

Asher Davison

Susan K. Boudreau

Daniel Seaver

Laura Baumgartner

**OTHER CONTRIBUTORS**

Kathaleen Burke

Richard Duquin

**CONTENT AND SCIENTIFIC REVIEW**

Peter J. Kelly, Emeritus Professor of Education and Senior Visiting Fellow, School of Education, University of Southampton, Southampton, England

Deborah Penry, Assistant Professor, Department of Integrative Biology, University of California at Berkeley, Berkeley, California

**RESEARCH ASSISTANCE**

Marcelle Siegel, Leif Asper

**PRODUCTION**

*Design and composition:* Seventeenth Street Studios

*Administrative assistance:* Roberta Smith and Anna Vorster

We would also like to thank Miriam Shein and Sylvia Parisotto for their contributions to this publication.

## FIELD TEST CENTERS

This course is a revision of *Science and Life Issues*. The following centers participated in field testing the original course or the revised materials. We are extremely grateful to the center directors and teachers who taught the program. These teachers and their students contributed significantly to improving the course.

### REGIONAL CENTER, SOUTHERN CALIFORNIA

Donna Markey, *Center Director*
Kim Blumeyer, Helen Copeland, Pat McLoughlin, Donna Markey, Philip Poniktera, Samantha Swann, Miles Vandegrift

### REGIONAL CENTER, IOWA

Dr. Robert Yager and Jeanne Bancroft, *Center Directors*
Rebecca Andresen, Lore Baur, Dan Dvorak, Dan Hill, Mark Kluber, Amy Lauer, Lisa Martin, Stephanie Phillips

### REGIONAL CENTER, WESTERN NEW YORK

Dr. Robert Horvat, *Center Director*
Kathaleen Burke, Dick Duquin, Eleanor Falsone, Lillian Gondree, Jason Mayle, James Morgan, Valerie Tundo

### JEFFERSON COUNTY, KENTUCKY

Pamela Boykin, *Center Director*
Charlotte Brown, Tara Endris, Sharon Kremer, Karen Niemann, Susan Stinebruner, Joan Thieman

### LIVERMORE, CALIFORNIA

Scott Vernoy, *Center Director*
Rick Boster, Ann Ewing, Kathy Gabel, Sharon Schmidt, Denia Segrest, Bruce Wolfe

### QUEENS, NEW YORK

Pam Wasserman, *Center Director*
Gina Clemente, Cheryl Dodes, Karen Horowitz, Tricia Hutter, Jean Rogers, Mark Schmucker, Christine Wilk

### TUCSON, ARIZONA

Jonathan Becker, *Center Director*
Peggy Herron, Debbie Hobbs, Carol Newhouse, Nancy Webster

### INDEPENDENT

*Berkeley, California:* Robyn McArdle
*Fresno, California:* Al Brofman
*Orinda, California:* Sue Boudreau, Janine Orr, Karen Snelson
*Tucson, Arizona:* Patricia Cadigan, Kevin Finegan

# Contents

**Evolution**

F

# Unit F

# Evolution

It was Kenya's fourth visit to the pet store. Ever since she decided she wanted a pet lizard for her birthday, she had tried to come every day. She still hadn't decided which lizard she would like to have—and her birthday was less than a week away!

"Excuse me, young lady, can I help you?" asked the sales clerk behind the counter.

"I want a lizard for my birthday," replied Kenya. "But I can't decide which one I like best. There are so many different kinds—and they look so different."

"Some of them eat different foods, too," added the sales clerk.

"I don't understand how there can be so many different kinds of the same animal," said Kenya. "It's amazing! I wonder how it happened."

• • •

Have you ever wondered about the amazing variety of organisms on Earth? How did they evolve? How are they related? Just as historians study the history of humans, some scientists study the history of life on Earth. They do this by gathering evidence, making connections, creating models, and testing theories. In this unit, you will learn to interpret the many sources of evidence that exist for the evolution of life on Earth.

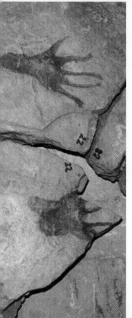

TALKING IT OVER

**W**hen the last member of a species dies without any surviving offspring, we say that that species has become **extinct**. Every species alive today is related to many other species that have already become extinct. Becoming extinct is not a sign of inferiority, but just another sign that ecosystems are constantly changing. In fact, it is estimated that 99.9% of all species that have ever lived on Earth are now extinct. Today, species that have such a small population that they are in danger of becoming extinct are called **endangered species**.

CHALLENGE

**What are the trade-offs in deciding whether to save an endangered species or to re-create an extinct one?**

*Extinct animals include dinosaurs and saber-toothed cats.*

*Endangered animals include tigers and gorillas.*

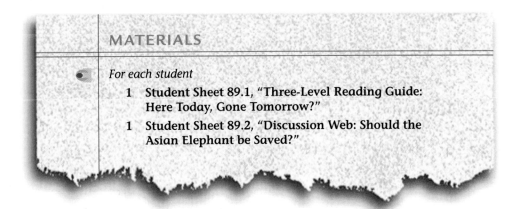

MATERIALS

*For each student*
1   Student Sheet 89.1, "Three-Level Reading Guide: Here Today, Gone Tomorrow?"
1   Student Sheet 89.2, "Discussion Web: Should the Asian Elephant be Saved?"

## PROCEDURE

*Use Student Sheet 89.1, "Three-Level Reading Guide: Here Today, Gone Tomorrow?" to guide you as you complete the following reading.*

### Mammoths and Elephants

You may know that dinosaurs became extinct about 65 million years ago, 64 million years before humans evolved. There is evidence that at least one enormous asteroid crashed into Earth at that time. Many scientists believe that this created huge clouds of dust that blocked out the sun for a long period of time. Plants and other producers form the base of the food web. A loss of sunlight would cause the death of many producer species, which, in turn, would cause the death of many consumer species, such as dinosaurs. By the time the dust settled and sunlight could reach Earth's surface, thousands of species, including the dinosaurs, had become extinct and most ecosystems were greatly changed.

One species that became extinct much more recently is the mammoth. If mammoths were still around, they would be close relatives of the elephants

living on Earth today. The entire bodies of some mammoths were trapped during the most recent ice age and have remained frozen ever since. Explorers have tasted mammoth meat, as have several curious scientists! Some scientists think that the tissue of frozen mammoths is in good enough shape to bring mammoths back from the dead.

Mammoths evolved 3 to 4 million years ago, about 60 million years after dinosaurs became extinct (Figure 1). Mammoths thrived and spread to North America about 1.8 million years ago. But about 10,000 years ago, all but a few small herds of mammoths died. The last mammoth died

FIGURE 1:
TIMELINE

around 4,000 years ago. There is no evidence that an asteroid or other catastrophic event brought about the extinction of the mammoths.

What did happen 10,000 years ago that caused this huge drop in the mammoth population? One possibility is that the mammoths could not survive the drastic changes in climate and vegetation that occurred when the last ice age ended. In addition, humans—who lived at the same time as the mammoths—were moving into new environments as their population grew. The end of the last ice age helped expand the range of humans into areas where mammoths lived. Increased hunting of mammoths by humans may have contributed to their extinction.

While mammoths and modern elephants are closely related, mammoths are not direct ancestors of modern elephants. In fact, until the mammoth became extinct, mammoths and elephants were alive in different parts of the world. Based on fossil remains, the common ancestor of both modern elephants and mammoths is estimated to have lived 4 to 5 million years ago. The fossil considered to be the first member of their order is dated at about 55 million years ago. Since then, scientists believe that there have been over 500 different elephant and mammoth species. Only two of these species are alive today: the Asian (or Indian) elephant and the African elephant. Figure 2 shows a "family tree" including modern elephants and several extinct relatives. Populations of both African and Asian elephants are declining, and the Asian elephant is considered an endangered species.

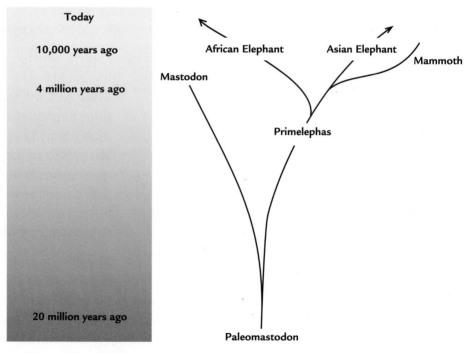

FIGURE 2: EVOLUTION OF MODERN ELEPHANTS

*African elephant*

*Asian elephant*

The Asian elephant is smaller than the African, with smaller ears and a slightly rounded or flat back. Asian elephants have a double-domed fore-head (African elephants have only a single dome). In addition, Asian elephants have a single "finger" on the upper tip of the trunk, while African elephants have a second on the lower tip.

Unlike African elephants, which all have tusks, only the male Asian elephants have them. In fact, even some of the male Asian elephants do not grow tusks! Killing elephants for their ivory is illegal in India and China. Still, most of the large-tusked male Asian elephants have already been killed for their ivory.

Asian elephants used to roam from Iran to southern Asia (see the map on the next page). In the early 1900s, approximately 250,000 Asian elephants lived in the wild. Today, it is estimated that no more than 50,000 Asian elephants are left. Their population has declined by more than 80% in less than 100 years! Without intervention, Asian elephants will most likely become extinct. By passing laws, raising money, creating wildlife pre-serves, and raising awareness, some people are working hard to save the Asian elephant.

Not all people are fighting to save Asian elephants. Asian elephants are forest animals. As the human population increases, forests have been cut down to build farms and villages. Today, most wild Asian elephants have been forced to live in hill and mountain regions. A single adult elephant eats about 330 pounds of grasses, roots, leaves, and bark each day, and these environments cannot always supply enough food. Elephant herds often seek out nearby farms that grow crops such as sugar cane and grains. These farms suffer crop loss, property damage, and even loss of life. In an average year, Asian elephants kill approximately 300 people in India alone.

Loss of habitat, combined with human hunting, has caused the decline in the Asian elephant population, a situation similar to that faced by the mammoth several thousand years ago. Should the Asian elephant be saved, or should this species be allowed to become extinct, just like the mammoth and millions of other species before it? Are people spending too much time, energy, and money trying to save endangered species? Or should efforts be increased, perhaps by going so far as to try to re-create extinct species, as has been proposed for the mammoth?

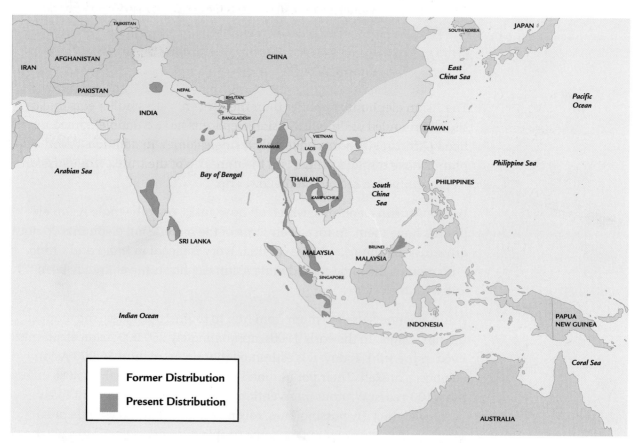

HISTORIC AND CURRENT RANGE OF ASIAN ELEPHANTS

## ANALYSIS

1. What are the similarities and differences between the extinction of mammoths and the possible extinction of Asian elephants?

2. Use evidence from this activity to explain why the mammoth could once have been considered an endangered species.

3. Some scientists would like to try to re-create a living mammoth by removing the DNA from a fertilized elephant egg and replacing it with mammoth DNA.

   a. Which species of elephant egg do you think scientists should try first?

   b. Do you think scientists should try to re-create a living mammoth? Explain.

4. Should people try to save wild populations of the Asian elephant? Support your answer with evidence and discuss the trade-offs of your decision.

   Hint: To write a complete answer, first state your opinion. Provide two or more pieces of evidence that support your opinion. Then discuss the trade-offs of your decision.

## EXTENSION

Learn more about attempts to save the Asian elephant from extinction and proposals to bring the mammoth back to life. Start at the *Issues and Life Science* page of the SEPUP website.

**M**any species have become extinct during the history of Earth. How can you know these creatures ever existed? The evidence is right under your nose—or your feet, to be more precise.

Our planet's thin outer layer, the crust, can be up to 40 kilometers (25 miles) thick. The crust is made up of many layers of rock that have been forming for over 4 billion years, and are still forming today. These rock layers can form when a volcanic eruption covers the land with lava, or when a flood spreads out a layer of mud. Lava, mud, or even sand can eventually harden into solid rock. New rock layers can also form over hundreds of years as sediment—sand, dirt, and the remains of dead organisms— gradually settles on the bottom of a lake or ocean.

Any new layer of rock can seal off the layer below it. Organisms trapped within these sealed off layers can become part of the rock itself. Any trace of life preserved in a rock is called a **fossil.** It can be an entire organism, a part of an organism, a footprint, a piece of feces, or a piece of shell, bone, or tooth.

CHALLENGE ⟹ **What can fossils tell you about organisms that lived in the past?**

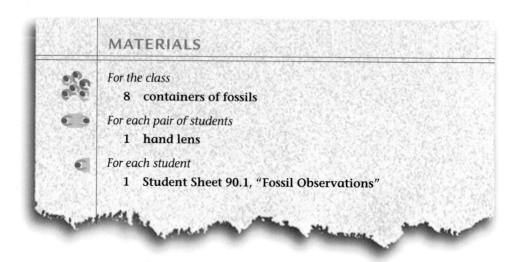

## MATERIALS

*For the class*
  8  **containers of fossils**

*For each pair of students*
  1  **hand lens**

*For each student*
  1  **Student Sheet 90.1, "Fossil Observations"**

## PROCEDURE

1. Work in a group of four. Collect a pair of fossils. One pair in the group should begin by examining one of the fossil specimens, the other pair begins by examining the other specimen.

2. Work with your partner to identify the unique features of the fossil. Be sure to look at both specimens of the species. Use the magnifier to help you.

3. On Student Sheet 90.1, "Fossil Observations," sketch the general shape and unique features of this type of fossil. Then record additional observations that are difficult to show in your sketch, such as color or size. Note that your group of four has two specimens of the same fossil. You can write observations on both of these specimens.

4. When directed by your teacher, exchange your pair of fossils with another group of four students.

5. Repeat Steps 1 through 4 until you have examined all eight types of fossils. As you continue to look at more fossils, observe similarities and differences among the different fossils.

## ANALYSIS

1. Review your notes on the eight different types of fossils.

   a. What can you infer about each of these? For example can you infer what habitat they lived in or whether they are related?

   b. Explain, using evidence from this activity to support your answer.

   c. What additional information would you like to have about the fossils?

2. In this activity, you were given a fossil to examine. What additional observations could you have made about the fossil if you had discovered it?

3. Choose one of the eight fossils you examined.

   a. Based on the fossil, describe what you think this organism looked like when it was alive. Include your evidence for your description.

   b. In what type of environment would you expect to find this organism? Explain your reasoning.

4. Although you probably have a vivid picture of dinosaurs in your mind, no one has ever seen a living dinosaur. All the evidence for the existence of dinosaurs comes from fossils.

   a. What details about the appearance and behavior of dinosaurs do you think would be easiest to determine from fossils?

   b. What details about the appearance and behavior of dinosaurs do you think would be hardest to determine from fossils?

**P**aleontologists (pay-lee-uhn-TALL-uh-jists) are scientists who study fossils. Fossils are rarely complete and are often just a shell, half a leaf, or a couple of bones. In some cases, the only evidence left by an organism is its tracks. Footprints and other types of animal tracks can be fossilized in the same way as actual body parts. But what can you find out from just footprints? Like detectives, paleontologists can use the information from fossil footprints to determine how an organism moved, how fast it traveled, what type of environment it lived in, and what it might have been doing when its footprint was formed.

**CHALLENGE** → **How can fossil footprints be used to study the behavior of animals that were alive millions of years ago?**

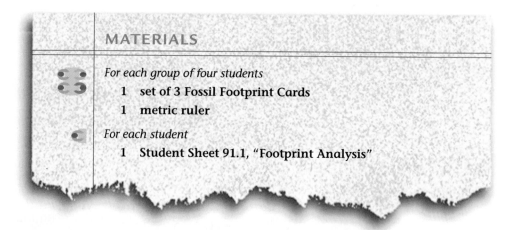

## MATERIALS

*For each group of four students*
- 1 set of 3 Fossil Footprint Cards
- 1 metric ruler

*For each student*
- 1 Student Sheet 91.1, "Footprint Analysis"

*Few fossil remains are as complete as this 10 million-year-old rhinoceros in Nebraska.*

## *Evidence Comes in Steps*

A fossil footprint site has just been discovered! You take a helicopter to the location in the hope that your expertise will be useful. The rest of the team is slowly brushing away layers of sediment to carefully uncover the footprints.

Your task is to use your observations to draw inferences and then develop a hypothesis about what happened to form the footprints. As the footprints are uncovered, there will be more evidence to examine. Remain open to new possibilities as the investigation continues.

# PROCEDURE

## Part A

1. Examine Fossil Footprint Card 1, which shows what the team has uncovered so far.

2. In your group, discuss what you think was happening while these footprints were being created. You do not have to agree, but:

   - If you disagree with others in your group about what happened, explain to the rest of the group why you disagree.

   - Listen to and consider other people's explanations and ideas.

3. Record your ideas in the first row of Student Sheet 91.1, "Footprint Analysis." Separate your ideas into observations and inferences. **Note:** Even though some of your inferences may conflict with other inferences, consider as many ideas as possible.

4. Time passes and more footprints are uncovered. Obtain Fossil Footprint Card 2.

5. Repeat Step 2. Then record your additional observations and inferences in the second row of Student Sheet 91.1. However, do not change what you wrote in the first row!

6. Time passes and a third section of footprints is uncovered. Obtain Fossil Footprint Card 3.

7. Repeat Step 2. Then record your additional observations and inferences in the third row of Student Sheet 91.1. Remember, do not change what you wrote in the first two rows!

8. Look back at all your observations and inferences. Try to think of the best possible explanation for how the footprints were formed. Record your strongest hypothesis in your science notebook. If you have two or more hypotheses in mind, record them all, but rank them from most likely to least likely.

9. Answer Analysis Questions 1 and 2.

*Fossil footprints*

## Part B

10. Hypotheses change as scientists gather new data. The information in Table 1 below has just come in from the fossil site!

| Table 1 | Average Depths of Footprints (Scenario 1) | | |
|---|---|---|---|
| | Card 1 | Card 2 | Card 3 |
| Larger footprints | 6.0 cm | 6.2 cm | 8.3 cm |
| Smaller footprints | 2.5 cm | 2.6 cm | —— |

a. What hypotheses would the data in Table 1 support?

b. Explain how these data could provide more evidence in support of one or more hypotheses.

11. Instead of the data from Table 1, imagine you just received the data in Table 2 below.

| Table 2 | Average Depths of Footprints (Scenario 2) | | |
|---|---|---|---|
| | **Card 1** | **Card 2** | **Card 3** |
| Larger footprints | 6.0 cm | 6.2 cm | 6.1 cm |
| Smaller footprints | 2.5 cm | 2.6 cm | —— |

a. What hypotheses would the data in Table 2 support?

b. Explain how these data could provide more evidence in support of one or more hypotheses.

c. What factor(s) might explain the difference in the depth of the footprints in the different scenarios?

## ANALYSIS

1. Why is it important for scientists—and people in general—to distinguish between observations and inferences when they develop a hypothesis?

2. Imagine that the team uncovered a fourth section of footprints. Draw what you predict this fourth section might look like. Explain how it would provide more support for the hypothesis you favor.

3. a. Think back to an activity in which you came up with hypotheses based upon evidence, such as Activity 74, "Observing Organisms," in the Ecology unit. Describe an example of an observation and an inference based upon that observation and explain how the two are different.

   b. Describe an example of an observation and an inference from a recent event in your everyday life.

MODELING

**A**s you learned in Activity 90, "Figuring Out Fossils," the history of Earth is divided into time spans. These time spans do not last any specific number of years. The beginnings and endings of the time spans are determined by fossils—either the appearance of new types of fossils that are not found in any older rocks or the disappearance of fossils that are commonly found in older rocks. With the help of radioactive dating technology, scientists have made good estimates of how many years each time span lasted.

CHALLENGE

**How long have organisms been living on Earth?**

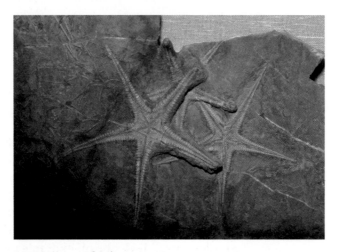

*Jurassic sea star fossils*

## MATERIALS

*For the class*
  2  sets of 8 fossils

*For each pair of students*
  1  set of 6 Time Cards
  1  metric ruler
  1  90-cm strip of paper

*For each student*
  1  Student Sheet 92.1, "Personal Time Scale"
  1  Student Sheet 92.2, "Major Divisions of Geologic Time"

# PROCEDURE

## Part A: Personal Time Scale, Geologic-Style

1. Look at the following list of events. Write the event that occurred most recently at the top of the column labeled "Order of Events" on Student Sheet 92.1, "Personal Time Scale."

   I started fourth grade.
   I ate or drank something.
   I learned to walk.
   I woke up.
   I was born.
   I took a breath.
   I started kindergarten.
   I learned to read.
   My parents were born.

2. Use the remaining spaces in the "Order of Events" column to write down the other events from most recent (at the top) to most distant (at the bottom).

3. In the column "Number of Years Ago," write the number of years ago that each event occurred (you can round off to the nearest year, or half-year). Like a paleontologist, count time backward from the present day. For example, if the event occurred 10 years ago, write "10 ya" as the time of the event. (The unit "ya" means "years ago.")

4. Think of a major event in your life that is important to you. (It may or may not already be described in your "Order of Events" column). Use this event to divide your time scale into two time periods by drawing a horizontal line to mark when the event occurred. For example, if you choose entering school as the major event, you could draw a line right below "I started kindergarten."

*These students were born about 14 ya.*

5. Name the two time periods that you just created. For example, if you drew a line at the time you first started school, the time period before that could be called "Pre-Schoolian."

6. As a class, compare the events that you and your classmates chose to divide your personal time scales into two periods. Work together to agree on a single event that was important to everyone in class. Agree on names for the time periods before and after that event.

## Part B: Geologic Time

7. Imagine that a paleontologist asks you to help her put in order some periods of time in the history of life. With your partner, read carefully the information on the six Time Cards and arrange them with the oldest on the left and the most recent on the right.

8. In your science notebook, record the order in which you placed the cards.

9. View the work of other student groups. Observe the similarities and differences between their orderings and yours. Discuss your choices.

10. Obtain Student Sheet 92.2, "Major Divisions of Geologic Time," and a 90-cm strip of paper from your teacher. Use the information on Student Sheet 92.2 to arrange the cards in the order scientists have determined from geologic evidence. In your science notebook, record any changes that you needed to make to your original order.

11. Follow Steps 11a–d to construct a timeline of the last 4,500 million years:

   a. Using Student Sheet 92.2, work with your partner to calculate the distance (in cm) that each time span will cover on your timeline.

   Hint: Since your timeline must represent 4,500 million years over 90 centimeters, first divide 4,500 by 90 to determine how much time each centimeter will represent.

*Mount Rainier formed approximately one million ya (1 mya).*

b. Draw a vertical line near one end of your long strip of paper and label it "The Origin of Earth."

c. Using "The Origin of Earth" as a starting line, use a ruler and your calculations from Student Sheet 92.2 to mark the boundaries between the time spans.

d. Label each time span with its name and each boundary with its defining event.

12. The figure below presents photos of the fossils you examined and sketched in Activity 90, "Figuring Out Fossils." In the appropriate time period on your timeline, draw and label a quick sketch or outline of each one.

A FEW FAMILIAR FOSSILS

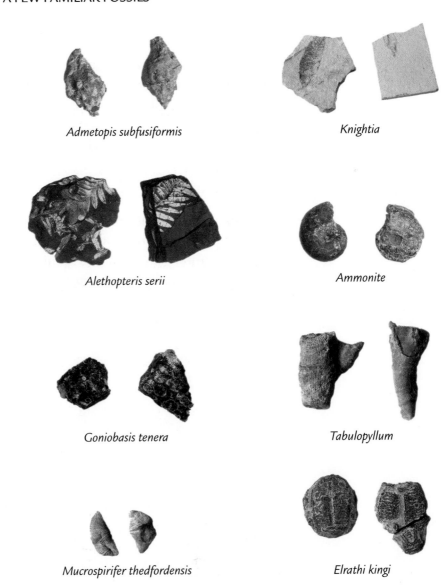

*Admetopis subfusiformis*

*Knightia*

*Alethopteris serii*

*Ammonite*

*Goniobasis tenera*

*Tabulopyllum*

*Mucrospirifer thedfordensis*

*Elrathi kingi*

## ANALYSIS

1. Think back to how you and your classmates divided your personal time scales into periods. How do you think scientists determined how to divide geologic time into its periods?

2. The total length of your timeline of Earth's history is 90 cm. Use your timeline to determine the fraction of Earth's history that:

   **a.** single-celled organisms have lived on our planet.

   **b.** multicellular organisms have lived on our planet.

3. **Reflection:** Imagine that no species ever became extinct. Do you think there would be more, less, or the same amount of diversity of life forms on our planet? Explain your answer.

## EXTENSION 1

Obtain a copy of a more detailed geologic time scale. Construct a timeline that represents only the last 550 million years. Label all the *periods* with their names and be sure to distinguish them from the *eras*. What additional information were you able to include on this timeline? What are the advantages and disadvantages of creating timelines for shorter time periods?

## EXTENSION 2

As a class, create a giant timeline that represents some of the major events (such as the first fossils of interesting life forms, mass extinctions, etc.) that have occurred during the 4.5 billion-year history of Earth. Stand at appropriately scaled distances from your classmates, and together hold up signs representing major events in the history of life.

In some places, such as the walls of a deep river canyon, hundreds of rock layers are visible, one on top of the other. As rock layers form, each new layer is deposited on top of an already existing layer. When you observe a sequence of rock layers, the top layer, along with any fossils it contains, is younger than any other layer in that sequence, and the bottom layer, along with any fossils it contains, is the oldest layer in that sequence. This is called the **law of superposition.**

A diagram representing a series of rock layers, such as the one on the right, is called a **stratigraphic column.** Stratigraphic columns can be made by looking at the sides of cliffs, or by looking at drill cores. A drill core is a cylindrical piece of rock removed from the Earth by a large drill, similar to the drills that are used to make oil wells. Drill cores can provide samples from many miles beneath the surface of the Earth.

*Rock layers in the Grand Canyon*

No single location contains a complete set of all the rock layers or fossils that exist on Earth. In order to study a particular fossil organism or find out which organisms lived during which geologic era, paleontologists must compare rocks from different places throughout the world. You will examine and compare four different drill cores, each representing the rock layers found on different fictitious continents.

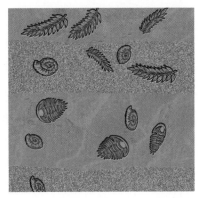

*Schematic diagram of fossils in rock layers*

CHALLENGE  **How can you determine which fossils are older, which are younger, and which are likely to be from extinct species?**

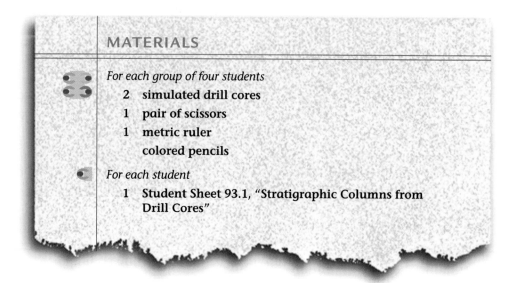

MATERIALS

*For each group of four students*
2   simulated drill cores
1   pair of scissors
1   metric ruler
    colored pencils

*For each student*
1   Student Sheet 93.1, "Stratigraphic Columns from
    Drill Cores"

## PROCEDURE

1. Examine your drill core. The top of each drill core is marked with its number.

2. Create a stratigraphic column by sketching in the boundaries of the layers and the fossils found within each layer in the appropriate place on Student Sheet 93.1, "Stratigraphic Columns from Drill Cores." Do this for both drill cores.

3. Based on the evidence within the layers of these drill cores, list the fossils in order from youngest to oldest.

4. When directed by your teacher, exchange your drill cores with a group that has two drill cores with different numbers.

5. Based on the appearance of the rock layers and the fossils found within each layer, match, or correlate, the layers from each core as best you can. Make a chart, similar to the one shown on the opposite page, that shows your correlation of the rock layers from the four different drill cores.

   Hint 1: You may want to cut out each column from the Student Sheet so that you can move them around as you try to match up the layers.

   Hint 2: Layers don't have to be exactly the same to correlate.

6. Use your correlation chart to list all four of the fossils in order from youngest to oldest.

   Hint: If you think a layer found in one drill core is the same as a layer found in another drill core, you can infer that those layers, and the fossils in them, are the same age.

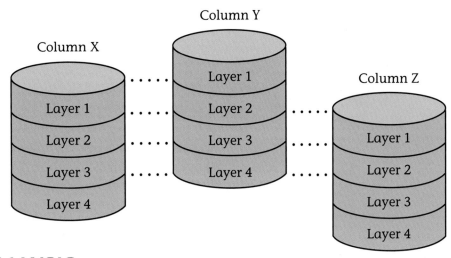

SAMPLE CORRELATION
OF STRATIGRAPHIC
COLUMNS

## ANALYSIS

1. Describe some of the difficulties you had trying to match evidence found in one drill core with evidence found in other drill cores. What additional evidence would have helped you make your correlations?

2. Based on evidence from all four drill cores, which, if any, of the organisms represented by the fossils may be from species now extinct? Explain.

3. Which fossil species could have lived at the same time?

4. Using the information below and the list you made in Step 6 of the Procedure, make a timeline that shows the time span when each species is believed to have been alive. Explain how you determined your answer and whether it is based on inference, observation, or a combination of both.

| Core | Layer | Geologic Era |
|------|-------|------------------|
| 4 | 1 | Early Cenozoic |
| 1 | 2 | Early Mesozoic |
| 3 | 5 | Middle Paleozoic |
| 2 | 5 | Early Paleozoic |

Hint: Refer to Figure 1 in Activity 89, "Mammoth Mysteries," for help in designing your timeline.

5. **a.** How does your timeline reflect the law of superposition?

   **b.** How do the timelines you drew in Activity 92, "Time for Change," reflect the law of superposition?

6. **Reflection:** Propose what might have caused the changes through time shown on your timeline. Explain.

**ROLE PLAY**

**P**lenty of fossil evidence shows that most of the species that have lived in the past are no longer alive today. It also seems that most of the species on Earth today were not always here. In other words, different species of organisms have lived at different times in Earth's history. New species have descended from earlier species, but have changed over long periods of time. These changes through time are called **evolution.**

But how does evolution happen? Two major theories were proposed during the 19th century. The first was disproved and abandoned, while the second has helped evolution become a central idea in modern biology. What would it sound like if the original experts met and discussed the problem?

**CHALLENGE**  ⟹  **How does evolution happen?**

---

**MATERIALS**

*For each student*

1  Student Sheet 94.1, "A Meeting of Minds"

---

## PROCEDURE

1. Assign a role for each person in your group. Assuming there are four people in your group, each of you will read one role.

### Roles

Charles Darwin, 19th century scientist

Isabel Matos, science reporter for Station W-EVO

Jean-Baptiste Lamarck, 19th century scientist

Wendy Chin, middle school student

2. Read the role play on the next pages aloud. As you read, think about what each character is saying.

3. Mark whether you think scientists today would agree or disagree with the statements on Student Sheet 94.1, "A Meeting of Minds."

4. Discuss the statements with your group.

# HOW DO SPECIES EVOLVE?

Isabel Matos: In today's episode of "Time Travel News," we have brought together two of the first scientists to publish ideas on how evolution occurs. Visiting us from the 19th century are Jean-Baptiste Lamarck and Charles Darwin. Monsieur Lamarck, let's start with you.

Jean-Baptiste Lamarck: I was one of the first to recognize that species evolve. In 1809, I proposed the first theory of how evolution occurs. Allow me to explain my theory. Let's begin by talking about giraffes. Wendy, why do you think giraffes have such long necks?

Wendy Chin: To reach leaves at the tops of trees, I guess. They have to be able to get food.

Lamarck: Quite right. I began to wonder how giraffes' necks became so long.

Wendy: I bet they evolved that way.

Lamarck: But how did this evolution occur? This is what I wanted to understand. My theory was that giraffes stretched their necks by reaching for leaves that were higher and higher on the trees. This made their necks longer.

Then, when they had babies, their babies had longer necks too. Look—this sketch helps explain my ideas.

LAMARCKIAN EVOLUTION

This is an adult giraffe.

The giraffe reaches for leaves slightly out of reach.

The use of the neck causes it to lengthen slightly.

The offspring of the giraffe also has a longer neck.

| | |
|---|---|
| Wendy: | Shouldn't a theory be based on evidence? |
| Matos: | Mr. Lamarck, did you ever see an adult giraffe grow its neck longer? |
| Lamarck: | Of course not. My idea was that the growth was very small, too small to measure in one generation. |
| Charles Darwin: | I'd like to explain another theory, called natural selection. Alfred Russel Wallace and I constructed this theory at about the same time. We also noticed that not all animals of the same type have the same features. Take horses, for instance. |
| Wendy: | Oh, I know what you mean! There are horses of different sizes and colors, but they are all one species and can interbreed. |
| Darwin: | Exactly—and the same is true of giraffes. Have you noticed that animals in the same species look different, or varied? This is important because, in the wild, some animals in each species usually die every year. Only animals that survive can give birth to offspring. Now, what feature of a giraffe might help it to survive and live to reproduce? |
| Lamarck: | Its neck, of course! As I said before, it must stretch from being used so vigorously. Giraffes can then pass on the longer necks to their children. |

*What differences do you observe in these giraffes of the same species?*

Matos: But Mr. Lamarck, modern scientists have found no evidence for your hypothesis that parents can pass *acquired* traits to their offspring. Consider professional wrestlers. They build muscles by lifting weights. But their babies are no stronger than other babies. If these babies want to have muscles like their parents, they have to pump a lot of iron too!

Darwin: But just like human babies, not all giraffes are the same. They have slight differences in all their characteristics, including neck length.

Lamarck: So you're saying any giraffe that happens to have a slightly longer neck can eat leaves that are higher in a tree than a shorter-necked giraffe can and therefore is more likely to survive.

Wendy: So the longer-necked giraffes are more likely to live longer because they can reach more food. If more of these giraffes live longer, they can produce more offspring!

Darwin: That's right. Animals with certain features, such as giraffes with longer necks, are more likely to live to adulthood and have more babies. We call that process **natural selection**. Here's a sketch of how it works

## DARWINIAN EVOLUTION (NATURAL SELECTION)

*Giraffes with longer necks tend to reach leaves more easily.*

*Longer-necked giraffes are more likely to eat enough to survive . . .*

*. . . and reproduce. The offspring inherit their parent's longer necks.*

Wendy: But why will the offspring of longer-necked giraffes have longer necks too?

Matos: Well, tall parents are more likely to have tall children, aren't they? The same is probably true of giraffes.

Darwin: According to my theory, each new generation of giraffes has, on the average, slightly longer necks than the generation before.

Lamarck: But not because they stretched their necks? Only because the longer-necked giraffes were more likely to survive and reproduce?

Wendy: I get it. Individual animals don't change, but over very long periods of time, the population of an entire species does.

Lamarck: But, Mr. Darwin, can your theory of natural selection explain why extinction occurs?

Darwin: I believe so. Consider the mammoth, which became extinct a few thousand years ago. Why didn't mammoths evolve and continue to survive?

Wendy: There are several theories about that. They became extinct during a time when the global climate was warmer than it had been before. The changing climate may have affected the mammoth's food supply, and human hunters may have contributed to the extinction.

Matos: So a species becomes extinct when it doesn't survive an environmental change. No individuals in the population have the traits necessary to survive.

Darwin: That's all it is. The **variation** in the population isn't enough to withstand environmental changes. In fact, sooner or later, most species become extinct.

Wendy: Let me get this straight. As time passes, species change, and we call this evolution. The way this occurs is by natural selection—some individuals in a population happen to be better suited to the environment and they're more likely to survive and reproduce.

Lamarck: As a result, the population as a whole over many generations comes to have an **adaptation**, such as a giraffe's longer neck.

Matos: Today, we know that we pass on characteristics like longer necks to our offspring through genes. Genes don't change because you exercise your neck.

Darwin: Tell us more about these genes.

Wendy: I learned about genes in school. Genes are things in our cells that we inherit from our parents. They cause us to have traits—the way we look and stuff.

Lamarck: Fascinating. I would like to learn more about this.

Darwin: Without this modern evidence, I hesitated to publish my theory for years, until Wallace sent me a brief paper containing the same ideas. Within a few years of our publications, scientists widely accepted the idea that species arise by descent with modification, or evolution.

Matos: Thank you, Mr. Lamarck and Mr. Darwin. Viewers, I hope you've enjoyed meeting people from our past. Join us next week for a scintillating conversation with Marie Curie, the first woman scientist to receive a Nobel Prize.

## ANALYSIS

1.  **a.** Compare and contrast Lamarck's and Darwin's theories of evolution: What are the similarities? What are the differences?

    **b.** Why do scientists find Darwin's theory more convincing?

2.  Ancestors of modern elephants had much shorter trunks than elephants do today. Use Lamarck's theory of evolution to explain how the trunks of elephants might get longer over many generations. Drawing a picture may help you to explain what you have learned.

3.  Use the Darwin/Wallace theory of natural selection to explain how the trunks of elephants might get longer over many generations. Drawing a picture may help you to explain what you have learned.

4.  **Reflection:** When antibiotics were first used, antibiotic-resistant bacteria were rare. Today antibiotic resistance is becoming more and more common. How is the problem of antibiotic resistance in bacteria an example of natural selection?

MODELING

In the last activity, you considered the interaction between the environment and a species over a long span of time. You saw that the location of leaves on trees could affect which giraffes survived. Over many generations, longer-necked giraffes would be more likely to reach the uppermost leaves on tall trees. This might make them more likely to survive, reproduce, and pass their traits on to their offspring. If this were to happen, longer necks would be called an adaptation to the tall-tree environment.

Adaptations that make a species more successful are not always traits that make the species stronger, bigger, or faster. For example, some adaptations decrease the chances that a species will be eaten by another species. Adaptations of this type include the skin colors of lizards, the spines of porcupines, and the scent glands of skunks.

**CHALLENGE**

**How do factors such as the environment and the presence of predators affect the process of natural selection?**

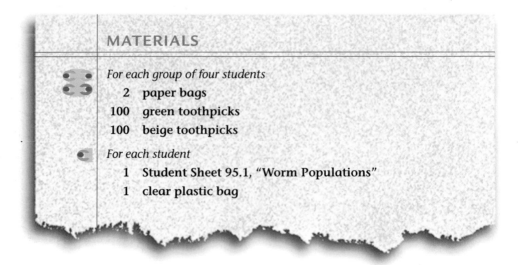

**MATERIALS**

*For each group of four students*
2   **paper bags**
100   **green toothpicks**
100   **beige toothpicks**

*For each student*
1   **Student Sheet 95.1, "Worm Populations"**
1   **clear plastic bag**

## *The Toothpick Worm Model*

Imagine that you are a bird that eats small worms. In this activity, toothpicks of two different colors will represent the worms that you eat.

## PROCEDURE

1. Label one of the paper bags "Worms" and the other "Reserve Toothpicks."

2. Each toothpick represents a worm. Count 25 green "worms" and 25 beige "worms" and place them into the paper bag labeled "Worms." This is the initial number of worms. These amounts are already marked for you in both tables on Student Sheet 95.1, "Worm Populations" (Table 1 is for green worms and Table 2 is for beige worms).

3. Place the rest of the toothpicks into the bag labeled "Reserve Toothpicks."

4. Shake the "Worms" bag to mix the worms.

5. As directed by your teacher, scatter the worms on the "ground."

6. You are going to play the role of a bird that eats worms. Your group must "eat" (pick up) 40 worms, and so decide how many worms each member of your group will "eat." You must pick up the first worms that you see, regardless of the color, and place them in the clear plastic bag, which represents the bird's stomach.

7. Count the total numbers of green and beige worms eaten by your group. Record these totals in Row 2 of each table on Student Sheet 95.1. Be sure to stay in the column for this generation.

8. *Some worms are still alive.* Subtract the number of worms that your group "ate" from the initial population in that generation. For example, if your group collected 18 green worms, there must be 7 green worms still alive on the ground (25 − 18 = 7). Record the numbers of surviving green and beige worms in Row 3 of each table on Student Sheet 95.1.

9. *Each living worm is reproducing.* On Student Sheet 95.1, multiply the numbers of green and beige worms still alive by 4. For example, if you had 7 green worms still alive, there would be a total of 28 green offspring worms (7 x 4 = 28). Record this number in Row 4.

10. Add one toothpick for each new green and beige worm into your paper bag labeled "Worms." For example, if your group had 7 green worms surviving on the ground, you would add 28 green toothpicks to the paper bag.

11. On Student Sheet 95.1, add Rows 3 and 4 of each table to calculate the final populations of green and beige worms. Record these numbers in Row 5 of each table. Record these same numbers in Row 1 in the columns for the *next* generation.

12. Repeat Steps 4–11 for Generations 2 and 3. If you have time, perform the simulation for further generations.

## ANALYSIS

1. **a.** Determine the ratio of green to beige worms in each generation. For example, the ratio of green to beige worms in Generation 1 is 25:25, or 1:1.

   **b.** Describe how the ratio of green to beige worms changed over the three generations.

   **c.** Why do you think this change occurred? Explain.

2. Imagine that you performed this simulation for another generation. What do you predict the ratio of green to beige worms would be? Explain your prediction.

3. Due to a drought, grass begins to dry out and die, leaving only dead grass stalks. What is likely to happen to the ratio of green to beige worms? Explain.

 4. **a.** In this activity, what effect did the environment have on the process of natural selection?

   **b.** In this activity, what role did the predator (bird) have in the process of natural selection?

5. What are the strengths and weaknesses of this activity as a model for natural selection?

6. **Reflection:** Why do you think earthworms are beige and not green?

## EXTENSION

Repeat the activity wearing a pair of sunglasses with green lenses. How are your results different?

MODELING

**D**uring the history of Earth, species have both evolved and become extinct. Why do some species survive to reproduce while others do not?

CHALLENGE ➡ **What role does variation play in the process of natural selection?**

## MATERIALS

*For each group of four students*

| | |
|---|---|
| 4 | plastic forks with 1 tine |
| 4 | plastic forks with 2 tines |
| 4 | plastic forks with 4 tines |
| 4 | plastic cups |
| 1 | number cube |
| 1 | flat tray or large bin |
| 1 | cup of "wild loops" |

*For each student*

| | |
|---|---|
| 1 | Student Sheet 96.1, "Forkbird Populations" |

*Why do these four different species of birds have such different beaks?*

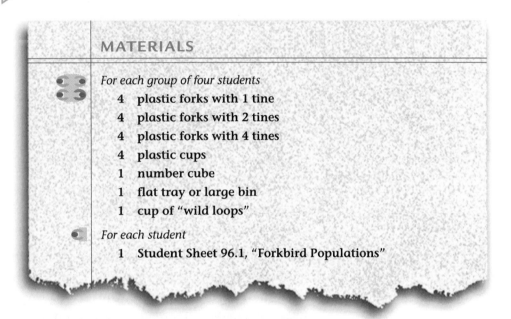

---

### The Forkbird Model

In this activity, you will role-play a single species called "forkbirds." Forkbirds feed by either spearing or scooping their food. During feeding time, each bird gathers "wild loops" and immediately deposits them in its "stomach" before gathering more food. Your goal is to gather enough food to survive and reproduce. This will allow you to pass your genes on to another generation. Occasionally, a forkbird offspring will have a genetic mutation that makes it look different from its parent.

---

## PROCEDURE

1. The initial forkbird population has beaks with only two tines. Each person in your group should begin the activity with a 2-tined fork. Record the initial population of each type of forkbird in Table 1 of Student Sheet 96.1, "Forkbird Populations."

2. Your teacher will tell you when feeding time begins, and then all of the forkbirds can feed.

3. When feeding time ends, count the number of wild loops eaten by each forkbird. Within your group, the two forkbirds that gathered the most food survive to reproduce. (If there is a tie for second place, then three forkbirds survive. The two forkbirds that tie should keep their forks and skip Step 4.)

4. The two surviving forkbirds should each toss the number cube. Use the table below to determine the type of beak of the offspring of each surviving forkbird. The group members whose forkbirds did not survive should now assume the roles of the offspring.

| Number Cube Key | |
| --- | --- |
| **Your Toss** | **Forkbird Offspring** |
| 1 | 1-tined forkbird |
| 2 | 2-tined forkbird |
| 4 | 4-tined forkbird |
| 3, 5, 6 | same as parent forkbird |

5. Record the new population of each type of forkbird in your group in the next row on Student Sheet 96.1.

6. Return all of the wild loops to the "forest floor" (tray or bin) to simulate the growth of wild loops.

7. Repeat Steps 2–6 for nine more rounds to represent additional generations.

8. Share your data with the class. As a class, record the population of each type of forkbird over many generations. Be sure to copy the class data onto Student Sheet 96.1.

9. Create a graph of the class totals of each type of forkbird over many generations. You can plot the data for all three types of forkbirds on a single graph. Be sure to title your graph, label your axes, and provide a key.

## ANALYSIS

1. Which type of forkbird was the most successful? Explain how the class data support this conclusion.

2. **a.** Look at your graph of the class results. Describe what happened to the number of each type of forkbird over many generations.

   **b.** In the forkbird model, mutations at reproduction were much more common than they are in real life. Imagine that the number of mutations was lowered, so that the vast majority of offspring had beaks similar to those of their parents. Predict what you think would have happened to the numbers of each type of forkbird in future generations.

3. How did the forkbird activity simulate the process of natural selection? Explain.

4. The forkbirds that you studied are a single species. Although they look slightly different, they are part of a single, interbreeding population. Imagine that a change in the food supply occurred.

   a. As a result of heavy rains, the major source of forkbird food is now soft berries, like blueberries. After many, many generations, how many types of forkbirds do you think will be in the population? Explain your reasoning.

   b. As a result of a drought, the major source of forkbird food is now sunflower seeds. After many, many generations, how many types of forkbirds do you think will be in the population? Explain your reasoning.

5. Did this activity model Darwin's or Lamark's theory of evolution?

6. What are the strengths and weaknesses of this activity as a model for evolution?

7. **Reflection:** The cheetah, an extremely fast and efficient hunter, is an endangered species. The few cheetahs alive today show very little variation. How does this help to explain why cheetahs are on the verge of becoming extinct?

**READING**

**I**n Activity 92, "Time For Change," you saw that the types of living organisms have changed throughout Earth's history. Where do all of the new types of organisms come from?

**CHALLENGE** What role do mutations play in natural selection?

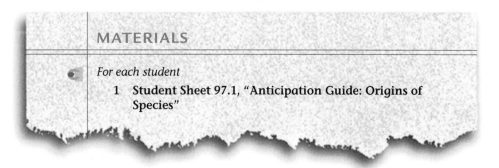

### MATERIALS

*For each student*

1 Student Sheet 97.1, "Anticipation Guide: Origins of Species"

*Three different species of bears*

# READING

*Use Student Sheet 97.1, "Anticipation Guide: Origins of Species," to prepare you for the reading.*

Each species has a particular role within its ecosystem. The angelfish is adapted to eating small aquatic worms. To people, most adult angelfish of a particular breed appear the same: they are all of similar size and coloration and eat the same types of food. But there is some variation—every angelfish is slightly different (see photo left). Consider other organisms that you might think are identical. What could you do to identify differences among individuals within the species?

*Variation Between Two Angelfish*

One way to look for variation is to examine physical features, such as color and shape. Often, features like the width or pattern of stripes on an angelfish are slightly different from one fish to the next. Since some physical differences are due to genetic differences, they can be passed along through the generations.

## STOPPING TO THINK 1

Think about similarities and differences among ten different people you know.

**a.** What are some physical features that are likely to be a result of genetic differences?

**b.** What are some physical features that may not be a result of genetics, but a result of some other factor(s), such as development from birth to adulthood?

**c.** What are some physical features that might be a result of both genetics and other factors?

In Activity 96, "Battling Beaks," you modeled a forkbird population that showed variation. Although all the forkbirds were from the same species, there were 1-tined, 2-tined, and 4-tined forkbirds. What was the source of these differences?

All genetic variation exists because of **mutations**. The reproduction of the genetic material does not always happen perfectly. As a result, occasionally an offspring has features that do not exist in the parents or even in the rest of the species. Some mutations are harmful. For example, a bird might be born with a beak of such unusual shape that the bird cannot feed. Such mutations are not passed on to the next generation, since the affected organism does not survive to reproduce.

In many cases, a mutation is neither helpful nor harmful. The 1-tined fork-bird from the previous activity was an example of this type of mutation. Even though it was not as successful as the 4-tined mutation, the 1-tined beak was neither helpful nor harmful when compared to the 2-tined beak. Since there was no advantage or disadvantage to this type of beak, the 1-tined forkbird did not die out in the population.

### STOPPING TO THINK 2

Imagine that you own a dog that recently gave birth to a litter of puppies. Your veterinarian informs you that one of the puppies has a genetic mutation.

a. Think of a mutation that the puppy could have that would be neither helpful nor harmful.

b. Think of a mutation that the puppy could have that would be harmful.

In some cases, a mutation is helpful. Imagine that a bird from a species that eats small nuts is born with a larger beak than the rest of the popula-tion. The larger beak allows this bird to eat large nuts as well as smaller nuts. If nuts became harder to find, this mutation could help this bird survive and reproduce. Any larger-beaked offspring might continue to be more success-ful than the rest of the bird population. After many generations, all of these birds might have larger beaks (see figure below). In the previous activity, the 4-tined forkbird was an example of a helpful mutation.

**EVOLUTION OF LARGER-BEAKED BIRDS**

*As a result of a helpful mutation occurring just once, an entire population of birds might look very different after many generations.*

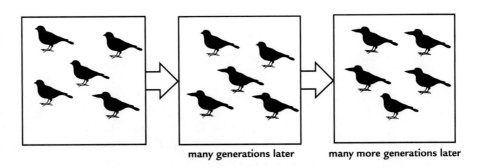

many generations later     many more generations later

In a new environment, natural selection might favor a mutation that is not favorable in the original environment. If this population eventually can no longer successfully reproduce with the population it came from, it is consid-ered a different species.

## STOPPING TO THINK 3

You may have heard someone who is wrapping a present say, "I wish I had another hand!" Explain why an organism cannot choose to have a mutation that would enable it to live more successfully in its environment. For example, could birds choose to have larger beaks? Explain your reasoning.

### THE GALAPAGOS

The fossil record provides evidence that many different species have lived during the history of Earth. But Charles Darwin was one of the first people to notice that living species also provide evidence for evolution. In the late 1830s, Darwin traveled on a ship called the *Beagle* that sailed around the world. He collected evidence and made careful observations of the natural world wherever the voyage took him. One of the places that the ship stopped was the Galapagos Islands, a chain of islands located in the Pacific Ocean, west of South America (shown at left).

In the Galapagos Islands, Darwin collected samples of many different species, including 14 species of finch (a small bird). All of the finches were similar, but the species varied in color, size, and beak shape. Darwin observed a relationship between the shape of a finch's beak and the food that it ate. Scientists had noticed that the beak of each species was particularly well-adapted to getting a specific type of food, such as a certain seed or insect (shown below).

### A FEW GALAPAGOS FINCHES

*Cactus finch*

*Large ground finch*

*Warbler finch*

Based on his observations, Darwin hypothesized that all 14 different finch species had evolved from one single ancestral species. He proposed that, thousands or even millions of years ago, a single species of South American finch migrated and began nesting on the islands. Over many generations, different adaptations proved more successful on one island than on another. Because each island is separated by some distance from others in the chain, the finch population on each island is relatively small and isolated. This allowed helpful genetic mutations to spread within a population—by natural selection—more quickly than usual. Eventually, changes in beak shapes, combined with the spread of other helpful mutations, resulted in enough differences that the various finches became separate species, each adapted for a different ecosystem role.

Today, scientists use genetic evidence to compare similarities and differences among species. By testing the genes of the various finches, scientists have shown that the finches are very closely related, providing more evidence that Darwin's hypothesis is correct.

## STOPPING TO THINK 4

Darwin identified 14 species of finch on the Galapagos Islands. Your friend says that this means only 14 mutations occurred within the finch populations. Explain whether you agree with your friend and why.

But you don't need isolated islands to produce new species. Remember the Nile perch of Lake Victoria in Africa, which you studied in the previous unit? One consequence of the introduction of these large fish into the lake was the extinction of up to 200 species of just one type of fish—the cichlid.

**SPECIES OF CICHLIDS**

How did so many species of the same fish family ever come to exist in a single lake? A single lake provides a surprising number of different places to live and ways to survive. Differences in the amount of light, wind, mud, sand, temperature, plants, predators, and insects produce a variety of habitats within one lake. Lake Victoria provides so many different habitats that over 300 different species of cichlids had evolved within the lake before the introduction of the Nile perch.

Are all of these cichlids really descended from a single ancestor? Every line of evidence suggests this is so. Modern genetic evidence indicates that all the cichlids in Lake Victoria evolved from a common ancestor within the last 200,000 years. That's a short period of time in terms of evolution!

## ANALYSIS

1. Are mutations always helpful? Explain.

2. How can mutations enable the evolution of a new species to occur? Use the story of the cichlids to help you explain your ideas.

3. Under ideal conditions, bacteria have a generation time of about 20 minutes. Humans have a generation time of about 20 years. Which would you expect to evolve faster? Why?

4. Complete the "After" column of Student Sheet 97.1, "Anticipation Guide: Origins of Species." Did your thinking change?

INVESTIGATION

Fossils have been found in Precambrian rocks 3.5 billion years old. But most have been found in rocks of the Paleozoic, Mesozoic, and Cenozoic eras, which are all less than 550 million years old. The types of organisms found in different rocks can provide important information about the history of life on Earth. The term **fossil record** refers to all of the fossils that have been found on Earth.

The fossil record has been used to classify fossils into families. A family is a category smaller than a kingdom, phylum, class, or order, but larger than a genus or species. For example, dogs are in the family Canidae, which also contains foxes, jackals, coyotes, and wolves. Lions are in the same kingdom, phylum, class, and order as dogs, but they are in a different family: Felidae. This family includes leopards, tigers, cheetahs, house cats, and extinct species such as the saber-toothed cat. You will investigate how the numbers of families in the fish, mammal, and reptile classes have changed over geological time.

CHALLENGE

**What can you learn about evolution by comparing the fossil records of fish, mammals, and reptiles?**

## MATERIALS

*For each student*
1   Student Sheet 98.1, "Graphs of Fossil Families"
1   set of colored pencils (optional)

## Classifying Carnivores

| Classification Level | Dogs | Lions |
|---|---|---|
| Kingdom | Animalia | Animalia |
| Phylum | Chordata | Chordata |
| Class | Mammalia | Mammalia |
| Order | Carnivora | Carnivora |
| **Family** | **Canidae** | **Felidae** |
| Genus | *Canis* | *Panthera* |
| Species | *familiaris* | *leo* |

## PROCEDURE

1. Table 1 below provides the history of all the families of fish currently known from the fossil record. When a fossil is found that does not belong to any family found in *earlier* geologic time periods, we call it a "first appearance." It is the first appearance of that family in the fossil record. When a fossil is found that does not belong to any family found in *later* geologic time periods, we call it a "last appearance." It is the last appearance of that family in the fossil record. Look at Table 1 and discuss the following questions with your partner:

   • Between which years did the greatest number of fish families appear in the fossil record? In what era was this period of time?

   • Between which years did the greatest number of fish families disappear from the fossil record? In what era was this period of time?

### Table 1: History of Fossil Fish Families

| Era | Precambrian | Early Paleozoic | | | Late Paleozoic | | | Mesozoic | | | Cenozoic |
|---|---|---|---|---|---|---|---|---|---|---|---|
| Time (mya) | >545 | 485 | 425 | 365 | 305 | 245 | 185 | 125 | 65 | 0 | |
| Number of first appearances | 0 | 25 | 43 | 162 | 67 | 13 | 52 | 33 | 84 | 299 | |
| Number of last appearances | 0 | 9 | 31 | 158 | 49 | 48 | 36 | 20 | 44 | 34 | |

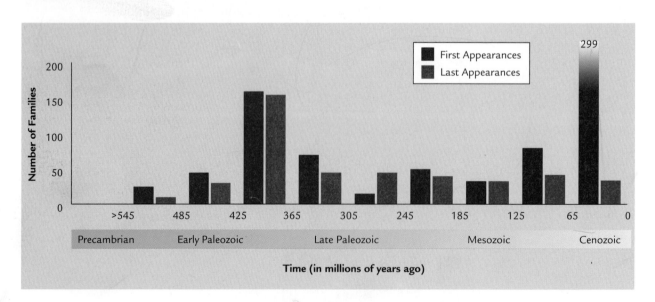

2. The double bar graph on the previous page is based on the data shown in Table 1. Look at the graph and discuss with your partner in what ways the graph makes the data easier to interpret.

3. Use the information in Table 2 to make a double bar graph for families of reptiles, similar to the one for fish shown on the previous page. Since you will be comparing graphs, be sure to use the same scale on the y-axis.

| Table 2: History of Fossil Reptile Families | | | | | | | | | |
|---|---|---|---|---|---|---|---|---|---|
| Era | Precambrian | Early Paleozoic | | Late Paleozoic | | Mesozoic | | | Cenozoic |
| Time (mya) | >545 | 485 | 425 | 365 | 305 | 245 | 185 | 125 | 65 | 0 |
| Number of first appearances | 0 | 0 | 0 | 0 | 3 | 67 | 95 | 68 | 97 | 35 |
| Number of last appearances | 0 | 0 | 0 | 0 | 1 | 57 | 93 | 46 | 84 | 26 |

| Table 3 : History of Fossil Mammal Families | | | | | | | | | |
|---|---|---|---|---|---|---|---|---|---|
| Era | Precambrian | Early Paleozoic | | Late Paleozoic | | Mesozoic | | | Cenozoic |
| Time (mya) | >545 | 485 | 425 | 365 | 305 | 245 | 185 | 125 | 65 | 0 |
| Number of first appearances | 0 | 0 | 0 | 0 | 0 | 0 | 6 | 14 | 33 | 404 |
| Number of last appearances | 0 | 0 | 0 | 0 | 0 | 0 | 2 | 8 | 33 | 262 |

4. Use the information in Table 3 to make a double bar graph for families of mammals, similar to the one for fish shown on the previous page. Since you will be comparing graphs, be sure to use the same scale on the y-axis.

*A familiar example of a fossilized reptile*

## ANALYSIS

1.  **a.** Use the graphs to place the three different classes in order, based on when they first appeared in the fossil record.

    **b.** What could this order tell you about the evolution of these types of species?

2.  **a.** What are some possible explanations for the disappearance of a family from the fossil record?

    **b.** How could Darwin's theory of natural selection explain the disappearance of these families?

3.  What could explain the appearance of a family in the fossil record?

### Table 4: History of Fossil Amphibian Families

| Era | Precambrian | Early Paleozoic | | Late Paleozoic | | | Mesozoic | | | Cenozoic |
|---|---|---|---|---|---|---|---|---|---|---|
| Time (mya) | >545 | 485 | 425 | 365 | 305 | 245 | 185 | 125 | 65 | 0 |
| Number of first appearances | 0 | 0 | 0 | 3 | 35 | 33 | 19 | 11 | 5 | 15 |
| Number of last appearances | 0 | 0 | 0 | 3 | 16 | 53 | 18 | 5 | 1 | 5 |

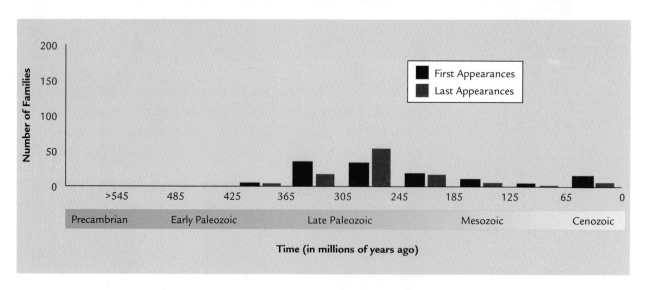

4. Look at your answer for Analysis Question 1. Where do you think scientists have placed the amphibian family?

5. **a.** The Cenozoic Era is often referred to as the "Age of Mammals." Using evidence from this activity, explain why.

  **b.** Based on evidence from this activity, what could you call the Mesozoic Era? Explain your reasoning.

  **c.** Look at the appearances and disappearances of families over time on all three graphs. Why is it misleading to label an era as the "age of" any particular class?

6. **Reflection:** Do you think the evolution of animals from aquatic fish to land mammals was inevitable?

**INVESTIGATION**

Whales, dolphins, and porpoises are mammals that live in the sea. Like all mammals, they are warm-blooded animals that give birth to live young and need air to breathe. DNA evidence shows that whales are closely related to hoofed land mammals such as hippopotamuses, pigs, cows, and sheep. All of these mammals are thought to have descended from a single species that lived millions of years ago and is now extinct. Besides DNA evidence, what other evidence suggests that these animals are related?

**CHALLENGE** ⟶ **How are modern and fossil skeletons used to investigate evolution?**

## MATERIALS

*For each pair of students*
1 set of 5 Skeleton Cards
1 metric ruler (optional)
1 Student Sheet 99.1, "Whale Fossil Chart"

### The Fossil Exhibit

You've just been hired as the assistant curator of the fossil collection of a museum. On your first day, you discover that the skeletons in the exhibit on the evolution of whales have all been moved to a new room and need to be arranged. Unfortunately, you are not a whale expert and the skeletons are not clearly labeled.

A local middle school has scheduled a field trip to the museum. It is very important that you arrange the skeletons properly before the students arrive. You decide to examine them to see if you can figure out how they should be arranged.

## PROCEDURE

1.  Compare the five Skeleton Cards. Based on similarities you observe, group the skeletons into two sets, each containing two or three cards. The set of skeletons containing Skeleton A should be called "Group 1." The other set of skeletons will be "Group 2."

Comparing Skeletons

|  | Similarities | Differences |
| --- | --- | --- |
| Group 1 skeletons:<br>A, _____ |  |  |
| Group 2 skeletons:<br>_____ |  |  |
| Group 1 skeletons compared with Group 2 skeletons |  |  |

2.  Create a table in your science notebook like the one shown above. In the first column, record which skeletons you put in each group.

3.  Compare the skeletons *within* each group. In your table, describe and record as many similarities and differences as you can.

4. Compare Group 1 skeletons with those of Group 2. In your table, describe and record as many similarities and differences as you can.

5. *It's time to figure out how to arrange the exhibit!* Use similarities and differences in the skeletons to arrange the cards in order. (While all five skeletons can be in a single line, they don't have to be.) Record the order in which you have arranged the skeletons.

   Hint: Place the two least similar skeletons on either side of your desk. Then arrange the other three skeletons between them.

6. *You're in luck! You discover a chart with information about the relative ages of the five skeletons.* Collect Student Sheet 99.1, "Whale Fossil Chart," from your teacher.

7. Compare the age data from Student Sheet 99.1 with the order in which you placed the skeletons in Step 5. If necessary, rearrange your Skeleton Cards. Record your final reconstruction of the museum exhibit in your science notebook.

## ANALYSIS

1. **a.** What kinds of skeletal changes appear to have occurred during the evolution of whales?

   **b.** What can you infer about the changes in habitat that occurred at the same time as these skeletal changes?

2. Use natural selection to explain how these changes (or one of these changes) could have occurred.

3. In this activity, you examined extinct and modern whale skeletons. How does the study of these skeletons provide evidence about how species are related?

4. Look again at Skeleton A. This is known as an ambulocetid (am-byoo-low-SEE-tid). The word *ambulocetid* means "walking whale." Where do you think the ambulocetids lived? Describe how you think they lived.

5. **Reflection:** Look at your answer to Reflection Question 6 from Activity 98, "Family Histories." Has your thinking changed?

## EXTENSION

Find out more about current research on whale evolution. Start at the *Issues and Life Science* page of the SEPUP website.

INVESTIGATION

Scientists use evidence such as similarities in skeletal structures and other physical traits to investigate evolutionary relationships. Thanks to advances in genetics and biotechnology, scientists studying evolution can now also use the genetic material itself.

Each cell in an organism contains the genetic information needed to perform all its functions, such as obtaining energy, moving, and getting rid of wastes. You may already know that the genetic information is located in DNA in the chromosomes found in every cell. DNA is made up of four chemicals whose names are abbreviated as A, T, G, and C. These chemicals are strung together like beads on a string. Differences in their order result in different messages. Think of these chemicals as letters in an alphabet: there are only 26 letters in the English alphabet, but there are millions of words. In a similar way, DNA contains millions of biological messages. The more similar the DNA, the more similar the messages used to run the organism.

*These scientists are analyzing evidence from DNA.*

CHALLENGE

**How does DNA provide evidence about how animals are related?**

## MATERIALS

*For each group of four students*

1   **Student Sheet 100.1, "DNA Samples"**
1   **Student Sheet 100.2, "Unusual Vertebrates"**
1   **Student Sheet 100.3, "Comparing Primates" (optional)**
1   **pair of scissors**

> ## *The Common Thread*
>
> You are an evolutionary biologist investigating relationships among different species. When a geneticist you work with offers to provide you with DNA samples from various animals, you do some background research. You find out that the samples are from a gene that is similar in all vertebrates. This means you can easily use them to compare species of vertebrates.

## PROCEDURE

### Part A: Comparing Vertebrate Classes

1. The two-page chart at the end of this activity shows how to classify vertebrates. If you did not complete Activity 76, "People, Birds, and Bats," from the Ecology unit of *Issues and Life Science,* your teacher will give you a Student Sheet with examples of some unusual vertebrates to classify.

2. Compare the five samples of DNA on Student Sheet 100.1, "DNA Samples." With your partner, discuss any similarities or differences that you notice among the samples.

3. Use the DNA samples to determine whether animals in the same class have more similarities in their DNA with one another than they do with animals in other classes. Record your ideas in your science notebook.

   Hint: First compare just two animals and count the number of differences in their DNA. You can make a table like the one shown below to record these counts.

Numbers of Differences Between DNA Sequences

|  | Mammal #1 | Mammal #2 | Mammal #3 | Reptile |
|---|---|---|---|---|
| Fish |  |  |  |  |
| Mammal #1 | —— |  |  |  |
| Mammal #2 | —— | —— |  |  |
| Mammal #3 | —— | —— | —— |  |

4. In Activity 99, "A Whale of a Tale," you examined evidence that whales are mammals. Look again at your DNA samples. Discuss with your group whether these samples provide additional evidence that whales are mammals.

## Part B: Gathering More Evidence

5. In Activity 76, "People, Birds, and Bats," you classified a number of vertebrates into different classes. Review how you classified four of these animals: the kiwi, platypus, armadillo, and bat.

6. A local biotechnology center provides you and the geneticist with DNA samples from these four animals. Use Student Sheet 100.2, "Unusual Vertebrates," to compare the DNA samples of these four animals with the DNA samples from Part A. In your science notebook, create a table similar to the one above to record your comparisons.

7. In your science notebook, record whether the DNA evidence supports or conflicts with the way that you had classified these animals. If you make any changes to your classification, be sure to record them.

## ANALYSIS

1. In this activity, you used DNA to evaluate relationships among animals. How does DNA provide evidence about how species are related?

2. Would you expect the DNA of a seahorse to be more like the DNA of a horse or the DNA of a trout? Use evidence from this activity to support your answer.

3. **a.** Look back at the evolutionary tree in Figure 2 of Activity 89, "Here Today, Gone Tomorrow?" Draw a simple tree that shows the evolution of reptiles, fish, and mammals.

   **b.** Explain how DNA evidence helps you draw evolutionary trees.

4. The first mammals evolved from a reptilian ancestor, 200 million years ago. Explain why it is not accurate to say that humans evolved from lizards.

## EXTENSION

Compare the human, chimpanzee, and rhesus monkey DNA sequences provided on Student Sheet 100.3, "Comparing Primates." Use this evidence to draw an evolutionary tree for these three types of primates.

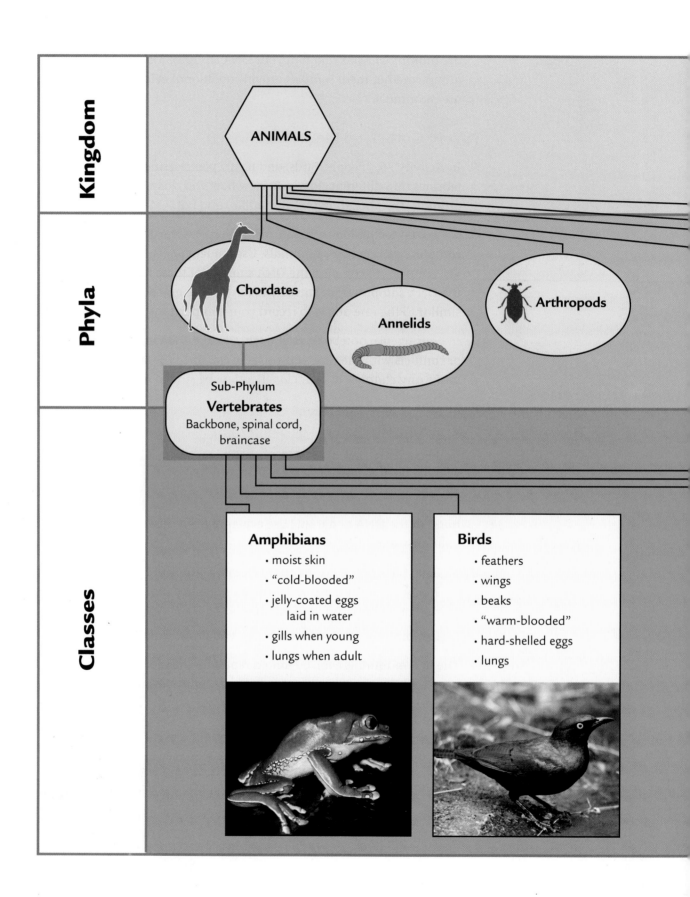

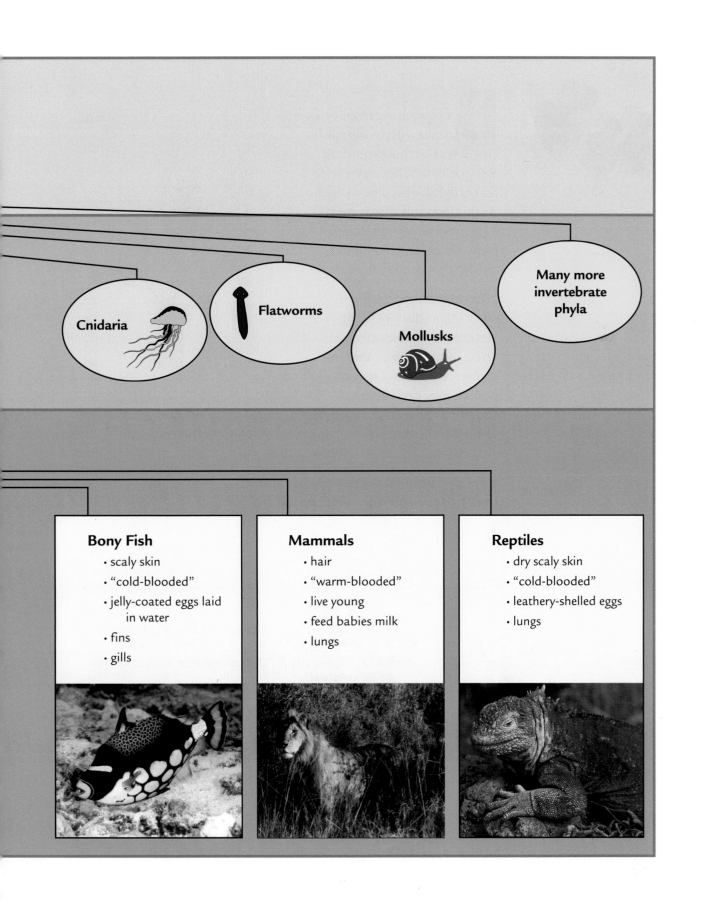

Cnidaria

Flatworms

Mollusks

Many more invertebrate phyla

**Bony Fish**
- scaly skin
- "cold-blooded"
- jelly-coated eggs laid in water
- fins
- gills

**Mammals**
- hair
- "warm-blooded"
- live young
- feed babies milk
- lungs

**Reptiles**
- dry scaly skin
- "cold-blooded"
- leathery-shelled eggs
- lungs

TALKING IT OVER

**B**y comparing fossil evidence with living species, it is clear that almost all the species that have ever lived on Earth have become extinct. As this diagram shows, most living species are descended from a small fraction of the species that have ever existed.

Why do some species survive while others disappear? Species die out for many reasons. These include environmental change, competing species, habitat loss, and disease. Human activity can contribute to each of these causes.

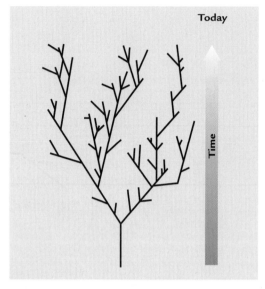

Today

Time

*Wherever a "branch" of this evolutionary tree of species ends, an extinction occurred (except at the present day).*

CHALLENGE

**How does natural selection help explain the extinction of the dodo bird and the success of the common pigeon?**

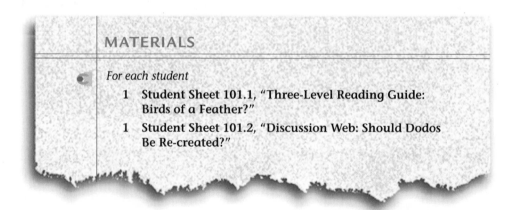

MATERIALS

*For each student*

1   Student Sheet 101.1, "Three-Level Reading Guide: Birds of a Feather?"

1   Student Sheet 101.2, "Discussion Web: Should Dodos Be Re-created?"

## PROCEDURE

*Use Student Sheet 101.1, "Three-Level Reading Guide: Birds of a Feather?" to guide you as you complete the following reading.*

## RELATED BIRDS, DIFFERENT FATES

The common pigeon seems to be everywhere—almost everyone has seen one of these birds. No one alive today has seen a dodo bird, and no preserved specimens of this extinct species exist. There are 27 orders of birds. Based on skeletal comparisons, the dodo and the pigeon have been classified in the same order for a long time. In 2002, scientists were able to take a DNA sample from a dodo that was preserved at a London museum. DNA analysis confirmed that the dodo is closely related to many modern pigeons. The pigeon and the dodo are evolutionary cousins!

### The Dodo Bird

Often portrayed as flightless, fat, slow, and stupid, the dodo bird (*Raphus cucullatus*) has become a symbol for something out-of-date or clumsy. Some people think it somehow fitting that the dodo species went extinct. How could natural selection have produced such a creature in the first place?

Dodos lived successfully for several million years on the island of Mauritius in the Indian Ocean (see the map, below). Migratory birds probably had settled on Mauritius long before, just as Darwin's finches did on the Galapagos Islands. Contrary to popular belief, evidence shows that the flightless dodo was a slender, fast-running animal (see photo next page). Although it com-

### LOCATION OF MAURITIUS

*Mauritius is a volcanic island about 10 million years old, about 500 miles east of Madagascar. Today, it is an independent country with a population of over 1 million people.*

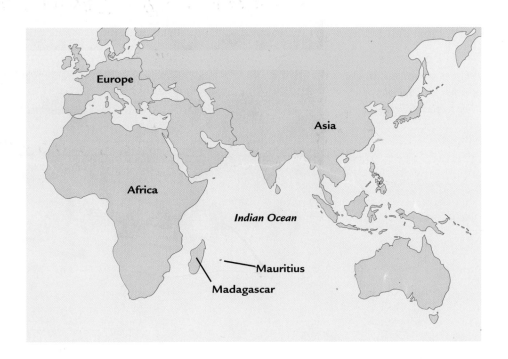

peted for resources with many other bird species, the 30- to 50-pound dodo had few predators on the island. Without predators, dodos could nest on the forest floor and eat fruit that fell from trees. Flight was unnecessary for survival and so, over many generations, the new species evolved to become flightless.

In 1505, Portuguese sailors became the first mammals to set foot on Mauritius. Soon, the island became a common stopping place for ships travelling between Europe and Asia. Because of its large size and inability to fly, the dodo became a hunting target for hungry sailors. Because dodo nests were on the ground, their eggs were easily found and eaten by the rats, pigs, monkeys, and other animals that accompanied the sailors. In addition, human settlers' need for cleared land and wood greatly reduced the size of the dodo's forest habitat. In 1681, less than 200 years after the first predators arrived on Mauritius, the last dodo bird was killed.

### WHAT REMAINS OF THE DODO

*Made of bones gathered from the island during the 1850s, this skeleton confirms that the dodo was flightless, but not that it was slow-moving.*

*Penguins, as well as kiwis and ostriches, are examples of living species of flightless birds.*

### The Common Pigeon

Native to Europe and Asia, pigeons now thrive on five continents. The common pigeon, or rock dove (*Columba livia*), was first domesticated by humans between five and ten thousand years ago. Early humans raised the birds for food, and pigeon meat is still a delicacy in many cultures. Later, pigeons were bred to race, to deliver messages, to do stunts, and for show (see below).

Perhaps even before becoming domesticated, pigeons discovered that human structures were convenient, safe places to nest. In addition, fields and marketplaces provided an easy-to-gather, year-round food supply. During their several thousand years of close association with humans, human-bred pigeons have escaped and mated with wild pigeons, sharing genes with them. As a result, pigeon populations found near people, known as feral pigeons, are quite different from wild pigeons. They can fly faster and for longer distances, breed earlier in life, produce more offspring, and live at a much higher population density. The remaining population of wild pigeons is decreasing, and may soon dwindle to zero. Meanwhile, the population of feral pigeons continues to grow.

**PIGEON DIVERSITY**

*Over many generations, through both natural processes and breeding, the pigeon species has evolved adaptations to many successful lifestyles associated with the human species.*

## ANALYSIS

1. If humans had never interacted with either the dodo or the pigeon, how do you think the history of each species would be different? Explain your reasoning.

2. Could the evolution of feral pigeons be described as the formation of a new species? Explain.

3. Use natural selection to explain how the flying bird that first settled on Mauritius might have evolved into the flightless dodo. In your answer, be sure to include the role of mutations.

4. Your friend argues that the dodo bird became extinct because it was a poorly adapted species, destined for failure. Do you agree? Explain.

5. Imagine that advances in science and technology allow genetic engineers to re-create living dodo birds and mammoths.

   a. Should mammoths be re-created and released into the Arctic ecosystem? Support your answer with evidence and discuss the trade-offs of your decision.

   b. Should dodos be re-created and released into the ecosystem of modern Mauritius? Support your answer with evidence and discuss the trade-offs of your decision.

   Hint: To write a complete answer, first state your opinion. Provide two or more pieces of evidence that support your opinion. Then discuss the trade-offs of your decision.

## EXTENSION

Find out more about extinct and endangered species. Start at the *Issues and Life Science* page of the SEPUP website.

# Index

A **bold** page number identifies the page on which the term is defined.

## Credits

Abbreviations: t (top), m (middle), b (bottom), l (left), r (right)

All illustrations by Seventeenth Street Studios.

"Talking It Over" icon photo: ©Michael Keller/The Stock Market

Unit opener (F-2, F-3): tl: Roberta Smith; tm: ©Charles Mauzy/CORBIS; bl: Roberta Smith; m: ©Kevin Schafer/CORBIS; mr: ©Jonathan Blair/CORBIS; bm: ©Lester V. Bergman/CORBIS; br: Donna Markey

F-4 tl: ©C.Iverson/Photo Researchers, Inc., tr: ©Bettmann/CORBIS, br: ©Kevin Fleming/CORBIS; F-7 tr: ©2001Manoj Shah/Getty Images F-12 ©Annie Griffiths Belt/CORBIS; F-14 ©Francesc Muntada/CORBIS; F-16 ©Kevin Schafer/CORBIS; F-17 ©2001 Lori Adamski Peek/Getty Images; F-18 ©Charles Mauzy/CORBIS; F-30 b: ©W. Perry Conway/CORBIS; F-33 bl: ©Gary W. Carter/CORBIS, br:©George Lepp/CORBIS; F-38 ©F. McConnaughey/Photo Researchers, Inc.; F-40 Images courtesy of Dr. Robert Rothman; F-41 l: ©Papilio/CORBIS, r: ©Sea World, Inc./CORBIS; F-58 t: ©Hulton-Deutsch Collections/CORBIS; F-59 l: ©2001 Cesar Lucas Abreu/The Image Bank, r: Annie Griffiths Belt/CORBIS; F-60 ©David & Peter Turnley/CORBIS

Front cover photo (DNA analysis): © 2008 Kevin Curtis/Photo Researchers, Inc.

# ISSUES

# Earth Science

&

## WEATHER AND ATMOSPHERE

SCIENCE
EDUCATION FOR
PUBLIC
UNDERSTANDING
PROGRAM

**S E P U P**

UNIVERSITY OF CALIFORNIA AT BERKELEY

LAWRENCE HALL OF SCIENCE **LHS**

INCORPORATED

RONKONKOMA, NEW YORK

**This book is part of SEPUP's middle school science course sequence:**

## Issues and Earth Science

Studying Soils Scientifically
Rocks and Minerals
Erosion and Deposition
Plate Tectonics
Weather and Atmosphere
The Earth in Space
Exploring the Solar System

## Issues and Life Science

Experimental Design: Studying People Scientifically
Body Works
Cell Biology and Disease
Genetics
Ecology
Evolution
Bioengineering

## Issues and Physical Science

Studying Materials Scientifically
The Chemistry of Materials
Water
Energy
Force and Motion

**Additional SEPUP instructional materials include:**
CHEM-2 (Chemicals, Health, Environment and Me): Grades 4–6
SEPUP Modules: Grades 7–12
*Science and Sustainability*: Course for Grades 9–12
Science and Global Issues Biology: Course for Grades 9–12

 This material is based upon work supported by the National Science Foundation under Grant No. 0099265. Any opinions, findings, and conclusions or recommendations expressed in this material are those of the authors and do not necessarily reflect the views of the National Science Foundation.

The preferred citation format for this book is
SEPUP. (2006). *Issues and Earth Science*. Lawrence Hall of Science, University of California at Berkeley. Published by Lab-Aids®, Inc., Ronkonkoma, NY

**SEPUP**
Lawrence Hall of Science
University of California at Berkeley
Berkeley CA 94720-5200

e-mail: sepup@berkeley.edu
Website: www.sepuplhs.org

Published by:

17 Colt Court
Ronkonkoma NY 11779
Website: www.lab-aids.com

**A Letter to *Issues and Earth Science* Students**

As you examine the activities in this book, you may wonder, "Why does this book look so different from other science books I've seen?" The reason is simple: it is a different kind of science program, and only some of what you will learn can be seen by leafing through this book!

*Issues and Earth Science* uses several kinds of activities to teach science. For example, you will observe and test the properties of soil, rocks, and minerals. You will examine a model of the way water moves earth materials to change the surface of the land. You will conduct a computer simulation to investigate the causes of earthquakes and volcanoes. A combination of experiments, readings, models, debates, role plays, and projects will help you uncover the nature of science and the relevance of science to your interests.

You will find that important scientific ideas come up again and again in different activities throughout the book. You will be expected to do more than just memorize these concepts: you will be asked to explain and apply them. In particular, you will improve your decision-making skills by using evidence to weigh outcomes and to decide what you think should be done about the scientific issues facing our society.

How do we know that this is a good way for you to learn? In general, research on science education supports it. In particular, the activities in this book were tested by hundreds of students and their teachers, and then modified on the basis of their feedback. In a sense, this entire book is the result of an investigation: we had people test our ideas, we interpreted the results, and we then revised our ideas! We believe the result will show you that learning more about science is important, enjoyable, and relevant to your life.

*SEPUP Staff*

**ISSUES & EARTH SCIENCE PROJECT**

Director (2003–2006): Barbara Nagle

Director (2001–2002): Herbert D. Thier

Coordinator: Janet Bellantoni

**UNIT E AUTHORS**

Manisha Hariani

Daniel Seaver

Sara Dombkowski

**OTHER CONTRIBUTORS**

Lee Amosslee, Janet Bellantoni, Kathaleen Burke, Ryan Chinn, Kevin Cuff, Asher Davison, Gayle Gutierrez, Kate Haber, Laura Kretschmar, Donna Markey, Linda Mead, Barbara Nagle, Mike Reeske, Suzanne Scott

**CONTENT AND SCIENTIFIC REVIEW**

Bill Martin, Chief Meteorologist, KTVU, Oakland, California

William Prothero, Professor of Geological Sciences, University of California at Santa Barbara, Santa Barbara, California *(Complete course)*

Zan Stine, Department of Earth and Planetary Science, University of California, Berkeley, California

**PRODUCTION**

Production Coordinator: Ayse Frosina

SEPUP Publications Coordinator: Miriam Shein

Design and Composition: Seventeenth Street Studios

Photo Research: Seventeenth Street Studios

Editing: Trish Beall

Administrative Assistance: Roberta Smith, Ezequiel Gonzalez

## Field Test Centers

The classroom is SEPUP's laboratory for development. We are extremely appreciative of the following center directors and teachers who taught the program during the 2003–04 and 2004–05 school years. These teachers and their students contributed significantly to improving the course.

### ATLANTA, GEORGIA

Geeta Verma, *Center Director*

Felecia Bell, Wanda Ellis, Lillian Harris, Patricia Lewis, Millicent McCaskill, Demetra McCoy, Melanie Robinson, Nicole Satchell

### BUFFALO, NEW YORK

Kathaleen Burke, *Center Director*

Delores Anderson, Dianne Johnson, Deborah Kimble, Steven Koch, Corean Lofton

### DALY CITY, CALIFORNIA

Andrew Coblentz, *Center Director*

Andrew Coblentz, Ken Klein, Catherine Macay, Benjamin Moser, Lucy Schoening

### GREELEY-EVANS, COLORADO

Ray Tschillard, *Center Director*

Joann Angus, Djems Domerson, Nick Durham, Christina Kauffman, Jason McLaughlin, Gemarie Romero, Ruby Sabzevari, Mark Wiegers

### LEMON GROVE, CALIFORNIA

Samantha Swann, *Center Director*

Jennifer Bates, Jim Haynes, Linda Schultz, Patti Sherillo, John Tessier

### PINELLAS COUNTY, FLORIDA

Dr. Chin-Tang Liu and Nancy Stitt, *Center Directors*

Shirley Green, Lisa Mackey, Jennifer Sinphay, Nancy Stitt

### WAKE COUNTY, NORTH CAROLINA

Michael Tally, Kim Gervase, and Catherine Norris, *Center Directors*

James Akins, Jon Corcoran, Karen Farnham, Jennifer Koch, Carla Steger

### WINSTON-SALEM/FORSYTH COUNTY, NORTH CAROLINA

Jim Bott, *Center Director*

Amelie Bartolino, Ed Beiles, Mary Kay Bell, John Cardarelli, Megan Clayton, Jennifer Sasser, Barbara Strange, Jane Trace

### VISTA, CALIFORNIA

Donna Markey, *Center Director*

Amy Alexander, Melissa Boeche, Nicole Buchanan, Dorothy Jones, Stacy Robe, Zamaria Rocio

# Contents

# Weather and Atmosphere

*E*

NOAA-15 AVHRR 1KM
August 29, 2005 @ 1148 UTC

MISSISSIPPI     ALABAMA

LOUISIANA

Gulfport    Biloxi

New Orleans

PROTEUS

N28108

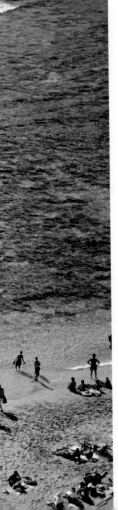

# Weather and Atmosphere

**H**ey, how about a little one-on-one basketball after school today?" Scott asked Marquel as they walked to class.

"I'm up for it," Marquel said. "But I don't think this sun will last."

"What do you mean?"

"This morning the meteorologist on Channel 5 predicted afternoon thunderstorms," said Marquel.

Scott looked out the window. "Really? It's sure sunny now."

"Yeah, but she says it is going to change," said Marquel, "and we've been having afternoon storms all week."

"I know, I was just hoping that today would be different. Rain really puts a damper on practicing my 3-point shot," said Scott.

"Do you remember last year being like this?" asked Marquel. "I don't think it was so rainy. The weather was so good that we could practice every day."

"I don't remember," said Scott. "But I do know that the next afternoon the sun is out I'll see you on the courts."

• • •

Weather affects what you wear, what you do every day, and even how you get from place to place. But do you know why it rains in some parts of the United States more than others? How would weather scientists describe the patterns of weather we experience each year? In this unit you will analyze weather, climate, and factors that affect weather and climate through the eyes of scientists who study the earth's weather and atmosphere.

**M**any people enjoy a warm sunny day or complain when it rains. But sometimes, bad weather can be more than an inconvenience. It can also pose a hazard. By knowing what the weather is likely to be, people can work to avoid such hazards.

CHALLENGE

**How does weather influence daily life?**

*Weather can vary from day to day. How would you describe the weather in each picture?*

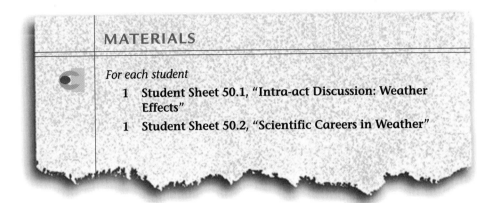

MATERIALS

*For each student*
1   Student Sheet 50.1, "Intra-act Discussion: Weather Effects"
1   Student Sheet 50.2, "Scientific Careers in Weather"

## PROCEDURE

1.  Carefully read the story that starts on the next page.

2.  Mark whether you agree or disagree with the statements on Student Sheet 50.1, "Intra-act Discussion: Weather Effects." Predict what you think other members of your group will say.

3.  Discuss the statements with your group. Have each person share his or her opinion about each statement and explain why he or she agreed or disagreed.

4.  Think about the different ways in which weather affected the students in the story. With your group, brainstorm about jobs that could be affected by severe or unexpected weather.

5.  On Student Sheet 50.2, "Scientific Careers in Weather," review some of the knowledge about weather that is required by four different scientific careers.

6.  During this unit, you will learn what skills and knowledge are needed for each of these four careers. Decide which set of skills interests you the most by selecting one of the careers. Discuss your selection with the rest of your group.

## BACK TO SCHOOL

It was the first day after Thanksgiving break. As Zoe walked down the hall, she saw her friends Sonia, Ray, and Luke.

"Hey Sonia, how was your break?" asked Zoe.

"Not bad," said Sonia. "We flew to my grandmother's house for a big family reunion. Everyone was waiting for us—my aunts, my uncles, and all of my cousins. We didn't get there until eight o'clock at night, and dinner was almost over."

"What happened?" asked Luke.

Sonia made a face as she replied, "That crazy snowstorm grounded our plane. The pilot said that it was too dangerous to fly. It must have been colder than 0 degrees Celsius (32 degrees Fahrenheit) because ice kept forming on the wings. The plane took off three hours late, after the storm was over."

"I remember," said Luke. "We had about 60 centimeters (24 inches) of snow on the ground after the storm ended. It was fun to walk around in the deep snow, but no one could drive anywhere, and most of the buses weren't running. I hated not being able to go to the movies."

"My vacation plans got messed up too," said Ray. "My uncle won one of those radio contests and took our whole family on a cruise. We were supposed to go to Puerto Rico, which is where my mother is from. The day after we left, a huge hurricane was moving through the Caribbean Sea. The ship went to Mexico to avoid the path of the hurricane."

"It's too bad you didn't make it to Puerto Rico," said Sonia.

Luke laughed. "Mexico still sounds pretty good. I'm surprised you're not more tan!"

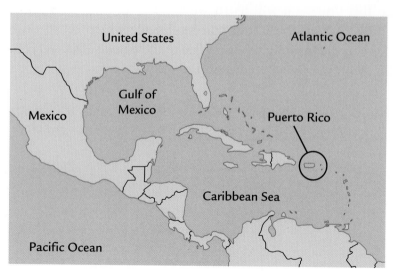

"It was the weather," said Ray. "Even though the hurricane passed us by, it was rainy and windy in the whole area. Whenever it cleared up a bit and I went out on deck, I had to dump water from the deck chairs! The wind speed was about 40 kilometers per hour."

"That's equal to about 25 miles per hour. That doesn't sound very fast," remarked Zoe.

Ray replied, "The wind was strong enough to form some large waves and cause a lot of spray along the sides of the ship. Because it was such a large ship and it had a stabilizer, it didn't cause any rocking. So I guess it wasn't so bad."

"Did you have fun over break, Zoe?" asked Luke. "It was your birthday, wasn't it?"

"Yeah, I had a good time," Zoe replied. "It was pretty low-key. I saw a lot of relatives, and I did get some nice gifts. I'm still waiting for my big present, though. I asked my parents for a digital camera. They went to buy it, but the one that I want wasn't in the stores. The delivery trucks bringing the camera shipment were delayed because of floods. I won't get the camera until next week."

"I heard heavy rains caused flooding out west," Sonia added. "It rained several centimeters in less than 24 hours, and it'll take several days for all of the roads to be cleared."

Sonia sighed. "It sounds like the weather affected everyone's break."

"Yeah, it's one of the few things no one can do anything about," said Luke. "Next thing you know, they'll tell us to expect a tornado over winter break!"

## ANALYSIS

1. How does weather affect your daily life? Provide at least two examples of situations when weather caused you to change your plans.

2. Use information from the activity to complete the following table.

Units Used to Measure Weather Data

|  | Metric Units | English Units |
|---|---|---|
| Temperature |  |  |
| Rainfall |  |  |
| Snowfall |  |  |
| Wind Speed |  |  |

3. Locate your state on the three risk maps shown on the next page. These maps, produced by the U.S. Geological Survey, are based on the numbers of hurricanes, floods, and tornadoes that have occurred in each region. Note: These maps do not include the states of Alaska and Hawaii.

   What is the level of risk:

   a. of hurricanes in your state?

   b. of floods in your state?

   c. of tornadoes in your state?

4. **Reflection:** What is the worst weather you have experienced? How did it affect you? Describe your experience.

Table 3: Monthly Weather Averages

| | Maximum Temperature | Minimum Temperature | Precipitation | Cloud Cover | Wind Direction | Wind Speed |
|---|---|---|---|---|---|---|
| January | | | | | | |
| February | | | | | | |
| March | | | | | | |
| April | | | | | | |
| May | | | | | | |
| June | | | | | | |
| July | | | | | | |
| August | | | | | | |
| September | | | | | | |
| October | | | | | | |
| November | | | | | | |
| December | | | | | | |

## ANALYSIS

1. Recall what you did on each of the five days that you collected daily weather data, and compare it to your data in Table 1, "Daily Weather Data." Which aspect of the weather most affected your daily life? How did it affect you?

2. Imagine that you are a meteorologist for a local radio station. Use your data from Tables 1 and 2 to create a radio weather report that summarizes the weather over the five-day period.

3. In your experience, is your area's weather in a particular month, such as January, the same from year to year? Explain.

4. Which type of weather data—daily or monthly—do you think is more useful for describing weather? Explain your reasoning.

**PROJECT**

**I**n April 1974, 148 tornadoes touched down in 13 states in a two-day period. At least 330 people died, 5,484 people were injured, and there was a total of $500 million in damage.

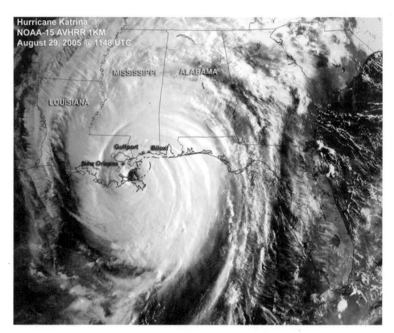

Hurricane Katrina
NOAA-15 AVHRR 1KM
August 29, 2005 @ 1148 UTC

MISSISSIPPI    ALABAMA

LOUISIANA

Gulfport   Biloxi

New Orleans

In 2005, Hurricane Katrina struck along the coasts of Louisiana, Mississippi, and Alabama. Everyone living in the area, including 1 million people from the city of New Orleans, Louisiana, was asked to evacuate to a safer place.

How can you tell if a weather disaster is likely to happen where you live? Although weather affects people on the ground, a lot of weather occurs in the atmosphere. The scientists who study the atmosphere, from the surface of the earth to several hundred kilometers above, are known as **atmospheric** (at-muh-SFEER-ik) **scientists.** They may collect and analyze data about current and past conditions. Areas that have had more hurricanes, floods, or tornadoes in the past are considered more likely to have these events in the future. In this activity, you will find out more about the severe weather that has occurred in your area.

## CHALLENGE

**How are weather disasters different from everyday weather?**

## PROCEDURE

### Part A: Designing the Survey

1. Work with your class to design a survey on weather disasters that have occurred in your area in the past 30 years. Begin by discussing the following questions with your class:

   • What would you like to know about weather disasters in your area?

   • How could people you know provide information about past weather disasters?

   • What questions could you ask to gather this information?

2. As a class, decide the following:

   **a.** What questions will you ask?

   To make your survey consistent, each student must ask the same set of questions.

   **b.** What kinds of responses are not relevant to your survey?

   Some people may have questions about your survey or may provide answers that are irrelevant. As a class, brainstorm possible survey responses that might cause problems, and discuss possible solutions.

   **c.** How will you compare or summarize the data that you gather?

   **d.** What population of people will you survey?

   Hint: Think about factors such as age or experience.

   **e.** How many people will you survey in total? How many people should each student survey? By what date?

3. Use the answers to each question in Step 2 to construct a class survey.

## Part B: Conducting and Analyzing the Survey

**4.** Conduct your survey as decided in class.

**5.** Share your survey results with the rest of your class.

**6.** As a class, compare and summarize the results of your survey.

## ANALYSIS

**1. a.** According to the class data, what type of weather disaster is most common in your area?

**b.** When did such a disaster last occur?

**c.** What can you do to prepare for such a disaster if it happens again?

**2.** Use your class data to create a bar graph of the number of times different types of weather disasters have occurred locally. Be sure to label your axes and to title your graph.

**3.** Look again at the risk maps on page E-9 of Activity 50, "Weather Effects." Did your class survey results support your local risk of hurricanes, floods, and tornadoes, as indicated by the maps?

**4.** Do you think that the survey was a reliable method for finding out what weather disasters have occurred in your area in the past 30 years? Why or why not?

**5. Reflection:** Which type of weather disaster are you most concerned about? Why?

*PROBLEM SOLVING*

The word **weather** is used to describe what's happening outside at a specific time and place, and it can change from day to day or even within a day. **Climate** (KLY-met) describes the average weather in a place over a fairly long period of time (usually at least 30 years). **Climatologists** (kly-muh-TOL-o-jists) are scientists who study the earth's climates. They use such factors as temperature and precipitation to describe different types of climate. For example, think about the climate of a desert as opposed to a tropical rainforest and how their temperatures and precipitation vary.

## CHALLENGE

**How do climates vary?**

*Climatologists study long-term weather trends, which may affect food-supply predictions, species survival, and human health. They may examine tree rings or collect sediments or ice cores (like the one pictured above) to find out more about the earth's past climates. Climatologists often use computer models to help them understand and predict climate changes.*

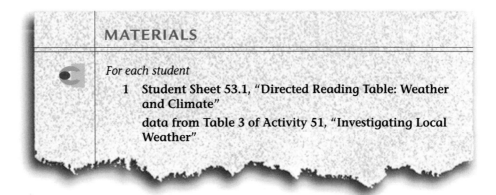

MATERIALS

*For each student*
1   Student Sheet 53.1, "Directed Reading Table: Weather and Climate"
    data from Table 3 of Activity 51, "Investigating Local Weather"

## PROCEDURE

1. Examine Figure 1, "Map of Climates of North America," shown on the next page. It shows some of the different climates found in this part of the earth.

2. Examine the photos and descriptions of the different climate types shown in Figure 2, "Climate Descriptions," on the next two pages. On Student Sheet 53.1, "Directed Reading Table: Weather and Climate," summarize the information about the different types of climates.

3. Work with your partner to:

   a. Locate your state on Figure 1.

   b. Record the climate type for your area in your science notebook.

   c. Determine if your observations and experiences match this description of the climate for your area. In your science notebook, describe any similarities or differences between the climate description for your area and your own observations.

   d. Compare the climate description with your data from Table 3, "Monthly Weather Averages," of Activity 51, "Investigating Local Weather." In your science notebook, describe any similarities or differences between the climate description for your area and your seasonal weather averages. (Your seasonal weather averages will be the average for several months during the same season. For example, in the United States, the summer season is typically from June through August.)

*(Procedure continues on page E-22)*

Figure 1: Map of Climates of North America

Key to climates
- Polar
- Severe
- Highland
- Mild
- Dry
- Tropical

Figure 2: Climate Descriptions

## POLAR

- Extremely cold and long winters, with only 2–4 months having temperatures above freezing
- Cool summers, with temperatures less than 10°C (50°F)
- Dry year-round, with very little precipitation (usually falls as snow)

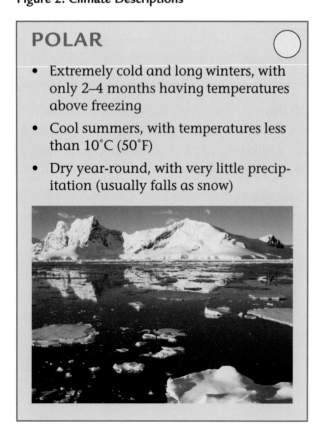

## SEVERE

- Warm summers, with temperatures over 10°C (50°F)
- Very cold winters, with at least one month averaging less than –3°C (27°F)
- Amount of precipitation varies

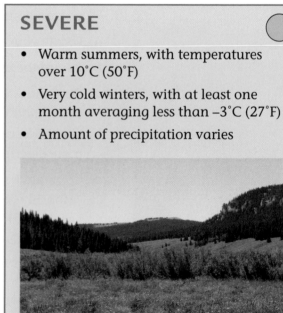

## HIGHLAND

- Very high mountains, such as the Rocky Mountains in the western United States
- Cold to cool year-round, with temperatures between –18°C (–2°F) and 10°C (50°F)
- Amount of precipitation varies, usually falling as snow in winter

## MILD

- Summers are warm or hot, with temperatures over 10°C (50°F)
- Winters are cool or cold, with temperatures below 18°C (64°F) but above –3°C (27°F)
- Moist climate, often with more precipitation in either the winter or summer

## DRY

- Hot days and cool nights year-round
- Maximum summer temperatures usually over 31°C (88°F)
- Dry year-round, with very little precipitation

## TROPICAL

- Hot year-round, with temperatures averaging over 18°C (64°F)
- Wet, with a total of more than 150 centimeters of rain in a year

4. Examine the three graphs on the next page. Each graph shows the average monthly temperature and precipitation for a specific place in the United States. In your science notebook, record which climate type you think each of the three places has and explain your reasoning.

5. Share and discuss your findings with the rest of your group. Remember to listen to and consider the ideas of other group members. If you disagree with someone's ideas, explain to the rest of the group why you disagree.

## ANALYSIS

1. What are the most common climate types in the United States?

2. Compare your responses on Student Sheet 53.1 to Figure 1, "Map of Climates of North America." How do temperatures vary with latitude? Support your answer with evidence from this activity.

3. What is the relationship between weather and climate?

4. Could areas with different climates have the same weather? Explain.

## EXTENSION

Graphs showing average temperature and precipitation for a particular area over a certain time period are known as *climographs* (KLY-moh-grafs). What does a climograph for your area look like? You can create your own climograph using the data from Table 3, "Monthly Weather Averages," of Activity 51, "Investigating Local Weather." First calculate the mean temperature for each month. Then use the temperature and precipitation data to create your own climograph.

**Figure 3: Climate Graphs Showing Average Monthly Temperatures and Precipitation**

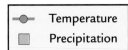

Temperature
Precipitation

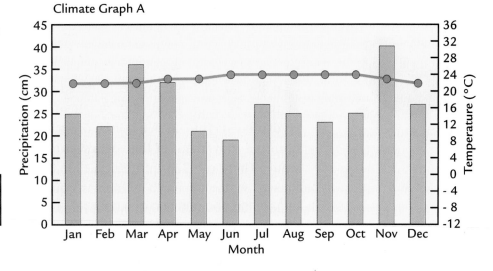

Climate Graph A

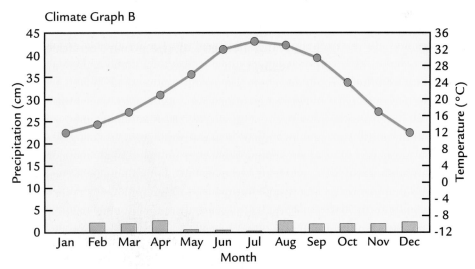

Climate Graph B

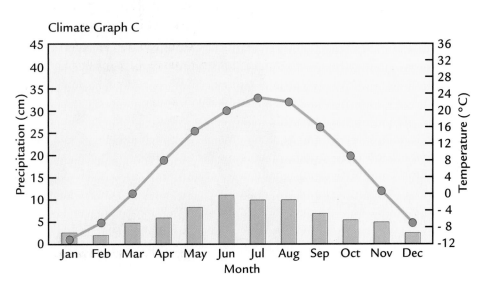

Climate Graph C

PROBLEM SOLVING

In the last activity, you considered some of the different climates that occur on land. But much of the earth's surface is water. **Hydrologists** (hi-DRAWL-o-jists) are scientists who study the distribution and movement of the earth's water. They have a lot of water to study! There are 326 quintillion (326,000,000,000,000,000,000) gallons of water on earth, which is equal to more than 1 sextillion (1,260,000,000,000,000,000,000) liters.

## CHALLENGE

**What percent of the earth's surface is water, and what percent is land?**

*Hydrologists who work for government agencies sometimes monitor the amount of water available in a particular area and how it is being used. Other hydrologists may work for private companies that specialize in water use or water chemistry. This hydrologist is testing for toxic chemicals.*

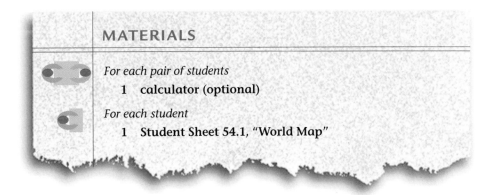

**MATERIALS**

*For each pair of students*
 1 **calculator (optional)**

*For each student*
 1 **Student Sheet 54.1, "World Map"**

## PROCEDURE

1. Copy and complete the following statement in your science notebook. Provide at least one reason to support your thinking.

   *I think that the percentage of the earth's surface that is covered by water is closest to:*

   *25% (¼ or 0.25)     50% (½ or 0.50)     75% (¾ or 0.75)*

2. Your teacher will give you a copy of Student Sheet 54.1, "World Map." With your partner, discuss how you will use it to determine the approximate percentages of water and land on the earth's surface. Briefly describe how you will make your estimate.

3. Calculate and record your estimate of the percentage of the earth that is covered by a) water and b) land.

4. Compare your estimates to those of the other half of your group. Discuss any major differences in your estimates.

5. Work with your group to label the following areas of land and water on Student Sheet 54.1:

| | |
|---|---|
| Africa | Atlantic Ocean |
| Arctic Ocean | Asia |
| Caribbean Sea | Gulf of Mexico |
| Australia | Indian Ocean |
| Europe | Pacific Ocean |
| North America | Southern Ocean |
| South America | |

6. Share your estimates from Step 3 with the class. Use the class data to calculate:

   a. the mean

      Hint: Calculate the **mean** by adding up all of the values and dividing by the total number of values.

   b. the median

      Hint: The **median** is the middle value after the data has been listed from smallest to largest OR largest to smallest. If the data has an even number of values, then the median is the average (mean) of the two middle values.

   c. the mode

      Hint: The **mode** is the value that appears most often.

7. Compare your initial thinking from Step 1 to the amount of water on the earth's surface that you calculated in Step 6a. Correct your statement (if necessary), and explain why your initial ideas were or were not correct.

## ANALYSIS

1. Look at your class data from Step 6, and discuss:

   a. Was your strategy a good way to estimate the percentage of the earth's surface covered by water? Why or why not?

   b. How could you make a better estimate?

2. The water on the earth can be found in many places, including lakes, rivers, icebergs, oceans, and even underground. Based on your work in this activity, where do you think that most of the water on the earth can be found? Explain your reasoning.

## EXTENSION

Use your response to Analysis Question 1b to revise your work from this activity. Calculate the percentages of water and land on the surface of the earth using your revised procedure. How does your revised data compare to your initial calculations? Which is more accurate? Why?

LABORATORY

**M**any factors influence weather and the different kinds of climates on earth. You will investigate some of these factors in the next few activities. One important factor is how land and water interact with energy from the sun. How does the energy from the sun affect different earth surfaces such as land and water? Design an investigation to find out!

## CHALLENGE

**How can you design an experiment to investigate how the sun's energy heats different earth surfaces?**

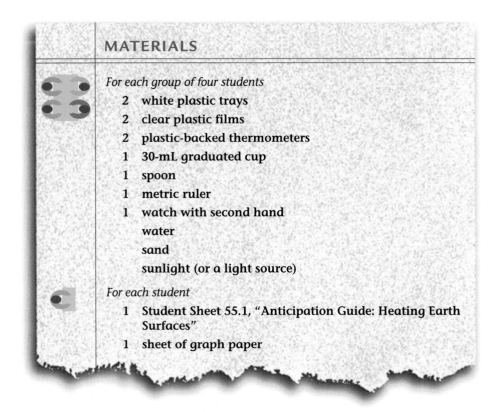

**MATERIALS**

*For each group of four students*

 2  white plastic trays
 2  clear plastic films
 2  plastic-backed thermometers
 1  30-mL graduated cup
 1  spoon
 1  metric ruler
 1  watch with second hand
   water
   sand
   sunlight (or a light source)

*For each student*

 1  Student Sheet 55.1, "Anticipation Guide: Heating Earth Surfaces"
 1  sheet of graph paper

## PROCEDURE

*Use Student Sheet 55.1, "Anticipation Guide: Heating Earth Surfaces," to prepare for the following activity.*

1.  Work with your group to design an experiment to find out:

    **a.** how different earth surfaces are heated by the sun's energy

    **b.** how the different surfaces then cool.

    When designing an experiment, think about the following questions:

    • What is the purpose of your experiment?

    • What materials do you need for the experiment?

    • How will you use these materials to investigate how different earth surfaces are heated and cooled? **Hint:** Think about how to keep everything the same except what you are testing.

    • What is your hypothesis? (What do you predict will happen?)

    • What data will you collect?

    • How will you record the data?

    • How will the data help you reach a conclusion?

2. Record your hypothesis and your planned experimental procedure in your science notebook. Be sure to decide what each person in your group will do.

3. Make a data table that has space for all the data you need to record. You will fill it in during your experiment.

4. Obtain your teacher's approval of your experiment.

5. Conduct your experiment and record your results.

## ANALYSIS

1. **a.** Create a graph of the data you collected. Remember to label your axes, title your graph, and include a key.

   **b.** Summarize the trends that you see in your graph.

2. Copy the table below. Calculate the changes in temperature for each substance you tested, and fill in the table.

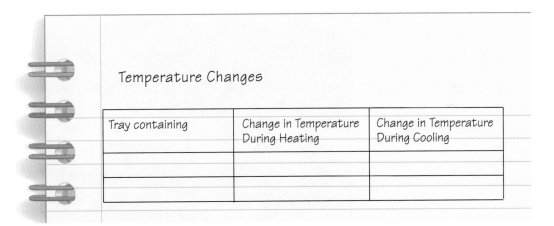

Temperature Changes

| Tray containing | Change in Temperature During Heating | Change in Temperature During Cooling |
|---|---|---|
| | | |
| | | |

3. What can you conclude about how land and water heat up and cool down? Support your answer with evidence from this activity.

## EXTENSION

Design an experiment to further investigate how different surfaces on the earth are heated by the sun's energy and then cool. You may want to investigate if the amount of land or water or different types of soil affect heating and cooling. Use these or other questions to design and conduct your own investigation.

PROBLEM SOLVING

In Activity 53, "Weather and Climate," you examined the range of temperatures found in North America and learned that different parts of the land on earth have different temperatures. But did you know that surface temperatures of the oceans also vary? Even if the ocean is several kilometers deep, the majority of the sun's energy is absorbed at the surface (approximately the top 400 meters). Both hydrologists and climatologists study changes in ocean-surface temperatures to learn more about the movement of ocean water and its effect on climate.

## CHALLENGE

**How do ocean temperatures vary over the surface of the earth?**

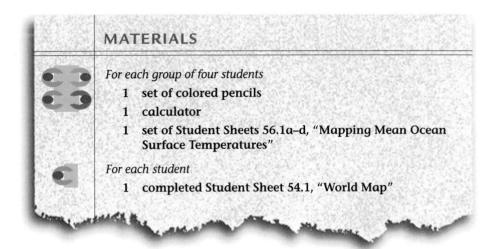

## MATERIALS

*For each group of four students*
1   set of colored pencils
1   calculator
1   set of Student Sheets 56.1a–d, "Mapping Mean Ocean Surface Temperatures"

*For each student*
1   completed Student Sheet 54.1, "World Map"

## PROCEDURE

1. Work with your group to complete a table like the one below. Record your results in your science notebook. **Hint:** To convert a temperature from Celsius to Fahrenheit, multiply it by 1.8 and then add 32.

Temperature Conversion

| Temperature (°C) | Temperature (°F) |
|------------------|------------------|
| 0                |                  |
| 5                |                  |
| 10               |                  |
| 15               |                  |
| 20               |                  |
| 25               |                  |
| 30               |                  |

2. Each person in your group will play the role of a climatologist studying the ocean temperatures on one part of the earth's surface. You may want to look at a completed copy of Student Sheet 54.1, "World Map," to help you identify different bodies of water. Decide who in your group will be the climatologist investigating water temperatures in and around the:

   a. northern Pacific Ocean and parts of the Arctic Ocean and Indian Ocean (Student Sheet 56.1a)

   b. northern Atlantic Ocean, Caribbean Sea, Gulf of Mexico, and part of the Arctic Ocean (Student Sheet 56.1b)

   c. southern Atlantic Ocean and parts of the southern Pacific Ocean and Southern Ocean (Student Sheet 56.1c)

   d. parts of the southern Pacific Ocean, Indian Ocean, and Southern Ocean (Student Sheet 56.1d)

3. Send each climatologist in your group to attend a "regional meeting" with the other groups' climatologists who are studying the same region.

4. At the regional meeting, examine the surface temperatures recorded on the section of ocean shown on your Student Sheet 56.1, "Mapping Mean Ocean Surface Temperatures." Fill in your map, using colored pencils and the Temperature Color Key.

5. At the regional meeting, discuss any patterns that you observe in your section of the map. You will present this information to your group. For example, you can discuss the temperature range, the relationship between temperatures and latitude, and any areas where high or low temperatures seem unusual.

6. Return to your original group and, one student at a time, present the patterns that you observed in your section of Student Sheet 56.1. Listen closely as other group members present their data.

7. Place the four sections of Student Sheet 56.1 together to form a single world map.

8. Discuss with your group any worldwide patterns that you observe in ocean temperatures.

   Hint: As you did in Step 5, you can discuss temperature range, relationships between temperatures and latitudes, and any areas of unusually high or low temperatures. Identify similarities and differences between individual sections of the map and the entire map.

## ANALYSIS

1. What is the temperature range of mean ocean surface temperatures on the earth?

2. How do temperatures vary with latitude? Support your answer with evidence from this activity.

3. Compare your answer to Question 2 above with your answer to Analysis Question 2 of Activity 53, "Weather and Climate." What similarities and differences do you notice?

4. Hurricanes start in areas where the ocean surface temperature is above 26.5°C (80°F). At what range of latitudes would you expect most hurricanes to begin? Explain.

ROLE PLAY

**Y**ou have learned that the sun's energy heats the earth, including the earth's oceans. In this activity, you will find out how climate is influenced by ocean temperatures.

## CHALLENGE

**How do oceans affect climate?**

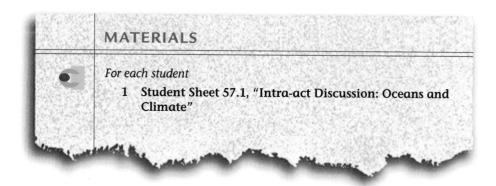

**MATERIALS**

*For each student*

1  **Student Sheet 57.1, "Intra-act Discussion: Oceans and Climate"**

## PROCEDURE

*Benjamin Franklin*

1. Assign one of the following roles to each person in your group.

   • Benjamin Franklin, 18th century scientist, inventor, and statesman
   • Dr. Tansy Makya, climatologist
   • Bo Nye, student moderator of "Time Travel News"
   • Dr. Leena Reddy, hydrologist

2. In your group, read the role-play aloud. As you read, think about what each character is saying.

3. Discuss how you think oceans affect climate.

4. Mark whether you agree or disagree with the statements on Student Sheet 57.1, "Intra-act Discussion: Ocean and Climate." Predict what you think other members of your group will say.

5. Discuss the statements with your group. Have each person share his or her opinion about each statement and explain why he or she agreed or disagreed.

## MAPPING OCEAN CURRENTS

**Bo Nye:** In today's episode of "Time Travel News," we will focus on ocean currents and climate. Our guests include a scientist, inventor, and statesman from the 18th century, Mr. Benjamin Franklin. Joining him are Dr. Leena Reddy, a hydrologist, and Dr. Tansy Makya, a climatologist.

I have heard that there is a current in the Atlantic Ocean that is slowing down. Some scientists say that this may cause changes to the climate of Ireland. How can that be?

**Dr. Leena Reddy:** All around the world, there are regular movements of large amounts of ocean water called **currents** (KUR-unts). Some of these currents move warm water from one place to another, while other currents move cool water.

**Bo:** It sounds like you're talking about rivers, not oceans!

**Dr. Reddy:** Some people describe currents as rivers that run through the ocean. Like rivers, these currents vary in width and depth, but you can't see them the way that you see rivers that run through land. They may be 100 to 1,000 kilometers wide, and flow on the ocean's surface or a couple of kilometers below the surface.

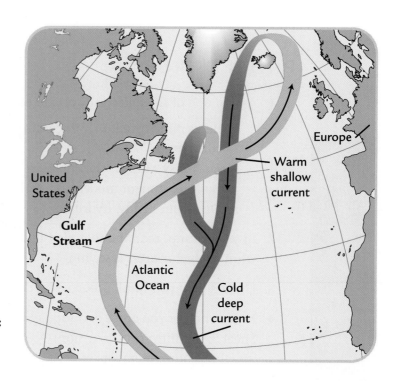

Ocean Currents:
The Northern
Atlantic Ocean

| | |
|---|---|
| Dr. Tansy Makya: | One really important ocean current is called the Gulf Stream. It is one of the strongest ocean currents in the world. It flows on the surface of the northern Atlantic Ocean and carries warm water from the Gulf of Mexico to northwestern Europe. |
| Dr. Reddy: | The warm water begins to cool as it travels north and eventually sinks. It becomes part of a cold deepwater current that then flows south from the northern Atlantic toward the equator. |
| Dr. Makya: | Measurements taken in 2005 show that this cold deepwater current appear to be slowing down. Ocean currents are like huge conveyor belts that move heat from one place to another. The slowing of one part of the belt may cause another part to slow down too. |
| Bo: | Let me see if I understand this idea. If the cold deepwater current is slowing, that could slow down the Gulf Stream. And if the Gulf Stream slows down, less warm water will reach Ireland and northern Europe. |
| Dr. Reddy: | Yes, but saying that this will lead to significant climate change in Ireland is an extreme prediction. There are no data showing that this will happen. |
| Bo: | Mr. Franklin, you were one of the first people to chart the Gulf Stream. What do you think? |
| Benjamin Franklin: | I'm afraid that I don't have enough information. In my day, we didn't have enough data to tell if ocean currents were speeding up, slowing down, or staying the same. |

Bo: I still don't understand how ocean temperatures near Florida could result in a change in the climate of Ireland.

Dr. Reddy: The sun's energy heats both land and water. You probably know that water heats and cools more slowly than land. As a result, oceans retain a large amount of heat. Ocean currents move some of this heat around the earth.

Dr. Makya: Wind blows some surface currents away from the equator toward the poles. A warm current like the Gulf Stream warms and moistens the air above it. The warm, moist air makes climates warmer and wetter than they would otherwise be.

Bo: Even to places that are far from the start of the current? Ireland is thousands of miles from where the Gulf Stream begins in the Gulf of Mexico.

Dr. Makya: Yes. Since the Gulf Stream carries warm water, it makes the climate of countries in northwestern Europe, like Ireland and England, warmer and wetter than other places of the same latitude.

Mr. Franklin: So you are saying that these countries have milder winters and warmer summers because of the Gulf Stream. If the Gulf Stream slowed down, less heat would be transferred, and both winters and summers in these places would be colder.

Dr. Makya: Exactly. The city of Tralee (TRAY-lee), Ireland has a mild climate because of the Gulf Stream. In January, it has an average temperature of 5°C (41°F). In comparison, Petropavlovsk (pet-ro-PAV-lofsk), a city of similar latitude in Russia, has a severe climate because it is

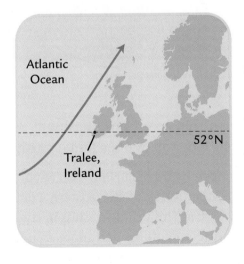

*These two places are at similar latitudes, but have very different climates.*

cooled by a cold ocean surface current that comes down from the North Pole. It has an average January temperature of –8°C (18°F).

Dr. Reddy:  You may have heard of El Niño (NEEN-yo). During El Niño years, the surface temperatures of the eastern Pacific Ocean become a few degrees warmer. This usually results in changes to local climates, like warmer air temperatures and more rain. It can also cause weather disasters, such as floods and droughts.

| | |
|---|---|
| **Bo:** | I never knew that oceans are so important to climate and weather! |
| **Dr. Reddy:** | Ocean currents not only affect climate, they also affect businesses like shipping and fishing. Ocean engineers are always working on new and improved instruments to collect data about currents that make ocean navigation easier. |
| **Mr. Franklin:** | When I was a postmaster in the mid 1700s, we would send letters to England by ship. It took about two weeks for them to reach England. But it would take three to four weeks for letters from England to reach an American port. One day, I received a letter from the head of the British postal service, asking why it took so much longer for mail to travel to the United States. |
| **Bo:** | But didn't he already know about the Gulf Stream? I read that in the early 1500s, Juan Ponce De León of Spain explored the waters around Florida. He wrote about seeing ripples in the ocean moving faster than the surrounding water. |
| **Dr. Makya:** | I understand that during Mr. Franklin's time, sailors familiar with the area knew approximately where the Gulf Stream flowed, but there were no accurate maps of the current. |
| **Bo:** | So, Mr. Franklin, how did you investigate the Gulf Stream? |
| **Mr. Franklin:** | In 1775, 1776, and 1783, I was on ships crossing the Atlantic. I took measurements of the water temperature, speed, and depth of the current two to four times a day by dropping a thermometer in the ocean. Then I recorded the temperatures on a map. I started to see a pattern of areas where the water was warmer and moving faster. |
| **Dr. Reddy:** | Mr. Franklin's measurements were used to construct the first scientific map of the Gulf Stream. |
| **Mr. Franklin:** | I also took daily air temperatures to help make maps of the Gulf Stream more detailed. Adding to my findings, fishermen and sailors told me about what they saw and experienced while sailing the Atlantic Ocean. |
| **Dr. Makya:** | What did they tell you? |
| **Mr. Franklin:** | The most fascinating stories they told were about catching huge fish originally from the Gulf of Mexico up north near North Carolina in the United States. They also described the color of the water in the Gulf Stream as more blue than the rest of the Atlantic Ocean. |
| **Reddy:** | Today, new technology is used to measure ocean current temperatures more quickly and more often. |

Bo: Are the measurements made with instruments on board ships?

Reddy: Some data are still collected that way. But most measurements are collected by instruments that scientists set afloat in the ocean. These instruments are dropped by boat or plane in specific places in different parts of oceans all over the earth.

Dr. Makya: Satellites pick up signals from these instruments and relay the data to scientists. With this data, we now have maps of temperature, speed, and salt content of different ocean currents. These maps can be updated every week or month.

Dr. Reddy: There are also instruments kept on board ships that link to satellites. People with smaller ocean-going boats sometimes buy these instruments so that they can download images of ocean currents to use for navigation.

Mr. Franklin: Amazing! Such accurate and up-to-date information must make sailing easier and safer.

Bo: I think so. How has this information changed people's understanding of ocean currents?

Dr. Reddy: Now we can see the details within large ocean currents. There may be smaller currents and different temperatures within a larger current as well, as you can see on this temperature map I brought.

*Scientists prepare a buoy for release at sea. Instruments attached to buoys collect data about the earth's oceans.*

**Surface Temperatures in the Atlantic Ocean**
*Red areas represent warmer water temperatures.*

| | |
|---|---|
| Dr. Makya: | We can also compare the speed, temperature and salt content of currents from year to year and tell, for example, if currents are slowing down. |
| Bo: | So the information collected from these instruments shows that the climate of Ireland may change? |
| Dr. Makya: | Not exactly. Temperature and water-speed measurements were collected in 1957, 1981, 1992, 1998, and 2004. In one study, scientists compared the five sets of data and concluded that the cold deepwater current flowing from the North Atlantic toward the equator has slowed down. |
| Bo: | So that's why they're projecting that the climate will change in Ireland? |
| Dr. Makya: | A slowing of the cold water current could result in the slowing of the Gulf Stream. This would mean less heat and a cooler climate for northern Europe. |
| Dr. Reddy: | That's one way to interpret the data. Another interpretation is that the slowing of ocean currents is a part of a cycle that reverses itself every 100 years or so. If that is the case, the current may again speed up, and the climate of Ireland would not change so much. |
| Mr. Franklin: | It sounds like we more data needs to be collected. |
| Bo: | So it does. We'll have to keep an eye on the latest news. In the meantime, a big thank you to our guests. Join us next week for another episode of "Time Travel News." |

## ANALYSIS

1. What kinds of data do you think scientists need to collect to determine if the climate of Ireland is changing?

2. How do techniques used to map ocean currents today differ from those used in the late 1700s?

3. What is the relationship between oceans and climate?

4. Look at the map below. Describe the likely effect of the California Current on the climate of California.

*The California Current is a cold water current that flows from north to south along the coast of California.*

## EXTENSION

Do you think you might be interested in a weather-related career? Go to the *Issues and Earth Science* page of the SEPUP website to find links to more information about careers in this field.

READING

**C**limates are described by the same conditions used to describe weather, such as temperature, precipitation, and wind. You now know that oceans have an important effect on climate, but oceans are only one of the factors that influence climates. In this reading, you will find out what other factors cause places to have different climates.

CHALLENGE

**Why do different parts of the world have different climates?**

# READING

*When reading, answer the Stopping to Think questions in your mind. They can help you find out whether you understand the main ideas.*

You examined a map of climates in the United States in Activity 53, "Weather and Climate." You may have noticed that the southern part of Florida has a tropical climate, with warm temperatures and lots of rain year-round. The northern part of Florida has a mild climate with much cooler winters. Why does climate vary so much from place to place? Many factors influence climate. Some factors, like the energy from the sun, are global and affect climates on every part of the earth. Other factors, like landforms, affect local climates.

## Energy from the Sun

The most important factor affecting the earth's climates is energy from the sun. The temperature of a place depends a lot on the sun's energy, because some parts of the earth's surface receive more intense sunlight than others.

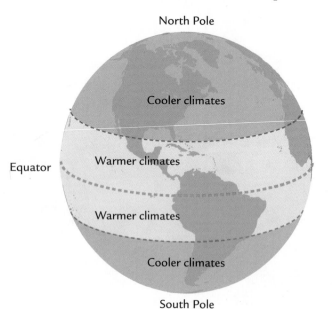

Some of the earth's warmest climates are along the equator. In general, the areas around the equator receive more of the sun's energy, while the North and South Poles receive less. In Unit F, "The Earth in Space," you will learn why this is so. The result is that areas around the equator have warmer climates, and areas around the poles have colder climates, as you can see at left.

## STOPPING TO THINK 1

Imagine holding a tennis ball in front of a heat lamp for five minutes. What do you predict will happen to the temperature along the "equator" of the ball compared to the top and bottom?

## The Role of Oceans

Another major factor influencing the earth's climates are oceans. This is because the water in the oceans holds a large amount of heat. Ocean currents transfer this heat from one part of the earth to another. Some surface currents move water as warm as 25°C (77°F), while other currents move water as cool as 10°C (50°F). Look carefully at the map below, which shows both warm and cold currents on the ocean surface.

The temperature of ocean currents affects the temperature and moisture content of air. Warm surface currents heat and moisten the air above them. This warm, moist air is carried to different parts of the world, where it makes climates warmer and wetter. Cold surface currents cause air to become cooler, resulting in cooler climates.

The movement of ocean currents depends on heat from the sun. Without the energy from the sun, ocean currents would stop and climates all over the world would be very different.

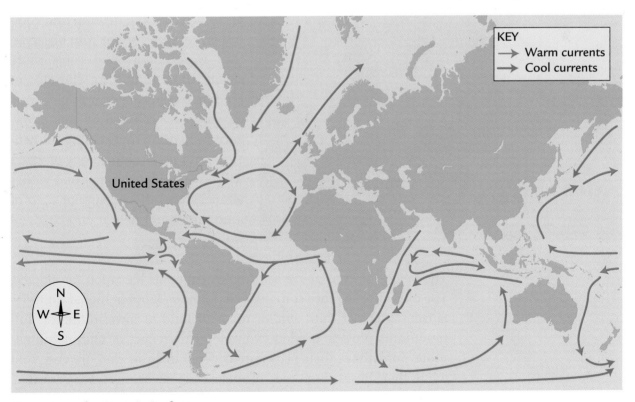

**Currents on the Ocean's Surface**

**STOPPING TO THINK 2**

a. Which coast of the United States is warmed by warm ocean currents? Hint: Look at Figure 1.

b. Which coast of the United States is cooled by cool ocean currents? Hint: Look at Figure 1.

c. Do you predict that the climate of southeastern states along the ocean (such as Georgia and North Carolina) would be warmer or cooler without ocean currents? Explain.

## Factors Affecting Local Climates

In Unit C, "Erosion and Deposition," you learned that the shape of the land and its closeness to water vary from place to place. Some features of local topography can affect climate. These include the presence of large bodies of water, the height of land above sea level, and large landforms such as mountains.

In Activity 55, "Heating Earth Surfaces," you investigated the differences between the heating and cooling of land and water. You observed that water heats and cools more slowly than land. The climates of land areas that are near large bodies of water are affected by this difference in heating and cooling. In general, land near a large body of water will have milder summer and winter temperatures than a similar area of land that is not near a large body of water.

The height of land above sea level is called its elevation, or *altitude.* The altitude of a place can affects its climate. Land at higher altitudes is usually colder than similar areas of land at lower altitudes. Tall mountains provide a good example of the effect of altitude on climate. Sometimes their peaks are covered in snow and are very cold while their bases, hundreds of meters below, are hot. For example,

Africa's Mount Kilimanjaro (shown above), is very close to the equator and has a tropical climate at its base and glaciers at its peak.

Landforms such as mountain ranges, hills, and valleys can also affect climate. When winds blow toward mountains, the air is pushed upward. As the air gains elevation, it cools and begins to release moisture that is in the air. This released moisture often forms clouds and then rain or snow. Because of this, the side of a mountain that is facing the most common wind direction is usually wetter, while the other side is usually drier.

## STOPPING TO THINK 3

What three factors affect local climates? Which of these factors do you think affect your local climate?

Climate and weather are a result of complex interactions between the sun's energy, surfaces on the earth, and the atmosphere. Today, many scientists are concerned that human activities are also affecting climates worldwide. Because of the number of factors that influence climate, it is not easy to determine if one factor is causing more change than another. Climatologists and other scientists study earth's climates in order to answer such questions.

## ANALYSIS

1. Which factors affecting climate were described in the reading in this activity?

2. Oceans can store large amounts of heat. How does this affect climate?

3. Imagine that the sun suddenly disappeared forever. What do you think would happen to the earth's climates? Explain.

4. **Reflection:** In this activity, you learned that many factors influence climate. If you were a climatologist, which factor would you most like to study? Why?

**LABORATORY**

Just like climate, ocean currents are affected by many factors. These factors include wind, water temperature, the shape of the ocean floor, and the rotation of the earth itself. The **salinity** (suh-LIN-ih-tee) of seawater is another factor driving ocean currents. Salinity is the amount of salt dissolved in water. In this activity, you will investigate how well solids dissolve in water compared to other liquids.

## CHALLENGE

**How well do different liquids dissolve the same solid?**

*In the Middle East, the Dead Sea is so salty that you can see areas of dried salt as well as water.*

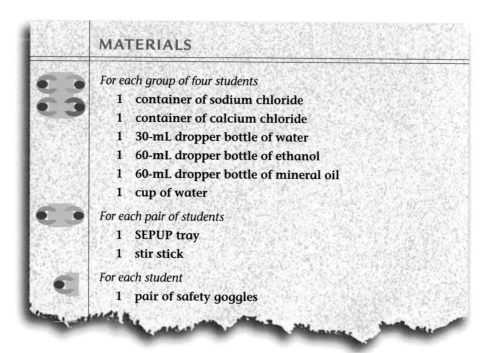

## MATERIALS

*For each group of four students*

1   container of sodium chloride
1   container of calcium chloride
1   30-mL dropper bottle of water
1   60-mL dropper bottle of ethanol
1   60-mL dropper bottle of mineral oil
1   cup of water

*For each pair of students*

1   SEPUP tray
1   stir stick

*For each student*

1   pair of safety goggles

### SAFETY NOTE

**Wear safety eyewear, and do not touch the chemicals directly. Follow all classroom safety rules. Wash your hands when you finish the activity.**

## PROCEDURE

1.  Carefully read the table below to review the different liquids and solids you will investigate in this activity.

| Mixing Liquids and Solids | | |
|---|---|---|
| Cup | Liquid | Solid |
| 1 | 15 drops of water | 2 level scoops of sodium chloride |
| 2 | 15 drops of ethanol | 2 level scoops of sodium chloride |
| 3 | 15 drops of mineral oil | 2 level scoops of sodium chloride |
| 4 | None | 2 level scoops of sodium chloride |
| 5 | 15 drops of water | 2 level scoops of calcium chloride |
| 6 | 15 drops of ethanol | 2 level scoops of calcium chloride |
| 7 | 15 drops of mineral oil | 2 level scoops of calcium chloride |
| 8 | None | 2 level scoops of calcium chloride |

2. Create a data table to record (a) your observations of the liquids in Cups 1–8 (b) your observations of each liquid and solid mixed together and (c) the amount of solid dissolved in each liquid.

3. Work with your partner and use Table 1 to add the correct amounts of three different liquids to Cups 1–3 of your SEPUP tray.

4. Observe the color, transparency, and odor of each liquid, and record your observations of Cups 1–3 in your data table.

5. Use the scoop end of your stir stick, as shown, to add 2 level scoops of sodium chloride to Cups 1–4.

6. Stir the mixture in each cup for exactly one minute, making sure to rinse the stir stick before placing it in the next cup.

7. Compare the amount of solid remaining in the cup to the amount of solid in Cup 4. Estimate the amount of solid that dissolved (all, some, or none), and record your observations in your table.

8. Use Cups 5–8 to repeat Steps 3–7, but when you come to Step 5, use *calcium* chloride instead of *sodium* chloride.

## ANALYSIS

1. A liquid that has a solid dissolved in it is called a **solvent** (SOL-vent). In this investigation:

   a. what are the solvents?

   b. in which solvent did the solids dissolve the most?

2. All water on earth contains some dissolved materials, usually salts. Ocean water is about 3.5% salt, with sodium chloride (table salt) being the most common dissolved salt. Calcium chloride is also found on the earth's surface. Would you expect to find calcium chloride in ocean water? Explain.

3. Water is sometimes called the universal solvent. Explain what you think this statement means. Support your answer with evidence from this activity.

4. Do you think most of the water on the earth is salt water or freshwater? Why?

## EXTENSION

How good a solvent is water? Design an experiment to find out. Consider investigating how much of a particular solid can dissolve in water or test other solids to see if they dissolve in water. Then present your results to the class.

READING

**W**ater is one of the most important natural resources. People need it for survival. Although the earth has a lot of water, it is not always in the right place or of the right quality for human use. Seawater, for example, has too much salt in it for people to drink. Hydrologists study how water moves around the earth so that they can help address people's need for water.

CHALLENGE

**How does water change?**

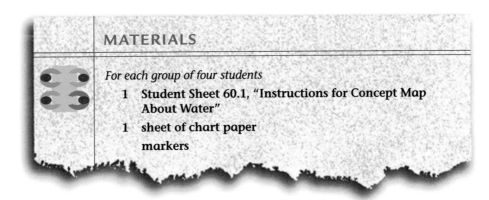

## MATERIALS

*For each group of four students*

1   Student Sheet 60.1, "Instructions for Concept Map About Water"
1   sheet of chart paper
    markers

# READING

*Work with your group to create a concept map that will help prepare you for this activity.*

### Water: Solid, Liquid, and Gas

Water can be found on the earth as a liquid, a solid, and a gas. Liquid water falls as rain or flows as a river. Sometimes water is frozen solid and falls to earth as snow, ice, or hail. When water is a gas, you cannot usually see it, but you can sometimes feel it.

When water is a gas, it is called **water vapor** (VAY-pur). If there is a lot of water vapor in the air, you may feel the air is damp or wet. **Humidity** (hew-MID-ih-tee) is the word meteorologists use to describe the amount of water vapor in the air. When it is very humid, there is a lot of water vapor in the air. It may take a long time for wet things to dry, and your skin may feel sticky and wet. Winds move water vapor from place to place.

### Clouds and Climate

Sometimes, water moves in a form you see every day—clouds. The **clouds** that you see in the sky are large collections of water, usually in the form of tiny droplets of liquid and solid water. When these droplets

*Like clouds, fog is also made up of tiny drops of water. If you have ever been in fog, you know what the inside of a cloud is like!*

become too heavy for air currents to hold them up, they fall down to earth as rain, snow, or hail.

Clouds both cool and warm the earth. Clouds can reflect the sun's rays back into space, causing temperatures to be cooler. Sometimes they act as a blanket over the earth's atmosphere, keeping it warmer. Depending on the time of day and the type of clouds, the result can be either a warmer or cooler surface. Areas with heavy cloud cover tend to be cooler during the day and warmer at night than they would otherwise be.

## Changing States of Water

Every second, somewhere on the earth water is changing its state and moving. Clouds, for example, are blown from one place to another, sometimes releasing rain that soaks into the ground. Because water changes state and moves around so much, it can sometimes seem like the earth has more or less water on it. This is not true. The amount of water on the earth stays the same.

Scientists have words to describe the different ways in which water can change from one state to another. Two familiar words used to describe water changing from one state to another are **melting** and **freezing.** Water melts when it goes from solid to liquid, and water freezes when it goes from liquid to solid.

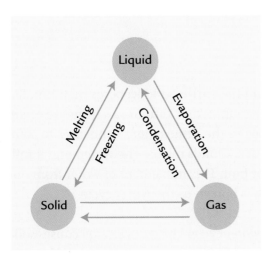

Liquid water becomes water vapor through a process called **evaporation** (ee-VAP-oh-RAY-shun). If you have ever left a glass of water on a counter and come back to find that some of the water has "disappeared," you have seen evidence of evaporation. The water hasn't disappeared; it has changed state.

Water vapor can also turn back into a liquid through a process called **condensation** (CON-den-SAY-shun). If you have ever seen drops of water appear on the inside of a car window or the outside of a glass, you have seen condensation take place. Condensation often occurs high in the sky, when water vapor condenses into tiny water droplets and forms clouds.

## The Water Cycle

Imagine water moving around the earth. Solid icebergs melt into liquid water that flows into the ocean. Water evaporates from the ocean into water vapor. Water vapor in the atmosphere condenses to form the tiny water droplets in clouds. Clouds release the water, and it falls back to earth as rain, snow, or hail. This movement of water from one state to another around earth is known as the water cycle.

Heat from the sun drives the water cycle. The sun's energy causes solid ice to melt into liquid water and liquid water to evaporate and become water vapor. Without the sun's energy, the water cycle would stop, and climates around the world would be very different. From evaporating the ocean water to melting snow, the sun plays an important role in the water cycle and the world's climates.

## ANALYSIS

1. Copy the three lists of words below.

| List 1 | List 2 | List 3 |
| --- | --- | --- |
| vapor | water | evaporation |
| liquid | solid | solid |
| solid | condensation | liquid |
| melting | vapor | vapor |
| water | liquid | water |

a. Look for a relationship among the words in each list. Cross out the word in each list that does not belong.

b. Circle the word in each list that includes the others.

c. Explain how the word you circled relates to the other words in the list.

2. The amount of water on the earth today is the same as it was 100 years ago. Use your knowledge from this activity to explain how this could be true.

**W**ater can be found in many places: on the ground, in the air, and below the earth's surface. Precipitation that falls on land may run off into lakes, rivers, or oceans, but some of this water will go below the earth's surface, where it is called **groundwater.**

About 50% of the water used in homes in the United States comes from water sources on the earth's surface, such as lakes. The other 50% of the water used in homes comes from groundwater. Some people have wells that connect directly to groundwater, while others receive water piped in from wells operated by local water districts. Because groundwater is so important to so many people, some hydrologists specialize in the study of groundwater. In this activity, you will investigate how water interacts with different materials in the ground.

## CHALLENGE

**How does water interact with earth materials?**

*A hydrologist collects groundwater for analysis.*

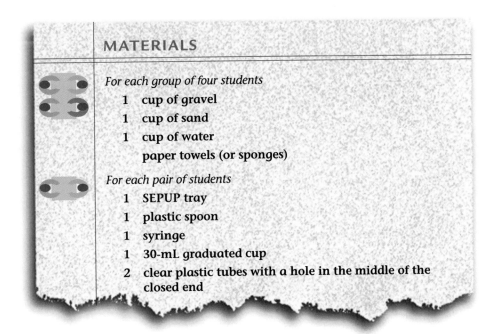

**MATERIALS**

*For each group of four students*

1 cup of gravel
1 cup of sand
1 cup of water
   paper towels (or sponges)

*For each pair of students*

1 SEPUP tray
1 plastic spoon
1 syringe
1 30-mL graduated cup
2 clear plastic tubes with a hole in the middle of the closed end

## PROCEDURE

1. In your science notebook, make a table like the one below.

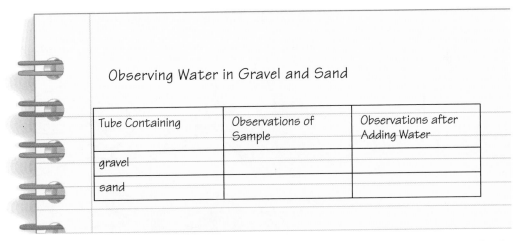

Observing Water in Gravel and Sand

| Tube Containing | Observations of Sample | Observations after Adding Water |
|---|---|---|
| gravel | | |
| sand | | |

2. Examine the samples of gravel and sand. Complete the second column of your table by describing and sketching the size and shape of the particles of each material as best as you can.

3. You will investigate how water travels through these two materials. In your science notebook, predict through which material water will travel more quickly. Explain your reasoning.

4. Fill your graduated cup to the 30-mL mark with sand.

5. Pour the sand into one of the clear plastic tubes.

6. Fill your graduated cup to the 30-mL mark with gravel.

7. Pour the gravel into the other tube.

8. Fill the syringe with 13 mL (equal to 13 cc) of water.

9. Carefully add the water to the 30-mL graduated cup.

10. Fill the syringe with another 13 mL of water.

11. Place the tube of gravel with its open end up over large Cup B of the SEPUP tray. Place the tube of sand with its open end up over large Cup C.

    Note: Hold the tubes steady so that they are not accidentally knocked over.

12. You and your partner will need to add water to both tubes simultaneously as shown below. Before doing this, read the following directions:

    • Use the syringe to add 13 mL of water to the gravel by slowly squirting the water onto the inside wall of the tube of gravel.

    • Use the graduated cup to add 13 mL of water to the sand by slowly pouring the water into the tube of sand.

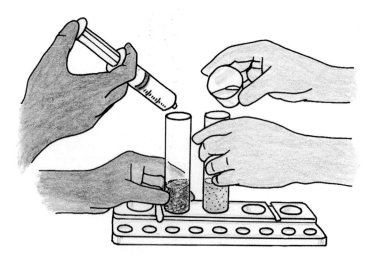

13. Record the time as you and your partner simultaneously add water to each tube.

14. Observe for five minutes what happens to the water in each tube.

15. Record your observations in your data table.

## ANALYSIS

1. Through which material did water travel more quickly? How did this result compare with your initial prediction?

2. Explain how this activity helps provide evidence that the amount of water on earth stays the same.

3. Materials such as sand and gravel often contain small amounts of salts. Based on your work in Activity 59, "Water as a Solvent," what do you think happens as water travels through these materials?

## EXTENSION

Where does your drinking water come from? Find out by going to the *Issues and Earth Science* page of the SEPUP website to find links to sites that provide local information. Or contact your local water district directly.

MODELING

Imagine taking all of the water at the earth's surface and pouring it into a single container. About 97% of it would be saltwater from the earth's oceans, seas, and salt lakes. The other 3% would be from all of the earth's freshwater, including water frozen in ice sheets, icebergs, groundwater, and water vapor in the air. The surface water in lakes, rivers and streams makes up only 0.03%!

$H_2O$ is an abbreviation for a molecule of water. A molecule is the smallest size particle of water that there is. Imagine that you could follow a group of water molecules over time. Your observations of these molecules would start right here in your town.

## CHALLENGE

**How does water move from place to place?**

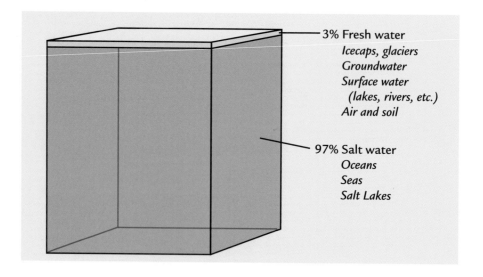

3% Fresh water
*Icecaps, glaciers*
*Groundwater*
*Surface water*
*(lakes, rivers, etc.)*
*Air and soil*

97% Salt water
*Oceans*
*Seas*
*Salt Lakes*

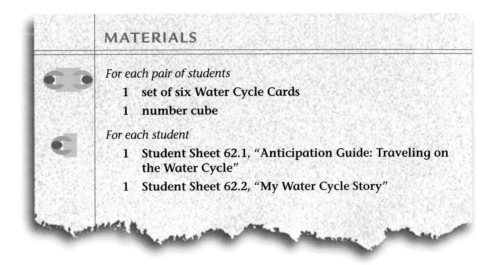

## MATERIALS

*For each pair of students*

1 set of six Water Cycle Cards

1 number cube

*For each student*

1 Student Sheet 62.1, "Anticipation Guide: Traveling on the Water Cycle"

1 Student Sheet 62.2, "My Water Cycle Story"

# PROCEDURE

*Use Student Sheet 62.1, "Anticipation Guide: Traveling on the Water Cycle," to help prepare you for this activity.*

1. With your partner, review the six Water Cycle cards.

2. Work with your partner to decide where your water adventure begins by selecting one of the Water Cycle cards as a starting place. Be sure to select a place that fits the location of your town. This is the card you will start with.

*Which parts of the water cycle can you see in this photograph?*

3. Record the title of the Water Cycle card on Student Sheet 62.2, "My Water Cycle Story."

4. With your partner, look at the Water Cycle card to see where your water molecules can be. Make a choice and record it on Student Sheet 62.2. In the third column, identify the state of your water (solid, liquid, or water vapor).

5. Roll the number cube. Look for the number you rolled on the Water Cycle card to find out where your water will go next.

   Note: Water can cycle back to the same place, so you may not use all six cards. When you get to one you have had before, choose a different form for your water.

6. Repeat Steps 3–5 for all the rows of Student Sheet 62.2. In the third column, identify the state of your water (solid, liquid, or water vapor) at each place in the story.

7. Each row of Student Sheet 62.2 is one part of the story of your water. Discuss with your partner:

   • Where in the world are your water molecules in each part of your story? Remember, your water first started in your town. Hint: If you are still having trouble, you may want to consult Student Sheet 62.3, "Story Ideas."

   • Describe what happened to your water molecules from one part of the story to the next. Be sure to explain exactly how your water changed.
   Hint: Did it move? If so, how? Or did something else happen, like a temperature change?

8. Based on your discussion, complete the last column of Student Sheet 62.2.

## ANALYSIS

1. On Student Sheet 62.1, you recorded your initial ideas about the water cycle. To complete Student Sheet 62.1:

   a. Use the following words to identify where water can be found in the picture:

      atmosphere          groundwater

      land                ocean

      organisms           precipitation

   b. Draw at least six arrows showing the movement of water from one place to another.

   c. Label places where each of the following is occurring:

      condensation        evaporation

      freezing            melting

   d. What changes did you have to make to your student sheet so that you could complete it?

2. The term "water cycle" is used to describe the movement of water on the earth. Do you think that your diagram on Student Sheet 62.1 is a good summary of the water cycle? Why or why not?

3. In this activity, you used cards and number cubes to model the water cycle. Do you think that this activity was a good model of the water cycle? Why or why not?

4. Expand your notes from Student Sheet 62.2 into a story that describes the journey of your water molecules. Your story should follow your water through at least five places. Be as creative and scientifically accurate as you can! Be sure to:

   • Describe or draw how your water molecules moved from one place to another.

   • Identify any changes in state (solid, liquid, gas) that occur.

On a rainy day, you see lots of clouds and watch rain fall to the ground. On other days, the sun shines brightly onto the earth. During a hurricane or tornado, high winds can blow everything in their path from one place to another. All of this weather in happening in the air that surrounds the earth. Learn more about weather and climate by investigating air.

## CHALLENGE

**Can you provide evidence that air is a substance?**

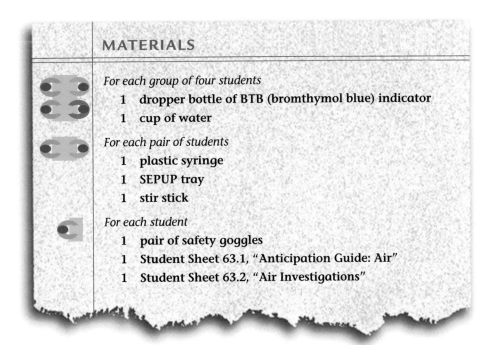

**MATERIALS**

*For each group of four students*

   1   **dropper bottle of BTB (bromthymol blue) indicator**

   1   **cup of water**

*For each pair of students*

   1   **plastic syringe**

   1   **SEPUP tray**

   1   **stir stick**

*For each student*

   1   **pair of safety goggles**

   1   **Student Sheet 63.1, "Anticipation Guide: Air"**

   1   **Student Sheet 63.2, "Air Investigations"**

**SAFETY NOTE**

**Wear safety eyewear, and do not touch the chemicals directly. Follow all classroom safety rules. Wash your hands when you finish the activity.**

## PROCEDURE

*Use Student Sheet 63.1, "Anticipation Guide: Investigating Air," to help prepare you for this activity.*

### Part A: What is Air?

1. Observe the air around you. Record your observations on Student Sheet 63.2, "Air Investigations." **Hint:** Think about color and odor.

2. Fill a plastic syringe with 20 mL (equal to 20 cc) of air by pulling the plunger up slowly.

3. Keeping the tip of the syringe about one centimeter (cm) from the skin on your partner's arm, push the plunger all the way down. Your partner should record his or her observations on Student Sheet 63.2.

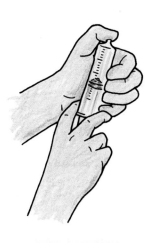

4. Fill the syringe with 20 mL of air by pulling the plunger back slowly. Hold your thumb tightly over the tip of the syringe and push the plunger all the way down, as shown at left.

5. Repeat Step 4, but this time lift your thumb off of the tip after pushing the plunger past 10 mL.

6. Record your observations on Student Sheet 63.2.

7. Switch roles with your partner, and repeat Steps 2–6.

## Part B: Is Air Always the Same?

8. Place 3 drops of BTB into large Cups A, B, and C of a SEPUP tray.

9. Use the syringe to slowly add 5 mL of water to each cup. Use the stir stick to mix the solution.

10. Record the initial color of each solution on Student Sheet 63.2.

11. Fill the syringe with 20 mL of air, and place the tip of the syringe into the solution in Cup B. Slowly push the plunger all the way down. Remove the syringe from the solution.

12. Repeat Step 11 one more time.

13. Have your partner do Step 11 twice more.

14. Carefully remove the plunger from the syringe.

15. Hold the top opening of the syringe several centimeters from your mouth (as shown at left), and blow into it for 10 seconds, until you are sure that the syringe is filled with air coming from your lungs. Quickly put the plunger back into the top of the syringe. You should now have 20 mL of air from your lungs in the syringe.

16. Place the tip of the syringe into the solution in Cup C, and slowly push the plunger all the way down. Observe what happens.

17. Switch roles, and have your partner repeat Steps 14–16.

18. Repeat Steps 14–17 one more time each.

19. Record the final color of each solution on Student Sheet 63.2.

20. Share your results, and discuss Analysis Question 1 with the rest of your group.

## ANALYSIS

1. Use your laboratory results to discuss the following questions:

   **a.** How can you describe air?

   **b.** Is air always the same?

   **c.** Look again at Student Sheet 63.1. Would you change any of your answers? How?

2. Do your observations from Part A provide evidence that air is a substance? Why or why not?

3. Look at your results from Part B. Is the air that comes out of your lungs the same as your classroom air? Explain.

4. Is air a substance or is it just empty space? Support your answer with evidence from this investigation.

COMPUTER SIMULATION

**Y**ou know the space around you as "air," and you may sometimes think of it as being empty. In fact, the air around you is a mixture of gases, including water vapor. Meteorologists call the air that surrounds the earth the **atmosphere**. To better predict weather and climate, scientists need to understand the atmosphere. You can find out what is in the earth's atmosphere by using a computer to simulate collecting air samples from different parts of it.

## CHALLENGE

**How does the earth's atmosphere vary?**

*This NASA aircraft can fly up to 20 km above the earth's surface. Atmospheric scientists have attached instruments to the bottom of the aircraft that can collect data on air temperature, water vapor, and air pollution.*

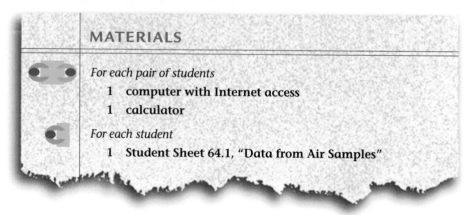

### MATERIALS

*For each pair of students*
   1  **computer with Internet access**
   1  **calculator**

*For each student*
   1  **Student Sheet 64.1, "Data from Air Samples"**

# PROCEDURE

1. Imagine releasing a balloon that can collect data about which gases are in the air, the air temperature, and the air pressure. Do you predict that the atmosphere would be the same at every altitude? Explain your ideas in your science notebook.

2. On a computer, go to the *Issues and Earth Sciences* student page of the SEPUP website, and select the link under Activity 64, "Earth's Atmosphere."

   • On the left side of the screen, you should see a list of atmospheric layers and the distance of each layer from the earth's surface.

   • You will gather data from three different altitudes within each atmospheric layer.

3. Select an atmospheric layer to investigate by clicking on the name of that layer on the left side of your screen.

4. Read Student Sheet 64.1, "Data from Air Samples," carefully. Be sure you understand where to record the data for the atmospheric layer you selected. Then write the name of that layer on the top of the data table that shows the correct altitude.

*A researcher in Antarctica launches a weather balloon that carries a package of instruments to an altitude of around 25 kilometers.*

5. Sample the atmosphere at three altitudes in this atmospheric layer by moving the cursor over the lower, middle, and upper altitudes. Record your data in the appropriate table on Student Sheet 64.1.

6. Repeat Steps 3–5 until you have sampled the air at all of the altitudes above the earth's surface.

7. Observe any patterns in the atmospheric data that you have collected. As you look over the data on different layers of the atmosphere, consider what stays the same and what changes.

Hint: Student Sheet 64.1 is set up so that the upper layers of the atmosphere are on the top and the lower layers are on the bottom.

8. Work with your partner to calculate the mean of each data set on Student Sheet 64.1.

9. In your science notebook, create a table to compare the mean data for the four layers of the atmosphere that you sampled. Be sure to create columns for each of the four gases that you sampled, the air temperature, and the air pressure. Label this table "Mean Atmospheric Values."

10. Discuss with your partner which data are the same for the different atmospheric layers and which data are different. Compare your data to the prediction that you made in Step 1, and revise your initial ideas as needed.

## ANALYSIS

1. Which layer of the atmosphere has:

   a. the most water vapor?

   b. the lowest pressure?

2. What remains the same in different layers of the atmosphere?

3. Scientists have divided the earth's atmosphere into different layers. What property of the atmosphere do you think these divisions are based on?

4. You collected data on four layers of the atmosphere. The atmosphere merges into outer space in an extremely thin upper layer known as the **exosphere**. Which of the five layers of the atmosphere do people live in?

**INVESTIGATION**

Today, the earth's atmosphere is a mixture of gases that includes nitrogen, oxygen, and water vapor. But the earth is more than 4.5 billion years old, and a lot of changes have happened in that time.

Atmospheric scientists and climatologists sometimes drill deep into the earth's surface to collect layers of ice and rock, as shown in the photo below. These layers provide information about what the earth's atmosphere was like hundreds of thousands of years ago.

**CHALLENGE**

**Has the earth's atmosphere always been the same as it is today?**

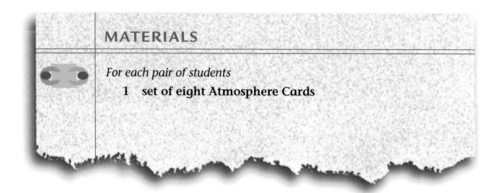

MATERIALS

*For each pair of students*
1 set of eight Atmosphere Cards

## PROCEDURE

1. With your partner, carefully read the information on each Atmosphere Card.

2. Work with your partner to place each card in order from oldest to most recent.

3. Compare how you ordered your cards with the way the other half of your group ordered them. Discuss similarities and differences in your arrangements.

4. With your group, work with one set of cards to place the cards in an order you all agree on, from oldest to most recent.

   Remember to listen to and consider the explanations and ideas of other members of your group. If you disagree with others, explain why you disagree.

5. In your science notebook, create a table like the one on the next page, and record your final order for the Atmosphere Cards. Complete the table by writing down information about the gases in the atmosphere and important events during that time.

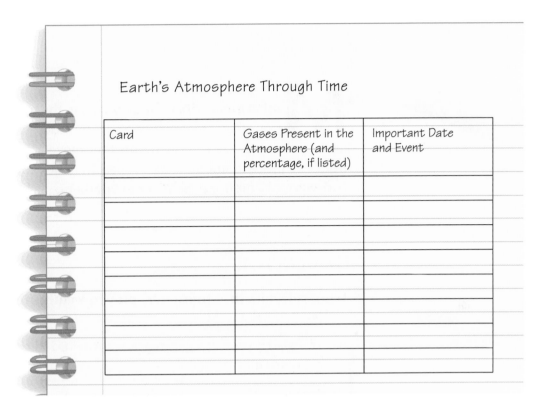

Earth's Atmosphere Through Time

| Card | Gases Present in the Atmosphere (and percentage, if listed) | Important Date and Event | |
|---|---|---|---|
|  |  |  |  |
|  |  |  |  |
|  |  |  |  |
|  |  |  |  |
|  |  |  |  |
|  |  |  |  |
|  |  |  |  |
|  |  |  |  |

## ANALYSIS

1. Look carefully at your completed table.

   **a.** How has the amount of carbon dioxide gas in the atmosphere changed over the earth's history?

   **b.** How has the amount of oxygen gas in the atmosphere changed over the earth's history?

2. What effect have living organisms (including people) had on the composition of the earth's atmosphere? Support your answer with examples from this activity.

3. **Reflection:** Do you think that the atmosphere will have different amounts of oxygen and carbon dioxide in the future? Explain your reasoning.

READING

**M**ost of the earth's weather occurs in the **troposphere** (TROH-poh-sfeer). In Activity 58, "The Causes of Climate," you learned that the ocean has currents that move warm and cold water from one place to another. The troposphere has currents as well. Air currents move air from one place to another.

CHALLENGE

**What role does the atmosphere play in weather and climate?**

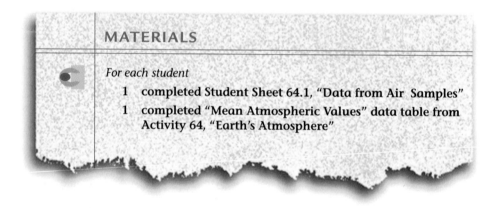

### MATERIALS

*For each student*

1   completed Student Sheet 64.1, "Data from Air Samples"
1   completed "Mean Atmospheric Values" data table from Activity 64, "Earth's Atmosphere"

# READING

*Use the "Listen, Stop, and Write" strategy to help you with this reading. Listen as your teacher reads aloud. Whenever he or she stops reading, close your book. Write down the main ideas you just heard.*

## Earth's Atmosphere

The atmosphere is the layer of gases that surrounds the earth. The main gases are nitrogen (78%) and oxygen (21%), with the remaining 1% made up of other gases including carbon dioxide, water vapor, and argon. Atmospheric scientists divide the atmosphere into five layers based on temperature differences (see the table below). Compared to the radius of the earth (6,370 km), the atmosphere is a very thin 262–382 km.

| Earth's Atmospheric Layers | | |
|---|---|---|
| **Atmospheric Layer** | **Approximate height above earth's surface** | **What happens in this layer?** |
| Exosphere | 120 km+ | The earth's atmosphere merges into space. |
| Thermosphere | 80–120 km | The space shuttle orbits the earth. |
| Mesosphere | 50–80 km | Meteors usually burn up. |
| Stratosphere | 12–50 km | Ozone layer absorbs some the sun's harmful ultraviolet radiation before it strikes the earth's surface. |
| Troposphere | 0–12 km | Most weather occurs. Cruising altitude of most commercial aircraft. |

## Atmosphere and Weather

Weather occurs in the troposphere. Air in the troposphere is heated from the ground up. The surface of the earth absorbs the sun's energy and heats up. The heated earth then heats up the air above it. Since some parts of the earth's surface heat up faster than others, this causes differences in air temperature and pressure, resulting in wind.

**Wind** is the horizontal movement of air. Air moves from areas of high pressure to areas of low pressure and can result in winds of different speeds. When there is very little or no difference between pressure in two neighboring regions, the air is calm and there is no wind. When there is a lot of difference in air pressure between two neighboring regions, strong winds can blow leaves off trees and push clouds across the sky. The fastest wind speed recorded to date is 513 km/hr (318 mi/hr) during a 1999 tornado in Oklahoma. In general, wind speeds tend to be higher in the daytime when there are greater differences in air temperature and pressure.

Heat is spread through the troposphere because air is slightly unstable. Unstable air can cause the moisture in the atmosphere to condense and clouds to form. On average, clouds cover 40–50% of the earth at any given time. Clouds and storms form when pockets of air rise and cool. They are carried through the atmosphere by wind. The more unstable the atmosphere is, the more likely you are to see clouds and more severe weather, such as storms.

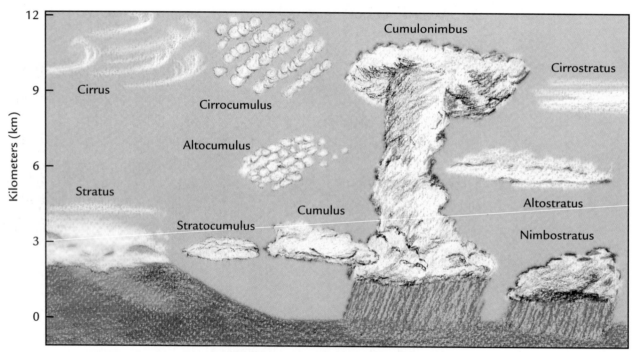

Clouds are described by their height in the atmosphere and their shape.

## Atmosphere and Climate

The way the earth's atmosphere interacts with the sun's energy and the oceans helps determine the earth's average temperatures and its different climate zones. Air heated at the equator eventually moves north or south to other climates. Some of the sun's energy reflects off the earth's surface and would be lost to space if there were no atmosphere. By trapping some of the sun's energy, the atmosphere helps maintain the different climates on earth.

The constant movement of air in the earth's atmosphere also ensures a steady environment for living organisms. Almost all living organisms require gases found in the atmosphere for survival. The interaction between living organisms and the environment means that the earth's atmosphere supports life and that living organisms continue to produce gases that become part of the atmosphere.

## ANALYSIS

1. What is the relationship between the earth's atmosphere and its weather and climate?

2. As an atmospheric scientist, you are asked to write an encyclopedia entry about the atmosphere. Use your work from Activity 64, "Earth's Atmosphere," and your knowledge about the atmosphere from Activities 65 and 66 to write a paragraph explaining the atmosphere and its layers. Be sure to describe significant similarities and differences among the different layers.

3. **Reflection:** In the past three activities, you have learned a lot about the earth's atmosphere. If you were an atmospheric scientist, what aspect of the earth's atmosphere would you most like to study? Why?

**LABORATORY**

**M**oving air is called wind. During hurricanes, winds can reach over 248 kilometers per hour (155 miles per hour). A tornado can have winds as fast as 512 kilometers per hour (318 miles per hour). The instruments pictured on this page are used to measure wind. Wind *speed* is measured by an **anemometer** (an-uh-MOM-ih-ter). Wind *direction* is measured by a **wind vane**.

## CHALLENGE

**How will you design instruments to measure wind speed and wind direction?**

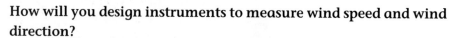

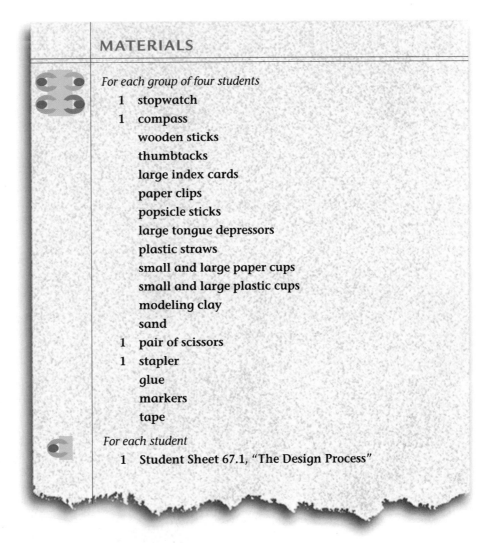

## MATERIALS

*For each group of four students*

1 stopwatch
1 compass
  wooden sticks
  thumbtacks
  large index cards
  paper clips
  popsicle sticks
  large tongue depressors
  plastic straws
  small and large paper cups
  small and large plastic cups
  modeling clay
  sand
1 pair of scissors
1 stapler
  glue
  markers
  tape

*For each student*

1 Student Sheet 67.1, "The Design Process"

## Part A: Creating a Design

1. Your group will make a wind vane and an anemometer. Decide which two members of your group will work on which instrument.

2. Review the list of materials that will be available to you. Discuss with your partner how you would like to build your instrument.

3. After you and your partner decide on a design, each of you should draw and label the parts of your design on your copy of Student Sheet 67.1, "The Design Process."

4. Exchange student sheets with the other pair in your group and review their design.

5. Work with your partner to provide feedback by identifying at least one strength of their design and one recommendation for improvement. Write your feedback on both their student sheets.

6. Exchange student sheets, and review the comments made by the rest of your group. Work with your partner to make any needed changes to your design, and record these on Student Sheet 67.1.

7. On Student Sheet 67.1, write a step-by-step procedure that explains how to use your instrument to measure the wind.

## Part B: Constructing Your Instrument

8. Build your instrument according to the design you sketched on Student Sheet 67.1.

9. Test your instrument by measuring wind (either outdoors or using a fan indoors).

10. Evaluate your instrument. If something did not operate according to plan or could be improved, record this on Student Sheet 67.1.

## Part C: Redesign and Refine

11. Based on your observations in Steps 9 and 10, discuss with your partner ways to redesign or improve your instrument.

12. Make any needed changes to your instrument.

13. Test your instrument again, and record on Student Sheet 67.1 any factors that did not go as planned.

14. Continue redesigning and refining your instrument until the deadline your teacher has set.

## Part D: Collecting Wind Data

15. Follow your teacher's instructions, and then take your instrument outside. Take three separate wind measurements with your instrument. Record your data on Student Sheet 67.1.

## ANALYSIS

1. Evaluate your group's two instruments by completing the following table.

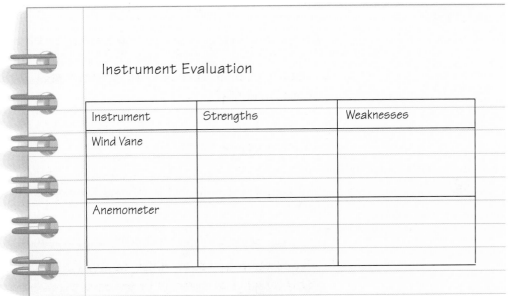

Instrument Evaluation

| Instrument | Strengths | Weaknesses |
|---|---|---|
| Wind Vane | | |
| Anemometer | | |

2. What do the more successful wind-measurement instruments have in common?

3. You designed and tested your anemometer and wind vane at school. Imagine using them on a ship, as Francis Beaufort did.

   a. What factors might be different on a ship than at school?

   b. Describe how you would adjust the design of your instruments so that they would work well on a ship.

COMPUTER SIMULATION

In Activity 58, "The Causes of Climate," you read about many different factors that influence global climate, including the sun's energy and ocean currents. In many places, the wind blows from one direction more than from any other. This direction is called the **prevailing wind**, and the pattern of prevailing winds also influences global climates.

## CHALLENGE

**What is the pattern of prevailing winds on different parts of the earth?**

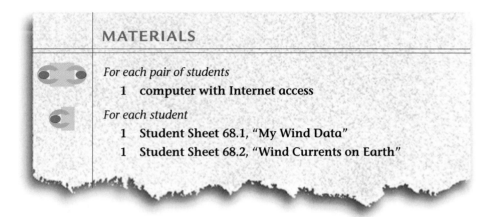

## PROCEDURE

1. Your teacher will assign you and your partner to a city. Record the number for your assigned city in the space provided on Student Sheet 68.1, "My Wind Data."

2. On the Internet, go to the *Issues and Earth Sciences* student page of the SEPUP website, and select the link under Activity 68, "Worldwide Wind."

3. Click on the number for your city.

4. You should see a list of dates. These dates represent days in which a local middle school science teacher measured the direction of the wind in this city.

5. Select a date, and examine the direction from which the wind blew that day. Note that the arrow itself represents the wind.

6. On Student Sheet 68.1, "Wind Data," draw an arrow showing the direction of the wind on that day and label it with the date, as shown below.

7. Repeat Steps 5 and 6 until you have collected all of the wind data for your city. If two or more dates have the same wind direction, write the second (and third and more) date(s) under the first date for that arrow. Record days without wind at the bottom of Student Sheet 68.1.

8. Work with your partner to determine the most common wind direction in your city. This is the prevailing wind.

9. Share your data with your class. Report the number of the region containing your assigned city and the direction of your city's prevailing wind.

10. On Student Sheet 68.2, "Wind Currents on Earth," draw arrows showing the prevailing winds for each of the regions that the other groups investigated.

## ANALYSIS

1. Look carefully at Student Sheet 68.2. Describe any overall pattern that you see.

2. Summarize global wind patterns by constructing a table to record the prevailing wind direction at different latitudes.

3. Look at the direction of the prevailing winds over North America. Based on the direction of the prevailing wind, would you expect weather systems over the United States to travel from east to west or west to east?

INVESTIGATION

**Y**ou have learned that meteorologists collect data about the earth's weather. They often use that data to construct weather maps. Meteorologists then use those maps to predict what the weather will be like in the next few hours, the next day, or for the next several days. This is known as a **weather forecast.**

When forecasting weather, meteorologists sometimes refer to **cold fronts,** which form when cold air moves in and replaces warm air. The cold air pushes the warm air up, forming high columns of clouds, as shown below. Cold fronts usually cause cooler temperatures. A **warm front** occurs when warm air moves in and replaces cooler air. Warm fronts bring in warmer temperatures. They also create cloudy conditions that usually last longer than the cloudy conditions produced by cold fronts.

**Cold Front**

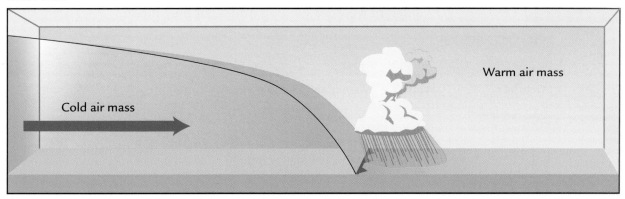

**Warm Front**

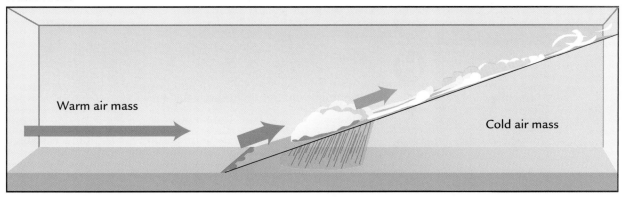

## CHALLENGE

What information is found on a weather map? How can a weather map be used to forecast weather?

### MATERIALS

*For each student*

1   Student Sheet 69.1, "Summarizing Weather Reports"
1   Student Sheet 69.2, "Map of Iowa"

## PROCEDURE

1.  Work with your group to review the information in the table below, "Weather Map Symbols." Make sure that you are familiar with the different weather symbols and what they mean.

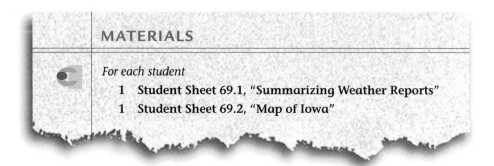

| Weather Map Symbols | | |
|---|---|---|
| **Weather** | **Symbol** | **Associated Weather** |
| Precipitation | | Rain, snow, fog, or other forms of precipitation |
| Cold front | | Cooler temperatures, possible precipitation |
| Warm front | | Warmer temperatures, possible precipitation |
| Low pressure | L | Cloudy skies, possible precipitation |
| High pressure | H | Clear skies |
| Hurricane | | Damaging winds, rain, possible flooding |
| Tornado watch | | Area where tornadoes may occur, possible severe thunderstorms |
| Tropical storm | | Very strong winds and heavy rains |

2. Your teacher will assign your group one of the weather maps for August 24–31 shown on pages 92–93.

3. Work with your partner to summarize the weather on this map. Identify:

   • weather fronts

   • precipitation

   • areas of high and low pressure

   • any unusual weather events, such as a tornado watch or a hurricane

   Be sure to discuss with your partner each type of weather and where in the country it is occurring. For example, if you were to begin to summarize the weather for August 24, you might say, "There is a cold front stretching from Arizona northeast up to Minnesota."

4. Work with your partner to write a weather report for your assigned day. You can do this by describing the weather that is associated with each weather symbol (see the table). As you summarize current weather conditions, make sure to describe:

   • weather fronts and possible changes in temperature

   • areas of precipitation

   • clear or cloudy skies due to changing pressure

   • any unusual weather events, such as a tornado watch or a hurricane

   In your science notebook, write your weather report in complete sentences and in the present tense, as if you were reporting the weather on television or the radio. For example, if you were to begin to summarize the weather on August 24, you could write, "The cold front stretching from the southwest up to Minnesota is causing cooler temperatures and may result in some precipitation."

5. Share your weather report with the other half of your group. Discuss similarities and differences in your weather reports, and make any needed changes.

6. Prepare one weather report to present to the class.

7. Read the statements on Student Sheet 69.1, "Summarizing Weather Reports." You will respond to these statements after listening to your classmates report on the weather for each of the eight days from August 24 to 31.

8. Have your group present its weather report and listen to other groups reports.

9. After listening to all eight weather reports, complete Student Sheet 69.1.

10. Based on the weather reports you heard, forecast the weather for Cleveland, Ohio for September 1. Describe likely fronts, temperature changes, pressure changes, precipitation, and severe weather that may arrive.

Hint: Look at the pattern of weather over the eight days. Use your knowledge of how weather moves across the United States to predict what type of weather is likely to occur in Cleveland.

**Locator Map for Cleveland, Ohio**

## ANALYSIS

1. **a.** Based on the patterns you observed in the weather maps, in what direction does weather generally travel across the United States?

   **b.** Think back to your work in the last activity. In what direction does the prevailing wind move across the United States?

   **c.** How does the movement of the atmosphere globally affect weather locally?

2. Below is weather data collected for Iowa on September 15. Your teacher will give you Student Sheet 69.2, "Map of Iowa." Use the information provided and your knowledge of weather maps to place the appropriate weather symbols on Student Sheet 69.2. Be sure to construct a key for your map.

   • Warm front extending from Lincoln, Nebraska northeast to Mason City, Iowa

   • Rain all along the warm front

   • Low-pressure system in and around Des Moines, Iowa

3. **Reflection:** People often complain about the unreliability of weather forecasts. Why do you think meteorologists are sometimes wrong about what the weather will be like?

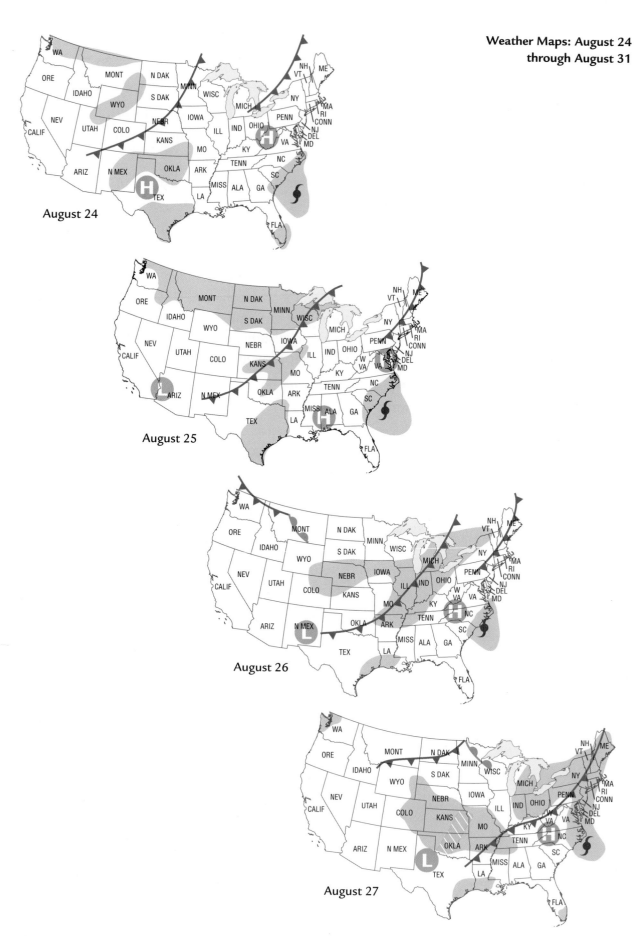

**Weather Maps: August 24
through August 31**

August 24

August 25

August 26

August 27

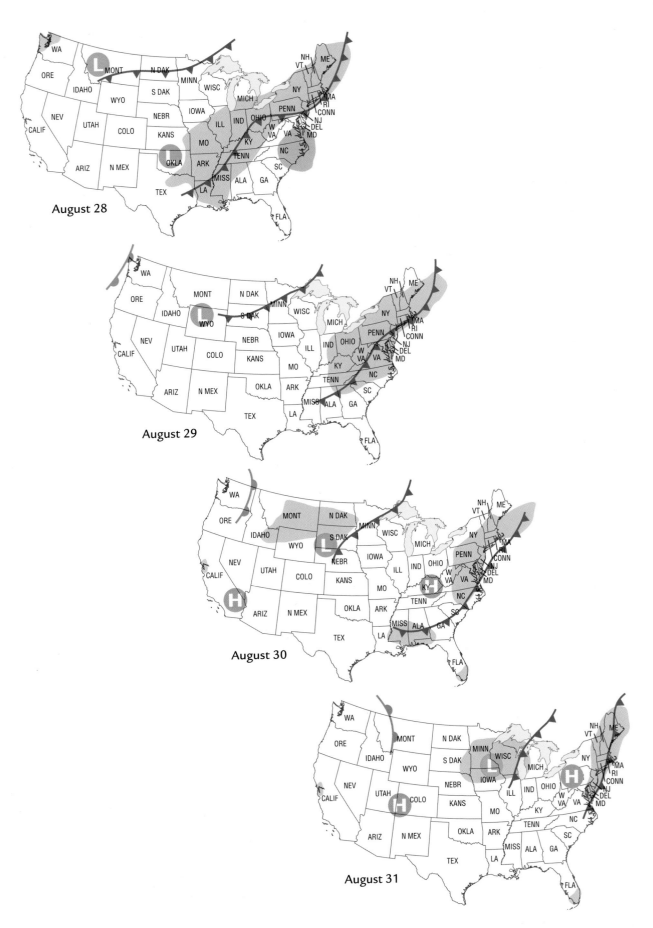

August 28

August 29

August 30

August 31

TALKING IT OVER

Over the course of this unit, you have learned about different aspects of earth's weather and atmosphere. Atmospheric scientists, climatologists, hydrologists, and meteorologists all study how the earth's weather, atmosphere, and climates work. Some of these scientists also study the interactions of humans with the earth's natural systems. In this activity, you will investigate the possible connection between the population of Sunbeam City and its weather and atmosphere.

*Imagine living in Sunbeam City, a rapidly growing city that has experienced population growth partly because of its sunny weather and dry climate. The economy is growing and many people are happy with the city's growth, but some city planners are concerned. They worry that the increase in population might cause changes to the weather, atmosphere, and water availability of Sunbeam City.*

## CHALLENGE

**Is the growth of Sunbeam City affecting its weather, atmosphere, and water availability?**

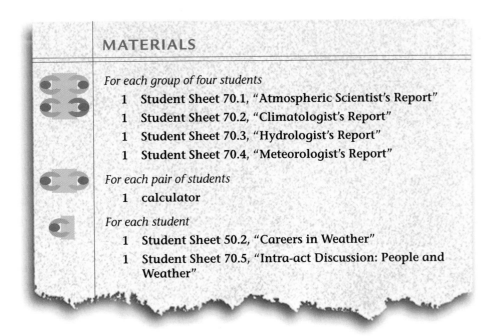

**MATERIALS**

*For each group of four students*

  1  Student Sheet 70.1, "Atmospheric Scientist's Report"

  1  Student Sheet 70.2, "Climatologist's Report"

  1  Student Sheet 70.3, "Hydrologist's Report"

  1  Student Sheet 70.4, "Meteorologist's Report"

*For each pair of students*

  1  calculator

*For each student*

  1  Student Sheet 50.2, "Careers in Weather"

  1  Student Sheet 70.5, "Intra-act Discussion: People and Weather"

## PROCEDURE

1. Look at the graph below. Discuss with your group how the population of the city has changed during the past 40 years, and what you think the size of the population will be in the years 2010 and 2020.

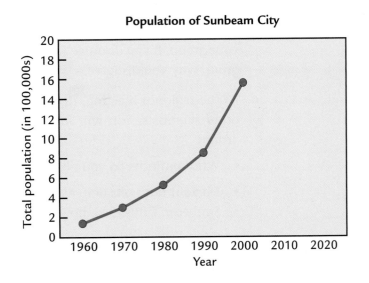

**Population of Sunbeam City**

2. Each person in your group will role-play a scientist studying the weather and atmosphere of Sunbeam City. Decide which person in your group will be the:

   - atmospheric scientist

   - climatologist

   - hydrologist

   - meteorologist

3. Have each scientist from your group attend a "regional meeting" with other scientists who are studying the same data. At the meeting, you will receive one of the following student sheets:

   - Student Sheet 70.1, "Atmospheric Scientist's Report"

   - Student Sheet 70.2, "Climatologist's Report"

   - Student Sheet 70.3, "Hydrologist's Report"

   - Student Sheet 70.4, "Meteorologist's Report"

4. At the regional meeting, read the summary on pages 98–101 that is most relevant to your type of scientist. For example, students who are role-playing atmospheric scientists should read the "Summary of Atmospheric Pollutants in Sunbeam City" on page 98.

5. Work with the other scientists at the regional meeting, and use the information in the summary to complete your student sheet.

   Remember to listen to and consider the ideas of other members of your group. If you disagree with someone, explain to the rest of the group why you disagree.

6. At the regional meeting, discuss the following questions with the other scientists. You will later present this information to your group.

   - What patterns do you observe in your data?

   - Do your data sets help explain why people would like to live in Sunbeam City? If so, how?

   - Compare your data to the population changes in Sunbeam City shown in the graph on page E-95. Do your data sets indicate that the weather, atmosphere, or water availability of Sunbeam City has been affected by an increase in its population? If so, how?

   - What will you tell scientists from other regions about your findings?

7. Return to your group. Present the data on your student sheet, pointing out any patterns that you observed in the data, and state your conclusions about the relationship between Sunbeam City's population growth and any changes in its local environment. Then listen as other group members present their data.

8. Work with your group to summarize the data by discussing the following questions:

   • Which data set(s) help(s) explain why people would like to live in Sunbeam City?

   • Which data set(s) show(s) that the weather, atmosphere, or water availability of Sunbeam City may have been affected by an increase in its population?

9. Mark whether you agree or disagree with the statements on Student Sheet 70.5, "Intra-act Discussion: People and Weather." Predict what you think other members of your group will say.

10. Discuss the statements with your group. Have each person share his or her opinion about each statement, and have them explain why he or she agreed or disagreed.

11. As a group, brainstorm all of the possible actions that the Sunbeam City planners could recommend to city residents to reduce the possible impact of people on the city's weather, atmosphere, and water availability.

12. Discuss the advantages and disadvantages of each option.

# Summary of Atmospheric Pollutants in Sunbeam City

**Carbon monoxide** is a colorless, odorless gas that forms during the incomplete burning of such fuels as gasoline, oil, and wood. In high concentrations it is poisonous to humans. More than half of the carbon monoxide released in the United States is from car exhaust. In cities, 85–95% of carbon monoxide in the air may come from car exhaust. In 2005, Sunbeam City's carbon monoxide releases were greater than the concentration limits set by the U.S. Environmental Protection Agency.

**Nitrogen oxides** are gases that form from the burning of fuels at high temperatures. Most of them are colorless and odorless, but one of them—nitrogen dioxide—is a brownish gas that can sometimes be seen in a smog layer above a city. These gases can form acid rain, ground-level ozone, and other chemicals that affect human health. More than half of the nitrogen oxides released in the U.S. are from car exhaust. Prevailing winds can blow nitrogen oxides over long distances.

**Sulfur dioxide** is a colorless, odorless gas that dissolves easily in water. It can be harmful to animals and humans, especially those with asthma, other lung problems, or heart disease. It forms from the burning of sulfur-containing fuels such as coal. More than 65% of sulfur dioxide is released from power plants that produce electricity. Sulfur dioxide can be blown over long distances, affecting air quality far from its original release.

**Particulate matter** refers to microscopic particles of solid and liquid chemicals, including metals, smoke, and even soil, that float in the air. The particles are small enough that people can inhale them into their lungs, sometimes causing health problems. Some particles are released into the air from human sources such as cars, power plants, and construction sites. Other particles are from natural sources and include dust and pollen. In 2005, the concentrations of particulate matter in Sunbeam City exceeded limits set by the U.S. Environmental Protection Agency.

| Release of Air Pollutants in Sunbeam City | | |
|---|---|---|
| **Air pollutant** | **1990 Release** | **2000 Release** |
| Carbon monoxide | 793,225 | 943,680 |
| Nitrogen oxides | 132,563 | 143,212 |
| Sulfur dioxide | 65,816 | 63,466 |
| Particulate matter | 123,458 | 234,650 |

# Climate Summary for Sunbeam City

Sunbeam City is located in a flat valley in the western United States. The valley is bordered on the east and west by mountains ranging in height from 610 to 3,048 meters (2,000–10,000 feet) above the valley floor. The city itself is approximately 3,048 m above sea level (2,000 ft). This altitude contributes to its cooler nighttime temperatures, which can be more than 15°C lower than daytime highs.

The prevailing winds, which are primarily from the south/southwest, can cause severe dust storms and sandstorms. Sunbeam City is 434 kilometers (270 miles) from the ocean, but the mountains block most of the precipitation that it might otherwise receive. Thunderstorms are rare, but can occur with the arrival of a low-pressure system.

Summer thunderstorms can cause flash flooding. In general, the region has a desert-like climate with very little precipitation year-round.

Sunbeam City has warm temperatures and more than 300 days of sunshine per year. Skies are usually clear, without much cloud cover. In the summer, daytime temperatures exceed 38°C (100°F). During summer nights, temperatures drop into the low 20s°C (70°F). In the winter, daytime temperatures average about 16°C (60°F). During winter nights, temperatures can drop as low as 2°C (36°F).

**Mean Monthly Temperature and Precipitation for Sunbeam City (1971–2000)**

|  | Jan | Feb | Mar | Apr | May | Jun | Jul | Aug | Sept | Oct | Nov | Dec |
|---|---|---|---|---|---|---|---|---|---|---|---|---|
| Temperature (°C) | 7 | 11 | 13 | 18 | 23 | 29 | 33 | 31 | 27 | 20 | 13 | 8 |
| Precipitation (cm) | 1.5 | 1.8 | 1.5 | 0.4 | 0.6 | 0.2 | 1.1 | 1.1 | 0.8 | 0.6 | 0.8 | 1.0 |

# *Hydrological Summary of Sunbeam City*

Historically, most of the water used in Sunbeam Valley came from groundwater. In 1980, the city passed a law that limited the amount of groundwater that could be removed each year. Today, Sunbeam City and the surrounding area get 10–15% of their water from groundwater and 85–90% of their water from Cross Country River. The river begins as snowmelt high in the mountains, which collects over hundreds of kilometers to form the river. The freshwater from the river is shared with seven nearby states.

Sunbeam City is allowed to use 370 billion liters of water per year from the Cross Country River. The only way for Sunbeam City to get more water from Cross Country River is to regularly pay one of the other states for its share of the water.

About 65% of the water used by Sunbeam City each year is used by households. Each home uses an average 800,000 liters per year. About 60% of this water is for outdoor use, such as watering lawns.

The remaining 10–15% of water used by Sunbeam City is mostly from groundwater. It collects from the rain and the snow that melts into the ground from the mountains surrounding Sunbeam City. It can take thousands of years for the water to travel from the mountaintops to the groundwater basin in the center of the valley, with precipitation from the mountains replenishing the groundwater at a rate of about 49 billion liters per year.

| Groundwater Use Since 1940 | |
|---|---|
| Year | Groundwater used (billions of liters per year) |
| 1940 | 26 |
| 1950 | 43 |
| 1960 | 59 |
| 1970 | 110 |
| 1980 | 92 |
| 1990 | 76 |
| 2000 | 92 |

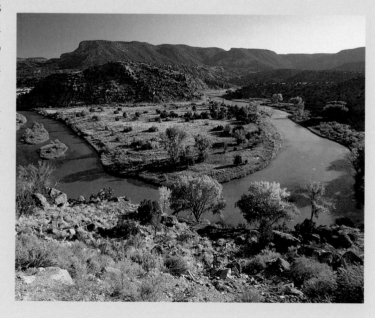

# Meteorological Summary for Sunbeam City

As the population of Sunbeam City grows, city planners and scientists wonder if it is becoming an "urban heat island." An urban heat island is a city or suburban area that experiences hotter temperatures than the surrounding rural areas. Heat islands can develop as cities grow and areas of natural vegetation are replaced by concrete sidewalks, roads, and buildings. Buildings and roadways absorb more of the sun's energy and can result in an increase in local surface and air temperatures. The U.S. Environmental Protection Agency reports that urban areas can be anywhere from 1° to 6°C warmer than surrounding rural areas.

The following temperature data sets were collected for Sunbeam City as well as the surrounding rural area to determine if the growth of the city is affecting its mean temperature.

**Mean Monthly Temperature (°C) in Sunbeam City**

|  | Jan | Feb | Mar | Apr | May | Jun | Jul | Aug | Sept | Oct | Nov | Dec |
|---|---|---|---|---|---|---|---|---|---|---|---|---|
| 1961–1971 | 7 | 11 | 10 | 17 | 23 | 29 | 33 | 30 | 26 | 16 | 8.5 | 8 |
| 1994–2004 | 8 | 11 | 13 | 18 | 23 | 29 | 33 | 31 | 27 | 20 | 13 | 8 |

**Mean Monthly Temperature (°C) in Rural Areas Outside Sunbeam City**

|  | Jan | Feb | Mar | Apr | May | Jun | Jul | Aug | Sept | Oct | Nov | Dec |
|---|---|---|---|---|---|---|---|---|---|---|---|---|
| 1961–1971 | 7.5 | 11 | 12 | 16 | 22 | 29 | 33 | 29 | 25 | 17 | 12 | 7 |
| 1994–2004 | 8.5 | 11 | 13 | 17 | 22 | 29 | 33 | 30 | 26 | 18 | 13 | 7 |

## ANALYSIS

1. Would a weather map provide more evidence about a possible relationship between population growth and changes in the weather and atmosphere of Sunbeam City? Why or why not?

2. Based on the evidence in the scientists' reports, is there any possible relationship between population growth and the weather, atmosphere, or water availability of Sunbeam City? Support your answer with evidence from this unit.

3. What do you think the people of Sunbeam City could do to reduce the possible effects of population growth on their weather, atmosphere, and water availability? Make a recommendation to Sunbeam City's residents, explaining what you think should be done and why. Be sure to support your recommendation with evidence and to identify the trade-offs.

4. **Reflection:** In this unit you learned a lot about weather-related careers and the kind of work that scientists in these careers do. Which of these careers is most interesting to you? What kinds of scientific questions or issues would you be most interested in investigating? Why?

## EXTENSION

Find more information about the weather-related career of your choice. You may want to investigate the type of education, training, and salary associated with this career. Begin by going to the *Issues and Earth Science* page of the SEPUP website for career-related links.

# Index

# CREDITS

Abbreviations: t (top), m (middle), b (bottom), l (left), r (right), c (center)

All illustrations by Seventeenth Street Studios / Valerie Winemiller.

Cover (front): volcano: Photodisc / Getty Images; magnifiers and rocks: LabAids®, Inc.; (back): student hands: Lab-Aids®, Inc.

"Problem Solving" icon photo: ©Thom Lang / Corbis
"Talking It Over" icon photo: ©Michael Keller / Corbis

Unit title (E1) © Royalty-Free / Corbis; Unit Opener (E2,E3) tl: National Oceanic & Atmospheric Administration (NOAA); cl: Juan Silva / Photodisc / Getty Images; bl: Tom Tschida / NASA Dryden Flight research Center Photo Collection; tr: © Royalty-Free / Corbis; br: © Royalty-Free / Corbis; E6: Image Source / Getty Images; E7 tl: Jim Reed / Digital Vision / Getty Images; bl: Richard Carson / ©Reuters / Corbis; E10 bl: Digital Vision / Getty Images; br: Joe Raedle / Getty Images News / Getty Image; E15: National Oceanic & Atmospheric Administration (NOAA); E16 bl: David W. Hamilton / The Image Bank / Getty Images; br: Ian Waldie / Reportage / Getty Images; E18: British Antarctic Survey / Photo Researchers, Inc.; E20 bl: Robert Harding / Digital Vision / Getty Images; br: Philip Nealey / Photodisc / Getty Images; E21 tl: Photodisc / Getty Images; bl: © Royalty-Free / Corbis; tr: Image Source / Getty Images; br: © Royalty-Free / Corbis; E24: Viktor Drachev / AFP / Getty Images; E25: Noboru Komine / Photo Researchers, Inc.; E30 c: © Royalty-Free / Corbis; b: © Royalty-Free / Corbis; E35: Tom McHugh / Photo Researchers, Inc.; E38 t: © Royalty-Free / Corbis; c: Gideon Mendel / Corbis; E40: Allen M. Shimada, NMFS / National Atmospheric and Oceanic Association (NOAA) / NOAA Corps Collection; E43: Martin Puddy / Stone / Getty Images; E46: Chad Ehlers / Stone / Getty Images; E47: Digital Vision / Getty Images; E49: Richard Ashworth / Robert Harding World Imagery / Getty Images; E53: Captain Albert E. Theberge, NOAA, Corps (ret.) / National Atmospheric and Oceanic Association (NOAA) / America's Coastlines Collection; E54: Jim Reed / Photo Researchers, Inc.; E56 t: D. Robert Franz / Taxi / Getty Images; cl: Caroline Woodham / Photodisc / Getty Images; cr: Juan Silva / Photodisc / Getty Images; E58: Stephen Ausmus / United States Department of Agriculture (USDA) / Agricultural Research Service (ARS); E63: Grant V. Faint / Photodisc / Getty Images; E66: © Royalty-Free / Corbis; E70: Tom Tschida / NASA Dryden Flight research Center Photo Collection; E71: British Antarctic Survey / Photo researchers, Inc.; E73: